Nabanga

A production of

The Oral Arts Project

Vanuatu Cultural Centre

The publication of this book has been an activity of the Oral Arts Project of the Vanuatu Cultural Centre, funded by the European Union.

The Oral Arts Project has the following objectives :

- the collection and transcription of the oral traditions of Vanuatu in association with the network of fieldworkers of the Vanuatu Cultural Centre ;
- the encouragement of a renaissance of oral traditions and story telling in association with the Titamol Association of story tellers ;
- the publication of oral traditions in literary form.

We would like to thank the European Union and its Programme of Support to Non State Actors, the Alliance Française of Port Vila and the Agence Universitaire de la Francophonie for supporting this initiative.

Already published:

Mashishiki and the flying woman: A tale from Futuna, 2003 (French, Bislama, English)
Book 1 - TAFEA Province

The story of the eel and other stories from Uripiv island, 2004 (French, vernacular, English)

Nabanga: Une anthologie illustrée de la literature orale du Vanuatu, 2004 (French)

Bimbingo: A tale from Erakor, 2005 (French, Bislama, English)
- Book 2 - SHEFA Province

Rat and Nambilak: A tale from Ambrym, 2005 (French, Bislama, English)
- Book 3 - MALAMPA Province

The logo of the Oral Arts Project is a sand drawing from Tomman island, Malakula. The traditional owners of the design have given us permission to use the design to promote the cultures of Vanuatu.

Nabanga

An illustrated anthology of the oral traditions of Vanuatu

Collected and transcribed by
Paul Gardissat

Translation into English
Kendra Gates
Sara Lightner

Original illustrations
Jacques Harry Tenene
Joseph Samuel Thomas

Editor:
Nicolas Mezzalira

Sub-Editor (English edition)
Josué Malwerssets Célestin

ISBN : 982-9032-09-4

Project team :

Aline Kapalu
Josué Malwerssets Celestin
Nicolas Mezzalira
Callixto Niowenmal
Ralph Regenvanu

Translation into English :

Kendra Gates
Sara Lightner

Cover artwork :

Painting by Deny Kaio
Logo of Nabanga newspaper by Ms Hayward
Logo of Oral Arts Project is a sand drawing from Tomman island

Proof reading :

Angelika Becker
Shu-Mei Denise
Elizabeth Hill
Michael Hill
Ted Hill
Anna Naupa
Anne Naupa
Beverley Sands
Tom Van Sebille
Jennifer West

Layout :

René Manceau

Printed in Vanuatu by Sun Productions

Disclaimer

The stories that you are about to read come from a strong oral tradition that exists in the archipelago of Vanuatu in the South Pacific.

We are publishing these texts - reproductions of newspaper articles and transcripts of audio tapes - exactly as they first appeared in the 1970's.

Except where noted, these stories were all published before the independence of Vanuatu, during the time of the Franco-British Condominium in the New Hebrides, and with the full consent of their traditional owners.

This book may have certain discrepancies due to differing versions of each story. Several stories exist in many different versions throughout the archipelago.

While reproduced faithfully, the stories in this book should not be used to support any scientific or political claims.

Acknowledgements

To the men and women who told us these stories :

Pelau of Namenimen, James Barton of Mota, Edgen Weting Asbal of Losolava, Sope Kalsrap of Pango, chief Tinol of Matantas, Titus Vatu of Atiripoï, Vincent Tabigerian of Melsisi, elder Donato of Lebukuvini, Fabiano Owa of Rentas, Marcel Tabi of the tribe of Wanmel, Claude Asal of Rentas, Johnson Tabiusu of Melsisi, Marsden Lolo of Longana, elder Taï de Lolopuepue, George Ruru of Lolovenue, Albert Tovutu of Fingalato, George Eiler of Lembinwen, Nase Robinson of Malvakal, Albano Rory of Vao, Danmelip Taso of Sanaï, Jacques Gédéon of Paama, Joseph Yona of Mabfilau, Shem Mwasoeripu of Makura, chief Tom Tipoamata of Tongoa, Kalotapa of Emae, chief Charley Tisamori of Marae, chief Kalfao of Moso, Kalo Manamuri of Mataso, Siviu Muerik of Mataso, Georges Kaltoï Kalsakau of Ifira, Charles Aïong of Ifira, Kalmermer of Pango, Liser Sablan of Erakor, John Iowan of Pango, assessor John of Tanna, chief Tuk of Tanna, Yapsen Kuras of Lonelapen, Véronique Runa of Aniwa, Willy Lakaï of Futuna, Jerry Taki of Erromango, and for all those other people who have contributed but are not mentioned.

to all of those, either near or far, who contributed to the realisation of this project :

David Nalo, Nina Sinsau, Timoti Natongtong, Marcel Melterorong, Jennifer Toa, Jimmy, Sero and Nikki Kuautonga, Sethy and Ralph Regenvanu, Shu Mei Denise, Thierry and Ida, Simone Leingkone, Sylvie Late, Peter Murgatroyd, Nancy Yona, Father Rodet, the French Embassy in Vanuatu, the Alliance Française of Port Vila, the European Union, the Agence Universitaire de la Francophonie, Jacques Gédéon, Vincent Bulekone, Léon Buroro Sacsac, Kirk Huffman, Didier Daeninckx, Eric Wittersheim, Lissant Bolton, University of Hawai'i Press, Philippe Métois, René Manceau, Marie-Léa Yoringmal, Numa Longga, Moses Jobo, the Nawita Association, the communities of Futuna, Manuapan, Uripiv, Sesivi, Melsisi, Walarano and Tomman island.

to the fieldworkers of the Cultural Centre ;

to the artists - traditional and contemporary - of Vanuatu ;

to the country that stands up.

This book is dedicated to Mateo and all the children of Vanuatu. *Faea i laet.*

Foreword

This book presents to the reader, for the first time in English, the complete collection of legends of Vanuatu that were broadcast on the radio or printed in the *Nabanga* and *Le Melanesien* newspapers during the last five years of the condominium of the New Hebrides, between 1975 and 1980. Almost all the texts published within these pages were produced by Paul Gardissat while he was working for *Radio New Hebrides*. While there, he broadcast a weekly legend that was then re-printed with illustrations in the *Nabanga* newspaper. Using stories told to him by individuals or those collected in the course of academic research by those interested in oral traditions (such as Jean Guiart), Paul Gardissat brought numerous stories to life in the form of French-language radio adaptations and their illustrated transcriptions. Among these are some of the most important oral traditions existing in the Vanuatu archipelago. We would like to thank him for his work as well as the confidence he invested in us by allowing unrestricted access to his archives. Every available broadcast and transcript was included in this compilation along with all original drawings. The transcripts that were originally published in Bislama were translated into English for the purposes of this edition and all others were translated from the original French into English. While assembling this edition, conservation and archival work was done to preserve the radio recordings of the original broadcasts. These are now available for consultation at the National Film and Sound Archives of the Vanuatu Cultural Centre.

Given the importance of some custom stories such as *The origin of clan names of Efate,* we have allowed ourselves the luxury of adding certain legends to those collected by Paul Gardissat. Additional legends from the islands of Epi, Paama and Erromango have been included in this edition so that, in the words of the great Sakora, "all islands might be reached." The previously unpublished legends are :

- *The legend of Titamol* and *The namele child* from Paama, told by Jacques Gédéon ;
- *The old woman and the bananas* and *The prisoner of the stone* from Epi, told by Joseph Yona ;
- *The marriage of kava and the coconut* from Erromango, told by Jerry Taki ;
- *The origin of clan names of Efate,* told by John Iowan.

The geographical origins along with the names of those who first told the legends have been included whenever possible. These names have been assembled in a comprehensive chart at the end of this book. We would like to apologise to those whose names could not be found, particularly during the period of the program *"Alors ...raconte!"* on *Radio Port Vila,* and thus are not mentioned here. We would also like to thank all those people, cited or not, who represent, along with their respective clans, the true authors of this book.

The reader will find two unique contributions at the end of the book. The first, *"The sailor and the children of Ambrym"*, is a translation of a text written especially for the French edition of this book by the French author Didier Daeninckx during a visit to Vanuatu in 2003. We would like to express our gratitude for this gesture and we hope that the subsequent reading of this text increases the memory of artistic generosity that he left behind in Vanuatu.

The second text is an article written by Dr Lissant Bolton, the Conservator of the Oceanic and Australian Collection at the British Museum in London as well as a long-time partner of the Vanuatu Cultural Centre. This article was originally published in 1999 in the journal *The Contemporary Pacific* published by the University of Hawai'i Press. Entitled *"Radio and the redefinition of Kastom in Vanuatu,"* it clarifies the context and the importance that the texts in this book had at the time of their first publication. Finally, this edition also includes a complete bibliography of the numerous publications (from handwritten pamphlets to scientific articles) having to do with the oral traditions of Vanuatu. This bibliography was compiled as part of the Oral Arts Project.

This is the first time that the oral tradition of Vanuatu, taken from a literary point of view, has been the subject of a work of this magnitude. Being a compilation of oral traditions - histories, myths and legends - this book is simply meant to help others discover, for their own pleasure, certain real and imaginary worlds that exist in the oral tradition of Vanuatu.

The only thing left to do is to wish you an excellent first meeting with the *lisepsep,* the winged people of *Siviritot,* the amazing mythical heroes and terrifying ogres of Vanuatu. We also wish that while diving into the Melanesian culture, you might, in the manner of the god Mauitikitiki, fisher of marvelous islands, bring back a little of the wisdom of Titamol and approach the soul of Vanuatu.

Nicolas Mezzalira
Editor

Oral Arts Project
Vanuatu Cultural Centre.

Preface

This large basket full of Kastom stories from all over Vanuatu collected by Paul Gardissat from the 1960s through to the early 1980s is an absolute treasure-trove. It is a basket full of riches, cultural identity and, yes, excitement. The scope and depth of many of these stories rivals stories produced by ancient societies from which Europeans trace their cultural heritage - and remember that what you are reading here is in modified form, translated from the rich traditional languages of Vanuatu into Bislama, French or English. Certain traditional concepts are so complex that it is often rather difficult to translate them into European languages - sometimes the vocabulary is lacking in the latter. Translation from language into Bislama often conveys the tone and flow of the story better than in English or French, but Bislama's vocabulary is also limited. However, this is a monumental work and is a worthy preliminary monument to Vanuatu's fascinating oral history, to its cultures, to ni-Vanuatu who provided the stories, to their ancestors, and to the years of hard work that Paul put into their collection.

Many ni-Vanuatu will be familiar with a number of these stories, or variants of them, if they are from their own cultures. Many older ni-Vanuatu will also be familiar with those stories that were broadcast, from the 1960s through to the early 1980s, by Radio Port-Vila/Radio Vila in Paul's immensely popular and influential 'Alors…Raconte!' and later 'Kastom, Kalja mo Tradisen' programmes. The immense amount of work that Paul and his colleagues put into these programmes is a measure of their love and respect for the peoples and cultures of Vanuatu. Other stories will be familiar to readers of 'Nabanga', the weekly French language newspaper that was published from 1975 until 1980, which regularly contained Kastom story contributions facilitated by Paul's tireless collecting, transcription, translating, editing and production. Sincere thanks should go to Paul and his colleagues in radio and newspaper and to those many ni-Vanuatu who provided the original stories for these contributions.

Bringing these stories together in this one publication is a major step in making this material available for ni-Vanuatu school students who can thus, at one sweep, get an insight into aspects of the historical traditions of our complex nation. Remember, though, that many of these stories exist in different versions which often vary from area to area, from clan to clan. This is only normal in complex cultures and this exists also overseas in historical context. For example, the differing versions of 'Genesis' and 'Flood' stories in Judaism, Christianity and Islam, bearing in mind that the earliest written versions of the themes of many of these stories, written on clay tablets by ancient Sumerian scribes a thousand years before the versions that have come down to us, present possibly a version of a 'parent stock' of history and belief from which later related cultures effectively modified and chose what was relevant to them. If you, as ni-Vanuatu, have been given by your family or culture versions of Kastom stories that differ from these printed ones, do not worry, this is normal - the sun produces many sunbeams, but is one; a rainbow has many colours, but is one; the hand has five fingers, but is one; thousands of hairs grow from one head; many yams can grow in one garden.

For outsiders or expatriates coming to the riches of Vanuatu oral tradition for the first time; although the cultures may be difficult for you to understand, many of the themes in these stories may be familiar to you if you have a knowledge of early stories from your own culture - spirits and the spirit world; devouring giants and ogres; creating gods; birds, animals or sea inhabitants that speak and whose behaviour mirrors the human world (or our world mirrors theirs); living nature - either stones, or trees, or vines or volcanoes or whatever; magical powers; heroic warriors; wise leaders; good and evil men and women; magical voyages; love; jealousy; warfare; combat; children; twins; trickery; forgiveness; ancestors and respect - the whole panoply of human life is here. Many of these stories follow certain almost universal themes but look at them and deal with them in our own Vanuatu ways. This is to be respected.

For ni-Vanuatu students again, use this collection as a guide to help inspire yourself to learn properly the Kastom stories you may be entitled to as a member of your family, your lineage, your clan, your village, your language and culture area and your land. Learn the stories in your proper language; learn what can and cannot be given out; learn to respect the tabus involved in learning and telling; learn that you may have to wait a long time to learn the deep things; learn that certain stories that mean one thing to young people can mean deeper things to those who know the codes that may be hidden in the stories; learn that many of these stories may have levels of meaning; learn that knowing your proper Kastom stories are the traditional way to prove your land ownership; learn that learning your language and stories is also one way to show respect to your ancestors, and that passing on these stories in the proper way to your children and grandchildren shows love for them as these will culturally protect and enrich them and enable them to respect you more. Learn that proper story-telling has its proper time and context - in the gardens as a child with your mother, aunt, or grandmother, during your initiation (if you are from such a culture), during kava preparation, in the evenings around the fire, or what-ever. Learn that story-telling, with the teller's facial expressions, gestures, imitations, songs (and possible associated sand drawings if you are from such a culture) and actions is one of Vanuatu's greatest 'arts'. Realise that some themes that sound similar to stories from overseas may actually be very different in Vanuatu: here I mention the numerous stories from throughout the country of people with wings - 'angels'. In Vanuatu, those that come to earth are usually women and their detachable wings are mostly similar to flying foxes' (fruit bats) wings, not necessarily feathered wings as in stories from outside the country. Remember that, since the 1970s, the Vanuatu Cultural Centre, through its Fieldworkers, has been amassing a vast collection of recordings of Kastom stories from throughout the nation; these are stored under strict conditions in the 'Tabu Room' and help to form a sort of 'safety bank' of such stories in case some stories are not passed on in the proper way. Remember that writing down a Kastom story actually results in only a partial version of it - these stories did not develop to be written down; they are part of an ancient, complex, living tradition that is passed down by word of mouth and should continue to be so. Writing them can help, but the real way to ensure these stories really live is to make sure they continue to be told in the proper way.

This book allows you, as ni-Vanuatu, to bend down and peek through part of the entrance of a large thatched hut full of traditional wealth. Use it as an introduction to learn who you really are. Learn that such Kastom stories are part of your real riches, more than modern money. Do not throw them away.

Kirk Huffman

Honorary Curator, Vanuatu Cultural Centre (Curator, 1977-1989).
Research Associate, Australian Museum, Sydney.
Honorary Associate, Macleay Museum, University of Sydney.
Member, Scientific Committee, Musee de Tahiti et des Iles, Punaauia, Tahiti.

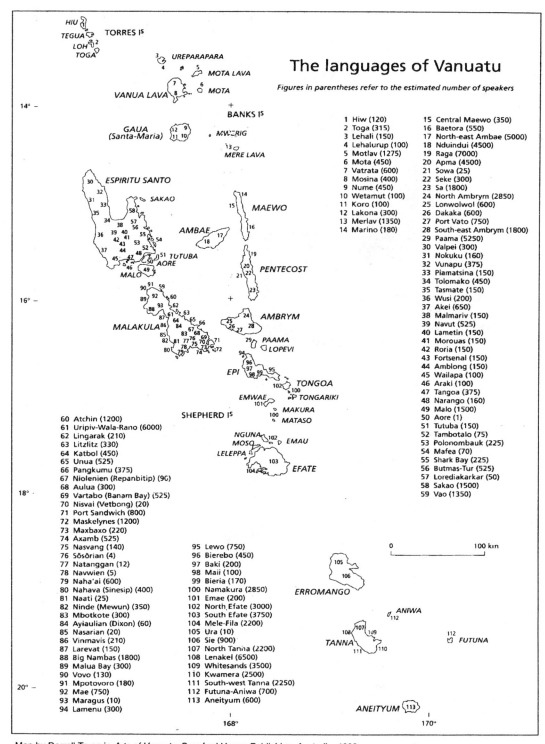

The languages of Vanuatu

Figures in parentheses refer to the estimated number of speakers

HIU
TEGUA
LOH
TOGA
TORRES IS

UREPARAPARA
MOTA LAVA
VANUA LAVA
MOTA
BANKS IS

GAUA
(Santa-Maria)
MWERIG
MERE LAVA

ESPIRITU SANTO
SAKAO
MAEWO
AMBAE
TUTUBA
AORE
MALO
PENTECOST

MALAKULA
AMBRYM
PAAMA
LOPEVI
EPI
TONGOA
EMWAE
TONGARIKI
SHEPHERD IS
MAKURA
MATASO
NGUNA
MOSO
EMAU
LELEPPA
EFATE

ERROMANGO
ANIWA
TANNA
FUTUNA
ANEITYUM

1 Hiw (120)
2 Toga (315)
3 Lehali (150)
4 Lehalurup (100)
5 Motlav (1275)
6 Mota (450)
7 Vatrata (600)
8 Mosina (400)
9 Nume (450)
10 Wetamut (100)
11 Koro (100)
12 Lakona (300)
13 Merlav (1350)
14 Marino (180)
15 Central Maewo (350)
16 Baetora (550)
17 North-east Ambae (5000)
18 Nduindui (4500)
19 Raga (7000)
20 Apma (4500)
21 Sowa (25)
22 Seke (300)
23 Sa (1800)
24 North Ambrym (2850)
25 Lonwolwol (600)
26 Dakaka (600)
27 Port Vato (750)
28 South-east Ambrym (1800)
29 Paama (5250)
30 Valpei (300)
31 Nokuku (160)
32 Vunapu (375)
33 Piamatsina (150)
34 Tolomako (450)
35 Tasmate (150)
36 Wusi (200)
37 Akei (650)
38 Malmariv (150)
39 Navut (525)
40 Lametin (150)
41 Morouas (150)
42 Roria (150)
43 Fortsenal (150)
44 Amblong (150)
45 Wailapa (100)
46 Araki (100)
47 Tangoa (375)
48 Narango (160)
49 Malo (1500)
50 Aore (1)
51 Tutuba (150)
52 Tambotalo (75)
53 Polonombauk (225)
54 Mafea (70)
55 Shark Bay (225)
56 Butmas-Tur (525)
57 Lorediakarkar (50)
58 Sakao (1500)
59 Vao (1350)

60 Atchin (1200)
61 Uripiv-Wala-Rano (6000)
62 Lingarak (210)
63 Litzlitz (330)
64 Katbol (450)
65 Unua (525)
66 Pangkumu (375)
67 Niolenien (Repanbitip) (90)
68 Aulua (300)
69 Vartabo (Banam Bay) (525)
70 Nisvai (Vetbong) (20)
71 Port Sandwich (800)
72 Maskelynes (1200)
73 Maxbaxo (220)
74 Axamb (525)
75 Nasvang (140)
76 Sösörian (4)
77 Natanggan (12)
78 Navwien (5)
79 Naha'ai (600)
80 Nahava (Sinesip) (400)
81 Naati (25)
82 Ninde (Mewun) (350)
83 Mbotkote (300)
84 Ayiaulian (Dixon) (60)
85 Nasarian (20)
86 Vinmavis (210)
87 Larevat (150)
88 Big Nambas (1800)
89 Malua Bay (300)
90 Vovo (130)
91 Mpotovoro (180)
92 Mae (750)
93 Maragus (10)
94 Lamenu (300)

95 Lewo (750)
96 Bierebo (450)
97 Baki (200)
98 Maii (100)
99 Bieria (170)
100 Namakura (2850)
101 Emae (200)
102 North Efate (3000)
103 South Efate (3750)
104 Mele-Fila (2200)
105 Ura (10)
106 Sie (900)
107 North Tanna (2200)
108 Lenakel (6500)
109 Whitesands (3500)
110 Kwamera (2500)
111 South-west Tanna (2250)
112 Futuna-Aniwa (700)
113 Aneityum (600)

0   100 km

Map by Darrell Tryon in *Arts of Vanuatu*, Crawford House Publishing, Australia, 1996.

13

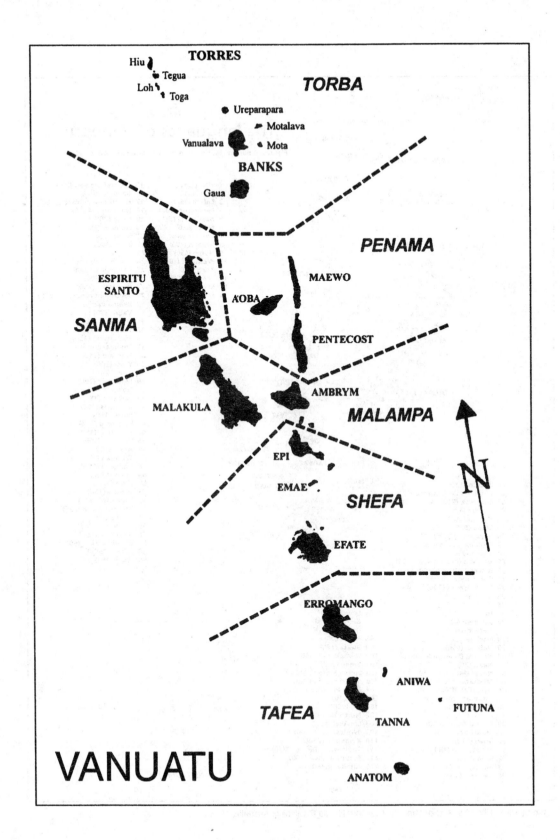

TORRES

Hiu

Tegua

Loh

Toga

TORBA

Ureparapara

Motalava

Vanualava

Mota

BANKS

Gaua

PENAMA

ESPIRITU
SANTO

AOBA

MAEWO

SANMA

PENTECOST

AMBRYM

MALAKULA

MALAMPA

EPI

N

EMAE

SHEFA

EFATE

ERROMANGO

ANIWA

TAFEA

TANNA

FUTUNA

VANUATU

ANATOM

TORBA Province

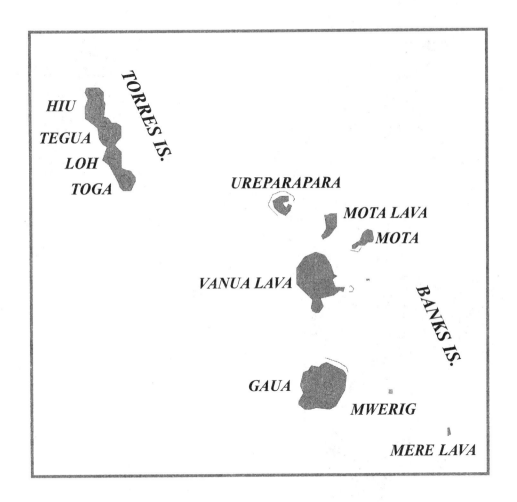

Maraptit the traveller
(Hiu)

While the navigator was heading north beyond the Banks, he saw the Torres archipelago suddenly appear with Hiu, the southern most island, profiled against the horizon, tall and majestic. Its summits were flat and its vegetation less dense than on other islands. The sand on Hiu's beaches shocked the explorer, who had just left Vanua Lava for the Torres, with their whiteness.

Here, while the sun plays on the vast beaches of radiant white sand and the sparkling blue-green sea, the brilliance becomes overwhelming. On this island lives Maraptit who is a lot like Kwat from Vanua Lava. We all know Kwat well: a spider helped him to free himself from dramatic circumstances. He forgave the treason of his eleven brothers to pull them from the snare of the diabolical Kwasvar from Gaua, whom he then catapulted into the heavens before returning to Vanua Lava, that highest of islands, to live in harmony.

On Hui, we have Maraptit: he is there on the beach near the water, looking at the sea in all its glory and thinking. His eyes are wide open, staring at the sea. He is attracted to the open water, and he turns his reveries to the blue line on the horizon. His neck is adorned with white stones and his big shoulders shine in the sun. His body is fully covered with tattoos that suggest an invincible strength. A simple vine is wrapped around his waist and magnificent pigs' tusks decorate his wrists. Everything about him breaths calm and strength.

All of a sudden, something broke the serenity; like an arrow in the sky, a sea bird shot up from the water. This startled our hero from his dreaming. The bird's cry broke the silence. Furious, he swore at the bird, which was hunting for fish. Maraptit then left the coast to rejoin his brothers.

Weary and disappointed, he arrived in the village. Today, the women were dancing.

"How boring their dances are!" he thought to himself.

It had been so different in his dream while looking at the horizon. He saw women a thousand times more beautiful and graceful, flocks of brilliantly coloured birds singing, and branches so heavy with splendid fruit that they hung to the ground. The whole of nature competed with itself to produce the best colours, songs, and riches.

Maraptit's brothers, sitting in the shade of a mango tree, remarked on his strange behaviour. They approached him and tried to get him to talk. He would say nothing. The dancing bored him.

Finally, to escape the spectacle, he said, "I am going into the bush to look for some *namambe*." He took his basket and left, his brothers following close behind him. They had already started to collect the chestnuts, each one trying to fill his basket first, when one of the brothers said, "While you're trying to fill your baskets, I'm going to hunt some *nautou*."

Maraptit interrupted and demanded that he stay with the others.

"Maraptit, you have been very strange for sometime now and certainly too strict with us," responded the youngest of the brothers.

Maraptit then revealed a few of his thoughts and told them of his desire to travel far from their island. They hadn't set foot off this island for two rainy seasons, and Maraptit wanted to go and see their brothers from Metoma. One of the brothers started to complain about the poor welcome that they had received on their last visit. However, his attention was suddenly attracted by some magnificent *namambe*. He shouted with joy.

"In the country where I was a little while ago, there was fruit much bigger than this," said Maraptit. He could not explain, though, what he meant and his brothers did not understand.

Their baskets finally full, the ten brothers returned to the village to take their harvest to Bubu, their grandfather, who then spoke to Maraptit.

"My son, I have found your behaviour strange for quite some time now. You cannot stay still, you go, you come, you give orders and then you leave. What is the matter?"

Maraptit kept his secret to himself but Bubu, wise with years, had understood what was eating at him. Without saying a word, Maraptit left to go and find his brothers. They all picked up their *natapae* boards, smooth, light, and slightly curved at the tip. Arriving on the coast, they made their way into the water. Each one tried to catch the waves before they began to unfurl and then quickly stretched themselves out on their boards and let the water take them. Maraptit, the strongest and the bravest, went the furthest because of his agility.

Hungry after all this exercise, the brothers went back to the village to taste their roasted *namambe*. They forgot to leave some for Maraptit who had just joined them. Anger got the better of him, and Maraptit dragged his brothers and their *natapae* boards down to the coast once again. Here, something extraordinary happened. Maraptit started to sing and with his song, he pushed his brothers towards the open sea.

"Have pity! Bring us back to dry land!" they cried.

Maraptit yelled back, "Now, hold on tight to your boards because we're going on a long trip!"

Maraptit from the island of Hiu in the Torres dreamt of going to the marvellous country beyond the horizon. Gifted with a divine power, he had seen an unknown and idyllic land and he sought to take his brothers there. Through simple songs, he was able to do this despite their resistance to being on the open sea.

"Take us back to the coast," begged the brothers. "Pity! Have pity, Maraptit! We are being pulled further out!"

However, Maraptit turned a deaf ear to their pleas. As soon as a wave would bring them close to land, he started to sing again and the waves pushed them back out. He wouldn't listen to them and so they set off on their big trip, carried by the waves. The water carried them all the way to the main land of Vanua Lava. When they finally put their feet on land, they cried out with pleasure, "Look at how full these trees are with fruit! What riches!"

"I told you so! This marvellous country is just as it was in my dreams," responded Maraptit. "All the trees here are laden with fruit but the inhabitants don't know that it is good to eat."

Attracted by the noise of dancing, they approached a group of people and asked them why they did not eat the fruit.

"Why, because this fruit isn't good," one responded.

Maraptit showed him one. "This is a *nakavika,*" he said. To his surprise, Maraptit started to eat it. The man then tasted the fruit.

"Why didn't we think of this earlier? This fruit is delicious!" said the latter. "Maraptit, you know everything. You are truly the best among us!"

Then, the brothers left and went into the bush. On the way, they saw a breadfruit tree loaded with young fruit.

19

"For me, for me!" they cried as they grabbed eagerly.

Maraptit watched them. He was the last to choose and only one poorly shaped and bruised fruit was left for him.

They then returned to the village and stayed several days. They had left their fruit on the tree but, now that they were ripe, each one went to get what they had reserved. They picked them, brought them back to the village, cooked them, and ate them. Maraptit, during this time, watched them without a word. His fruit stayed on the tree and continued to grow and grow. The bruised part fell off by itself and now the fruit was perfect.

"Mine is ripe," said Maraptit. "Let's go get it."

Arriving at the base of the tree, he asked one of his brothers to climb up and pick it. The brother obeyed, picked the fruit, and they brought it back to the village. Once they got there, Maraptit started to call the birds, his echo carrying the call very far.

"Birds, my friends, come, I need to speak to you. Birds! Birds! Come quickly!"

The call echoed through the forest and each bird took flight in its turn. The first to respond to the cry was the *nawimba*.

"Who are you?"

The bird, in a birdly fashion, introduced itself. Maraptit spoke to it.

"You are the *nawimba*. Can you not take me back to my home?"

But the *nawimba*, very upset, could not help our hero.

"And you? Who are you?" he asked the parrot. "You are the parrot. Can you not take me back to my home?"

But the parrot could not help either.

"You, come closer. You are the flying fox. Can you take me back to Hiu?"

But the flying fox could not. "How could I do that?" it asked.

Then, Maraptit turned to another bird. "You, come here. Take me back to my island!"

"I am too small," responded the latter, "Look at my height, my wings!"

All the birds chorused, "We are sorry, Maraptit, but we are unable to help you."

All of a sudden, like an arrow from the sky, a *nasiko* shot up.

"You, be kind, my dear *Nasiko*. Could you take me to Hiu, the island of my ancestor?"

The *nasiko* accepted. Quickly, Maraptit grabbed his breadfruit in the house and arranged its stem like one arranges leaves to plug the end of a bamboo carrying water. Then he said to his brothers, "Now, get inside this fruit. We will stay inside until we reach Hiu. The *nasiko* will take us."

Each one rushed in. Maraptit then told the bird, "Now, *Nasiko,* plug up the fruit and take us."

The *nasiko* took the stem of the fruit in his beak and flew away. Soon, he arrived on Ureparepara. "Can you hear those people dancing? Is this not your island, Maraptit?"

"No, *Nasiko,* it is further still," he answered.

The *nasiko* took flight again until he reached Toga. "Listen to those people dancing and singing. Is this not your home?"

"No, *Nasiko,* it is further still," Maraptit answered.

Then Loh appeared on the horizon. "Those people dancing, would they not be yours?"

"No, further still," repeated Maraptit.

The trip continued on to Tegua. "Are you sure that this is not your island?"

"No, *Nasiko,* still a little bit further."

Finally, Hiu could be seen in the distance. "Maraptit, here is your island, I am sure."

"Yes, my good *Nasiko,* this is the island of my ancestors, my happy and most dear island. You can let us go now."

The *nasiko* opened his beak and let the fruit go. It burst when it hit the ground; Maraptit and his brothers were free. Attracted by the noise, the whole village came running. For ten days, they had waited for the brothers and then they had cried and killed pigs. Now that they had found them alive, they couldn't believe their eyes and cried with joy.

Maraptit the traveller exclaimed, "There is no place like home!"

This legend was told to me in Bislama by Pelau
from the village of Nanenimen on the island of Hiu in the Torres Group.
Paul Gardissat .

Nabanga n°103-104 (April 1979)

The legend of Kwat
(Mota)

On the 8th of June 1707, while Captain de Quiros was sailing between the islands of Vanua Lava, Mota, and Mota Lava, he was sure that he would discover Espiritu Santo. His ship, "La Capitana," had just left the islands that would later take the name of his co-captain, Captain Torres. He navigated his ship around these islands because de Quiros found them much too small to be interesting. He was hoping to find larger islands further away.

Captain de Quiros guessed as well that these islands would not be easy to approach. Nevertheless, he saw smoke issuing from the sides of mountains, and other such things that should have peaked his curiosity. He wrote in his ship's log: "...island baptised Portales de Belen, by me, Pedro Fernandez de Quiros, the 8th of June, in the year of our Lord 1707. "La Capitana," all sails to the wind, pursued its course, heading towards Gaua to enter next, on the holy day of Saint Philip and Saint Jacques, the big bay of Espiritu Santo.

The Captain had viewed Vanua Lava with disdain, finding it too small. Yet, in the language of the Banks, Vanua Lava means "the big land." Between the Solomon Islands and Espiritu Santo, there is no other island as large. It is the island of big rivers, the island where sulphur covers the flanks of Suratmati, the highest of mountains, the island where crocodiles hide in the mangroves and muddy waters without ever attacking man. On this mysterious island lived a man whose name was Kwat.

Kwat lived with his twelve brothers and one day, as everyone seemed to be bored, he suggested, "We could cut down some wood to make canoes."

"That's an idea!" said one of the brothers. "That way we could go from island to island."

"We could take long trips," added Kwat, "to go visit Tagaro, instead of staying here being bored and fighting."

This idea had come to him because he wanted to travel. Kwat had heard tell of a powerful being named Tagaro that lived on a very high island, Omba. His twelve brothers also wanted to see other places and other men, so they agreed to Kwat's idea. That evening, while they slept, they dreamed about their future adventures. As soon as the sun had risen, at the first cry of the roosters, Kwat and his twelve brothers got up, took an axe, and went to cut down tree trunks.

Each brother chose his own with which to make his canoe. None of them went far from the house and all chose very soft wood, except Kwat who was more courageous and a harder worker than the others. He went to the highest summit of the highest mountain, the Suratmati. He went to work on the best wood for canoes: the *nananara*.

22

He spent the whole day chopping to fell the tree. In the evening, all the brothers went to the *nakamal* to discuss their day's work. Kwat was surprised to hear that the bush offered such soft wood that would be easy to shape into a canoe. He explained that he had gone very far to find a very good tree.

The next day, each brother left to hollow the trunk that he had cut. Kwat climbed the mountain once again. Once on top, he was stupefied to see that his trunk was not lying on the ground. The tree that he had chopped down was once again standing. With great anger, Kwat took up his axe and went at the *nananara* again. It was not until he had finished his work that this man from Vanua Lava returned to his home.

The brothers were already seated around a bonfire in the *nakamal* when Kwat arrived. Everyone commented on his worried expression and fatigue. One of the twelve then asked him, "How is your canoe coming along?"

Kwat responded, "I don't understand at all what has been happening. I was in the middle of the bush. I chose the most beautiful *nananara*. I chopped it down. This morning, I went back to the same place that I had left the tree. I didn't find anything. The tree had been put back together. It was upright once again. I chopped and chopped all day long. Now, the *nananara* is on the ground, but I'm worried about tomorrow. And you, are your canoes well underway?"

The other canoes were almost finished. While the brothers were talking, a spider went creeping towards the *nananara* in the black of night. It gathered together the pieces of the felled tree and set it upright once again.

The next day, Kwat left again to go find his tree. Arriving at the place, he felt his anger rising, his anger against this invisible enemy that was destroying his work. The *nananara* reached straight up into the sky. Kwat started to chop at the tree aggressively. Then, he decided to spend the night near the tree. To guard his work, he hid himself behind another big tree. He waited.

In the light of a moonbeam, Kwat saw the spider arrive. It started its work and soon the *nananara* was again how Kwat had first seen it. The man jumped from his hiding place and threw himself at the spider to kill it.

"Don't kill me, Kwat!"

"Why should I not kill you when you do nothing but hurt me? This is the third day that I have worked hard and the third time that you have undone everything I have worked for."

"Kwat," responded the spider, "have confidence in me. I won't hurt you anymore. Go back to your house and you will receive a wonderful surprise."

The next morning, each brother went to get his canoe to bring it to the beach. However, Kwat said that he had not yet even begun his canoe. He had to return to the mountains to work. Once there, to his big surprise, he found a beautiful canoe perfectly fashioned.

"The spider kept its promise," he said, impressed by the craftsmanship of the work before him. Truly, this was a wonderful canoe. Kwat touched it, stroked it, and then gave a magical cry! A river appeared before him and took him and his canoe right to the shore. Seeing him, Kwat's brothers said, "Well, well, well. You've lied to us: your canoe is ready!"

"I didn't know that the spider would hollow it out so quickly in only one night!" responded Kwat.

"You really had us going with your stories!"

The brothers felt cheated. Each one wanted to try out his own canoe. The first brother pushed his into the water and barely had enough time to jump in and paddle when it was overturned by the first wave: it was too light. The second one did the same in his turn and had hardly gone a couple of metres when it too turned over and sunk. Thus, each of Kwat's brothers had made canoes either too light, poorly constructed, or unstable and each was overturned by the waves. However, Kwat's canoe floated perfectly and because it was carved, it cut through the waves with an admirable speed. His brothers were jealous and angry; they went back to their houses without saying a word. But, in their heads, they were all asking the same question: how could they get their hands on Kwat's canoe?

The brothers met in the dark of the night.

"He thinks that he's better than us," said one of the brothers to the others. "But wait! Tomorrow, we'll take him to hunt pigeons in the *nandarao*. There are many pigeons in this tree. While he's busy hunting..."

In this way, Kwat's brothers set their trap. The next day, the brothers suggested to Kwat that they all go hunting for *notou* in the big *nandarao* deep in the forest. As soon as Kwat had climbed into the tree, the brothers ran back to the village. They put Kwat's wife and his bananas into his canoe. Then, they all got in. While they were paddling, one of the brothers gave a magical cry to make the *nandarao* grow very high. The tree started to push its way into the sky.

24

Kwat yelled, "What's happening? I don't want to be so high up. Don't abandon me, my brothers!"

The brothers, however, were already far from Vanua Lava. They were paddling in the direction of Lakona and to taunt Kwat they blew into a conch shell. Kwat heard them and sighed, "I've been tricked once again. They've left with my canoe and my wife! What will become of me high up in this *nandarao?"*

Luckily, the spider heard Kwat's lamenting. It asked him, "What are you doing perched in this tree?"

Kwat knew that the spider was his friend and that it would help him out of this situation. Even though he was a little ashamed of his position, Kwat asked the spider for aid. The spider explained to him, "I will weave a web on which you can climb down."

Kwat used the web like a ladder and climbed down from the tree. He went to find his mother, Rowul. "Mother, where is my wife?"

"Your brothers took her with them."

This was exactly what he had feared. Furious, he ran to the shore and picked up a coconut with two rotten "eyes." He said to his mother, "I'm going to go inside this coconut. You must count the waves. On the fourth one, throw the coconut into the sea." Rowul did as Kwat had asked.

While floating, the coconut slowly gained on the stolen canoe in which the twelve brothers sat. One of the brothers saw it and picked it up to eat. When he brought it to his mouth, he became conscious of a nauseating odour.

"Ugh," he exclaimed, "this coconut smells rotten."

"Let me smell it," demanded one of the other brothers.

He too found the odour repugnant. As the coconut passed from brother to brother, each found the coconut to be completely rotten. Thus, they threw it back into the sea. This rotten smell was actually a clever trick by Kwat. He didn't want his brothers to open the coconut and find him inside. Therefore, each time a brother brought the coconut to his nose, Kwat squeezed his bum against the "eyes" of the coconut and farted.

Once back in the water, Kwat arrived on the island of Gaua well before his brothers. He sat down under a pandanus to wait. When the canoe beached on the island, Kwat's wife saw her husband sitting nearby and she cried with joy. Seeing Kwat, the brother's held their distance. They grumbled amongst themselves, "It's not possible! How could he be here?" They were ashamed of the way that they had behaved.

Kwat did not hold a grudge against his brothers or ask them to explain their actions. However, he did give a magical cry that cracked the stolen canoe in two. "Now," said Kwat, "you have done enough stupid things. I ask you to follow me and to listen closely."

Each of the brothers obeyed him, hanging their respective heads. In this way, they arrived at the house of a man that was, in reality, half man and half devil. His name was Kwasvar. He was particularly ugly and his favourite food was *laplap* made with human flesh. Seeing this family from Vanua Lava arrive, he was very welcoming and kind.

"Come and make yourself at home in my house," he said, "I will sleep in the *nakamal*. Good night!"

However, Kwat had understood the danger. "If we sleep here," he explained to his brothers, "Kwasvar will come and eat some of us. Let's take advantage of his absence to hide. I'll open the beam of the house and we'll all sleep inside."

Everyone scrambled up into the beam, which then closed around them so that when Kwasvar came at midnight to kidnap some of them, he found no one. On the contrary, they were all there in the morning! Where had they spent the night?
"We spent the night in the beam of your house," said Tagarolbong, who had the biggest mouth among the brothers.

"Why can't you keep your mouth shut?" cried the other brothers.

"What a wonderful idea you all had! The beam is the quietest place," responded Kwasvar with a smile.

Kwasvar played the perfect host. Together, they were preparing the evening meal when Kwat suggested, "We should mix our taro with saltwater. That way the *laplap* would taste better. Here, brother, why don't you get us some water in this bamboo?"

"A very good idea," commented Kwasvar.

In secret, Kwat whispered to each of his brothers, "Don't go to the sea. Go to the forest and climb the ironwood tree." And this is what the first brother did.

When he did not see his brother come back, Kwat exclaimed, "I don't understand. It's been too long since my brother went to get the saltwater. He must have gotten lost. You, our brother, you must try to find him. And you, our other brother, take this bamboo and go get some water."

The two brothers left like the first one and climbed into the ironwood tree. Nobody came back. Then, Kwat said to one of the brothers that had stayed behind, "They must be amusing themselves on the beach. Go and find them."
Each time, Kwasvar acquiesced, "Yes, that's a good idea."

Thus, all the brothers left and went to climb the tree. Finally, Kwat said to Kwasvar, "You are an imbecile," and he sprinted towards the tree. Kwasvar suddenly realized the trick that had been played on him and he ran after Kwat brandishing the *nalnal* that he used to kill pigs. While running, Kwat had picked up a *por,* which is *"laplap* bag" in the language of Vanua Lava. The two ran around and around the *kwaranis,* that pit of burning hot stones where everything is baked. Kwat opened the pit without being caught and one by one put the steaming taros into the *por*. Finally, when his bag was full, he took off towards the tree with Kwasvar hot on his trail.

Kwat started to sing and the tree pushed its way up towards the sky. Then Kwat requested of the tree, "Lower yourself until you touch the ground of Vanua Lava."

The tree bent itself double and the men from Vanua Lava jumped to the ground. Kwat let all of his brothers jump down ahead of him while he stayed behind to fend off Kwasvar. When Kwasvar wanted to jump down as well, Kwat told him, "No! We don't want you here. You were too rude to us. You'd be better off in the sky."

The ironwood tree sprang back up and catapulted Kwasvar high, high into the sky. Kwasvar, terrified, gave a demented scream.

This legend was given to me in the vernacular by James Barton of Mota.
John Atkin translated it into Bislama. Adapted by Paul Gardissat.

Nabanga n°91-93 (1978)

The devils' nasara from Sarevugvug
(Vanua Lava)

One day, a man from Tagtan took some bananas and went to meet a friend from Surlau. The same day, the man from Surlau had a similar idea and followed the shore all the way to Tatgan. This was how the two men met halfway between the villages of Tagtan and Surlau. They promised each other that the next day they would take a picnic to a place called Kwarang Pura, situated on top of a big rock. Meanwhile, while the two men were discussing their plans, a passing devil heard them.

He said to himself, "I'm going to introduce myself to the man from Tagtan and he will become my friend. I'll make myself look like his friend from Surlau and I'll take him to the *nasara*. We'll dance with all the devils and this will give him a good glance of the underworld."

The next day, just as the two men had planned, the man from Tagtan left his house in search of his friend. However, the devil from the day before had already waylaid the man from Surlau and taken on his appearance. When the two men finally met up, the man from Tagtan didn't suspect a thing: he didn't even realise that he was in the company of a devil. The two started walking, following the shore until they got to Kwarang Pura, the place where they had decided to have a picnic. The two men started to bow fish. The human shot and often missed his target. The devil, though, never missed his prey. After having finished fishing on the reef, the two went all the way to the gardens in the bush and started to unearth yams. The white ones were for the man and the red ones were for the devil. They set to cooking them with the fish until everything was ready. The devil then divided the food into two portions. While eating, the brave man noticed that his neighbour did not chew his food. It was thus, by observing his neighbour out of the corner of his eye, that he realised that he was in the presence of a devil and not a man. He wasn't too worried, however, and continued eating.

Both of them were full when the devil said to the man from Tagtan, "It's almost nighttime. Come, I want to invite you to be my guest this evening. Let's go dance with the other devils at the top of the hill. I call it Sarevugvug, or the devils' *nasara.*"

The two men started to climb the hill when the devil again spoke to the man, saying, "Let's take along some of those little mushrooms that glow in the dark."

The two of them picked many mushrooms and placed them in a taro leaf which they then filled with water. The mushrooms began to show like stars in the night sky. The devil spoke again.

"We should also bring a dry branch from the breadfruit tree. Break it in two and carry it with you."

Then the devil and the man went to dance with the demons. While they were dancing, the other devils smelled the scent of a fresh man.

They said, "Hey! There is a man dancing among us this evening! Yum-yum! He smells good! We should capture him and eat him!"

However, the devil that had taken on the appearance of the man from Surlau responded, " No, look! There is no one else except us, the inhabitants of the Underworld. What if we closed our eyes to help us concentrate on the dance a little more?"

Turning towards the man from Tagtan, the devil whispered, "You must keep your ears well tuned. If not, you'll end up in their empty stomachs. All the devils have their eyes closed right now, but things will get a little more complicated later on. If you ever hear the signal given by one of the devils to open your eyes, you should take out the taro leaf and shake it. This will make all the mushrooms glow and tremble on the leaf. The devils will see them and think they are the eyes of one of their own. And if ever the signal is given to shake your bones, you should take out the pieces of wood and smack them against each other. They'll hear the noise that you make and think that it is their own bones groaning and creaking."

The man followed all the advice that the devil had given him. The dance was quickly reaching its most intense point when one of the devils stepped forward to give a signal.

"Alright, everyone open your eyes!"

As planned, the man lifted up the taro leaf full of water and mushrooms. The devils, amazed by the intense luminosity, exclaimed, "Oh, yes! He's definitely one of ours! Definitely!"

Then, everyone started dancing even harder. Again, one of the devils stepped forward to give a signal.
"Alright, let's shake our bones!"

At this signal, the man banged his sticks together. The devils, having noticed nothing out of the ordinary, said, "Very good! And now we need someone to play the *tamtam.*"

The kind devil then said to his friend the man, "I'm going to go now and sing a very long song. During this time, all the elders, all the men and all the women, all the children, all the boys and all the girls, indeed, all the devils from this island will start dancing. This will be the only time that you'll be able to escape with your bones intact. You should run as quickly as you can!"

The man took the advice of his friend the devil. The devil started to sing. Every devil started to dance. At the same time, the man snuck off. He started to run for his life.

He ran like a crazy man, following the shore that led to his house. There was no sand on the shore, only big black rocks. He ran, jumped and climbed, scaling rock after rock. From time to time, he hid, breathing hard and listening for his eventual pursuers. He was almost out of breath and sweating hard, but he kept running because his house was in sight.

It was then that the devils' dance ended. Every one of the devils could smell fresh man now. The kind devil felt that he could no longer hold off the other demons. He said, "You're all crazy! We were dancing with a man!"

One of the devils jumped to his feet and went after the man. Hunger, mixed with anger, gave him wings and he arrived very quickly at the man's village. The very moment when the devil was going to attack in all his fury, the man slipped into his house and banged the door shut.

The devil found himself in front of a closed door. He was furious, but the only thing to do was to turn around and go back to where he came from. He walked all night long, and it was only in the early morning that he trudged into Sarevugvug, the devils' *nasara*.

This legend was told by James Barton from the Banks.
It was collected and transcribed by John Atkin.
It was originally published in Bislama.

Nabanga n°14 (25/10/75)

Wenagon and his two daughters
(Gaua)

Once upon a time, on Gaua in the Banks islands, there was a man named Wenagon. Wenagon means "joker." This man had twin daughters approximately ten years of age. This sly man spent his life playing mean tricks on his neighbours. One day, he wanted to have a laugh at the expense of his daughters, so he pretended to fall gravely ill. Seeing this, the twins started to light a big fire to warm their father who appeared to be trembling with fever.

Several minutes later, Wenagon sat up feebly and said, "Please my daughters, go fish some shrimp from the first pool of water in the stream. Don't go near the second pool or the third. Scoop out all the water in the first pool and you will easily fill your baskets with shrimp."

Picking up their baskets, a sort of tool with two compartments that made fishing easier, and a scoop made from coconut palm, the girls started walking up the hill that lead to the pools in the stream. After they had left, Wenagon got up from his bed. Then he took off his robe and picked a *nasorsor* flower that he then fixed to the bamboo wall of his hut. He took off running, completely naked, towards the stream. He took a shortcut that only was only known to him and so arrived very quickly at the first pool in the stream. Wenagon then dove into the water and hid himself under a large black stone. A moment later, the twins arrived at the pool. They immediately started to scoop out the water. When they had finally emptied the pool, they filled their baskets with thousands of shrimp. All of a sudden, they heard a noise coming from under the big black stone. One of the girls bent down to examine a hole hidden under the stone.

She cried out, "Hey! Come and see! It's a huge eel! Bring a big stick!"

The other sister brought the stick and they tried to harpoon the big eel. When the stick jabbed him for the first time, their father, hidden under the stone, jumped. In doing so, a bit of his hand became visible to the girls. When the stick jabbed him a second time, Wenagon exposed just a little more of his hand. At the third jab, the man jumped again and his hand became completely visible to the two girls. Seeing this, the terrified twins ran like the wind to their own house. Wenagon then came out of his hiding place, took up the baskets of shrimp abandoned by his daughters, and followed his shortcut to the house once again. Arriving just a moment before the girls, he lit a big fire in the kitchen, rolled in the ashes, and pretended to be sick again.

When the girls arrived completely out of breath, he said to them, "Hey! You two, where's the fire? Why are you so out of breath?"

"We saw a monster!"

"A monster! What did it look like?"

"It looked like a hand!"

"You must have seen a giant eel!"

"No, we're telling you the truth. We saw a monster! We saw his hand come up from under the big black stone in the first pool of the stream."

A little while later, when they were preparing dinner, the girls realised that the shrimp they were cooking were those that they had fished from the stream. They then understood that the hand that they had seen in the pool was that of their father. Fed up with his antics, they went to their father and made him understand that they were old enough to live alone. Wenagon burst into tears and begged them not to leave.

"I'm begging you! Don't leave me! The three of us should stay together! I'm begging you! Don't go!"

"We're sorry, father. But you have already humiliated us enough. We're old enough to get by without you now."

Wenagon took two big baskets full of shell money and handed them to the girls by way of reconciliation. However, the twins were not interested in money. Instead, they gathered up their possessions and went to live far from their father. This is why Wenagon, "the joker," finished his life alone.

This legend was told by Edgel Weting Asbal from the village
of Losolava on Gaua in the Banks.
Originally appear in Bislama.

Nabanga n°26 (10/04/76)

SANMA Province

SANTO

MALO

The Namalao Cave

(Santo)

Once upon a time, there was a young married couple. Both of them were relatively happy. However, before getting married, the woman had met another man and she couldn't stop thinking about him. One day, an idea hit her like a lightning bolt.

"How could I get rid of my husband? That's it! I've got it!"

Across from Big Bay there was a cave full of birds. These birds were called *namalao* and are occasionally known to eat small chickens. In order to catch them, men often went to this big cave on the side of a hill: the *Namalao* Cave. To catch this bird, one must climb all the way to the top of a hill and then attach a vine to a big tree trunk that is just above the entry to the cave. Then the vine must be lowered into the mouth of the cave. This is the only way to get inside to hunt the *namalao*. Once they have been caught, the birds must be secured by their feet with little vines. Someone must be waiting on top to pull up the vine at the right signal. This is how *namalaos* must be hunted.

The woman was thinking of this hill and the cave in particular.

Some time later, she said to her husband, "I would really like to eat some *namalao* today."

"Sorry," he responded, "if you had told me yesterday, I would have gone. But today, it is too late. I think it would be better to put that off until tomorrow..."

"But... it's still early... and I really have a craving!"

So they set off together. They walked through the night and into early morning until they reached the *namalao* refuge. They climbed to the top of the hill, cut a vine, attached it to the trunk of the big tree and let it fall into the hole. The man was careful to cut many little vines and take them with him in order to bind the birds.

Then he said to his wife, "You wait here for me. I'll catch the *namalao,* attach them with these vines and then call up to you. When I do, you pull up the rope."

The woman responded, "Yes, I'll do everything you tell me to do."

The man then lowered himself into the cave. As soon as he was inside, he saw three sleeping *namalao.* He caught and bound them and then headed back to the mouth of the cave. However, to his great consternation, he found that the vine had fallen to the floor. The man was at a loss. How would he climb back out of the cave? He could only vaguely see the entrance to the cave and so, very sad, started to cry. At the bottom of his hole, he started to think, "The only thing left for me to do is to wait here." Hunger pangs started to bother him and so he killed a *namalao* and ate it. He did this until there weren't any *namalao* left. Finally, without either water or food, he fell to thinking about how to save his life. Suddenly, he had an idea.

He told himself, "I'm going to try to catch a lot of *namalao*. That way, I can tie them together and they can fly me out of the cave to the top of the hill." And, without stopping to pause, he started to capture the *namalao* until he had close to one hundred.

Days soon became weeks until the man had spent more than three months trapped at the bottom of the cave. He was only skin and bones. Hunched over, he could neither talk nor call out. He couldn't even moan. He had, though, been able to assemble all the birds into one group attached at the wings by vines. When he was ready, he shook the cords and the birds flew out of the cave with the man trailing behind them.

But there were too many *namalao*. Some wanted to fly to the west, others towards the east. They couldn't decide in what direction to fly. The man, still holding on to the birds, only rose and fell in the sky. This is how he was able to grab on to a coconut palm. He climbed to the top of the tree and, looking down, realised that he was looking into his uncle's garden. Then, he freed the *namalao* that had saved his life.

The man was left alone on the palm tree. A little while later, he saw someone approaching. A man was coming towards him to dig up some *kumala*. From his perch, the man in the tree looked at the approaching man but could not call out. His voice had disappeared. Suddenly, he realised that the man coming towards him was his uncle. Yes! There was the tattoo on his arm that he knew so well. The man in the tree picked a green coconut and threw it at his uncle's feet. The uncle heard the coconut fall and was surprised to see that the fruit that had fallen was still green.

He called out, "Hey! Who's making these coconuts fall? A flying fox? This coconut is still fresh!"

He then lifted his head and saw the man sitting in the palm tree.

"Who are you? Are you a man or are you a devil?'

The man didn't say anything and continued to stare at his uncle. He then picked another green coconut, drew his uncle's tattoo on it, and threw it to the ground. When the uncle finally realised that it was his nephew who had disappeared without a trace, he climbed up into the tree. He put his nephew over his shoulder, climbed down, and went to his house.

Arriving there, he said to his wife, "This man needs something to eat and drink."

In his uncle's house, the man started to regain his strength as well as his voice. As soon as he could speak, he told the story of how his wife had betrayed him. The uncle called all the men in the village to his house and told them what had happened.

He said, "Tomorrow, in the middle of the night, all the strong men will come with me. We'll go to the village of this woman and kill all the men, all the women, and all the children. There must be no survivors."

The next day, all the strong men followed the uncle. In the middle of the night, they arrived at the woman's village. They went into the first house that they saw and started to yell. A child woke up and looked at them. The men cut his throat. They did the same to all the women and all the men. Before the nephew went into his wife's house, he called to her. When she woke up, she knew who was outside. The *namalao* man wanted to speak with her. When she stood beside her true husband she was very surprised and very, very sorry. But it was too late. The man asked her a first question. The woman then had her legs broken and finally cut off. The man asked her a second question and her two arms were broken. When he asked the last question, the woman's neck was snapped and her head fell to the ground.

Finally, the man went to join the others to finish the massacre. They did not stop until every person in the village was dead. The next day, a large feast was held in honour of the man who came to live in his uncle's village.

Even today, if you go to Big Bay at Biapot, on the side of the hill, you can still see the *namalao* cave!

The story that you have read was written in Bislama by Elda Sope Kalsrap from Pango
at the Presbyterian College of Tangoa in South Santo.

Having appeared originally in Bislama,
this story was translated into English for this edition.

Nabanga n°21 (1976)

The tamed lisepsep of Santo
(Santo)

A man from Santo wanted to leave his native village to go and live in a neighbouring village. Naturally, he couldn't take all of his belongings so he left his herd of pigs in his native village. Because it broke his heart to have abandoned them, he returned each morning to bring them some food. The animals became accustomed to seeing him. Every day, at the same time, they would gather together, ready to be fed. The man didn't even need to go looking for them. This lasted for a long time. The man would have liked for it to last even longer, but he didn't take into account a certain *lisepsep*.

One lovely morning, the man came as usual to see his pigs and his native village. So accustomed was he to this daily ritual, that he noticed immediately if anything was out of place. Something was indeed wrong. No pigs came to be fed. He called to them, yelled with all of his strength, but nothing. Bitterly disappointed, he took the basket of food destined for the pigs and left. While walking, he convinced himself that nothing serious had happened. It was possible that one of the pigs had died and the others stayed close to it rather than coming to eat their daily meal. Maybe later in the day the pigs would be hungry.

"I will return and leave the basket and all the food. It would be stupid for my pigs to go hungry like this."

The man returned as he said he would and left the basket. He walked back to the neighbouring village, but he still felt uneasy. The missed morning ritual wasn't normal; it just wasn't natural. There must have been something extraordinary behind it. Impatience, winning the day, pushed the man to return to his native village. Nothing could compare to his surprise when he saw his herd rush towards him. However, his astonishment grew when he saw that all the food had already been eaten.

"This is absolutely incredible. My pigs are hungry but there isn't any food left from what I had put here for them! Well, we'll see about this!"

The next day, the same thing happened, and again every day thereafter for three days. It was too much. The man searched the surrounding area looking for the key to the mystery. Looking down, he saw a footprint, a footprint like that of a child.

"Ah, I understand! It's a *lisepsep* that is playing this horrible trick on me. Well, we shall see what we shall see."

In the village where he now lived, the man warned the men that a *lisepsep* was happily eating all of his pigs' food.

"You understand that this cannot last. My herd will die of hunger. I suggest that we go in search of the *lisepsep* quickly, tomorrow for example."

The decision seemed wise. The next day, very early, the man headed up a group of sixty men from the village. Once they arrived in the other village, the chief of the group looked for his pigs. He didn't see them. After a week of this, he had become used to it. He began calling and yelling with all of his might. Nothing. So he climbed up a *namambe* and hung his basket full of provisions for the pigs. He descended very quickly and acted like he was going back to the other village. But as soon as he was at a suitable distance, he quickly hid in the bushes with his sixty companions. During this time, the *lisepsep* was doing all he could to stop the pigs from approaching the tree where the basket was hung. But seven minutes later, believing the man to be far away, the dwarf decided to free the animals that arrived at a gallop under the *namambe*.

In the bushes, the look-outs cried, "There are the pigs! The *lisepsep* must be close behind."

Sure enough, the *lisepsep* came charging towards the tree on the back of a big pig. Very quickly, he jumped to the ground and climbed the tree like a cat. He sat on the branch where the basket still hung, and started to eat. The provisions, ample enough to feed a herd of swine, quickly filled him up. It was at this moment that the men decided to grab the *lisepsep*. Slowly, walking on their tiptoes, the men approached the tree. Their goal was to stop the dwarf from coming down. However, one of the men became frightened.

"No, I don't want to go! A *lisepsep* is supernatural, and we never know what it will do. No, I won't go! I'm too afraid."

The plan was ruined. The man who owned the pigs made the decision to send two volunteers up the tree to try and catch the dwarf who was drowsing happily after his meal. Courageously, the two men climbed the *namambe,* but at the moment that they were to surprise the *lisepsep,* he saw them! He gave a malicious laugh and in one jump, landed safely on the ground, well beyond the men waiting at the foot of the tree.

Unfortunately for him, the dwarf fell precisely into the bag that the coward had left behind. Having followed this scene with their eyes, the man that had led the whole village threw himself at the bag and tried to grab the dwarf by the feet. Lively and agile, the latter was able to grab the man's head. The other men from the village leapt to their friend's aid. But what can one do against a *lisepsep* that is as big as a seven year old child but as strong as a herd of pigs? The battle raged, but the men seemed vanquished from the start.

Yet, a man from the village remembered what he had heard on the island. He had been told that to defeat a *lisepsep,* one must cut his hair! He would lose his power at the same time as his hair. Why not try? Without waiting, he grabbed a knife.

"Hold it, men! Let me do it. I will get to the end of this dwarf."

The men backed off. In one gesture, the man threw his knife and the blade shaved off the *lisepsep's* hair. The dwarf fell to the ground, emptied of all strength. He retained his malicious and sly air, but he was, at present, inoffensive. The sixty men escorted him all the way to their village, savouring their victory. But on the way, the *lisepsep* said strange things.

"It is true that I am your prisoner and that you have won against me and that I am without strength. But I can be very useful to you. However, you must respect certain rules. You must never let me sleep on the ground, let me choose my own lodgings, and you must never play the flute or the *tamtam*. If you do exactly as I have told you, you will not regret it."

At first, the men from the village laughed at this speech, but little by little they realized that maybe it should be taken seriously.

"After all, this dwarf has already shown us his strength. It's true that he might be useful. We have only to follow his advice. Let him choose his own shelter, and maybe he will help us!"

The dwarf, overhearing the men's discussion, reminded them, "You must never play the flute or touch the *tamtam*. Don't forget, no flute, no *tamtam*."

The *lisepsep* chose to reside in a large *tamtam*. He would have been forgotten if strange things had not started happening. A man had but to say, "I feeling like eating fish," and the next morning he would find the fruits of a miraculous catch in his hut. If a woman wanted to go to the river to wash some clothes, she didn't have to lift a finger. The dwarf took care of it. Or if a garden needed to be weeded, the *lisepsep* started working without having to be given a single order. The village became a virtual paradise. Men and women lived in harmony, free of any material woes. All this could have lasted a very long time, but...

One day, a man from a neighbouring village came to visit his friends. They spoke a long time about the *lisepsep* whose reputation had become known all over Santo. However, no one had told him about the *lisepsep's* recommendations. The story of the dwarf's exploits lasted a long while, so long that the quickly falling night surprised the stranger. He did not want to return to his village through the bush at night. It was so dark in there that no star could pierce the blackness. Thus, he accepted his friends' invitation to sleep in the village.

Very early the next morning, an earthquake abruptly woke them. Everyone was used to the tremors that came from time to time, but this one was particularly violent. The man from the neighbouring village became frightened. He rose hastily and ran towards the large *tamtam* and began to beat it. This was the custom when something bad had happened.

But alas, he had done just what the *lisepsep* had always forbidden. Wakened abruptly, the lisepsep jumped out of his lodgings. Someone had beaten his *tamtam!* Supple and agile, he lunged towards the stranger and hit him so violently that the man fell to the ground unconscious. The dwarf then took advantage of the situation to escape into the bush.

The whole village despaired. They had just lost their good luck charm because a stranger had ignored their new custom. It was too bad! The men pursued the *lisepsep* through the bush, but he was already very far away. Arriving at the shore, the *lisepsep* followed the reef into the deep water. The men saw him and without hesitating, plunged into the water in an attempt to catch him. But in turn, the dwarf dived and disappeared forever. The men searched a long time, but they could find no trace of him.

When they had returned to the village, the men cried and lamented bitterly the loss of such a precious companion. The *lisepsep* was never seen again in Santo. But maybe, if you dive, you will come upon him. He will surely pull a few tricks to amuse himself, but if you know how to catch him by cutting his hair, he will do many wonderful things for you. And if you are this lucky, follow his advice and don't let any friend remain unaware of his recommendations. If you do, you will lose him like the inhabitants of Santo, and a *lisepsep* is not easy to find!

Broadcast "Alors...Raconte!" Radio Port-Vila

Maliu the fisherman and the giant eel
(Santo)

A long time ago, on the island of Santo at the foot of Tabwemasana, there was a river in which everyone liked to swim. This river was a special favourite for divers. One day, a young man named Vanao decided to go diving in this very river. He stayed for a long time, appreciating the fresh, clear water. Suddenly, he saw an interesting stone. He dived to the bottom of the river and, giving in to his intense curiosity, lifted up the stone. There, he found a gigantic eel. It was so big that Vanao was afraid to kill it. Quickly, he got out of the river, ran up the bank, and hurried home. When he reached to his village, Vanao told everyone about his discovery.

"We must go look for Maliu," the villagers said.

Though old, Maliu was still considered the best diver in the area. No one had ever been able to rival his feats. So, it was decided that he would be the man to kill the gigantic Santo eel. Maliu arrived the next day, having been told by a friend that some people wanted to meet with him. He seemed very confident.

"Alright! We shall go to the foot of Tabwemasana right away. Then, we shall see what this is all about!"

Preparations were made. Pandanus baskets were filled with important staples: taro, *manioc,* yams and bananas. There was so much food that the men could have withstood a siege. It must be said that the men were not overly anxious to get under way.

Finally, they arrived next to the river and pitched camp on the bank. The food was spread out on a big, flat stone. A few men went to find some dry wood with which to make a fire. Unconcerned with these domestic tasks, the old Maliu was getting ready to dive. His goal was simple: dive directly to the large stone, uncover the giant eel and kill it so that people could once again dive in the river without being afraid. The old man jumped into the water. The men on the bank waited a long time for him to resurface. As the minutes ticked by, their worry grew. The diver could no longer be seen and time was slipping away like the waters in the stream. Forty five minutes had gone by when one of the men cried out.

"Look! Blood! There's blood over there!"

All along the bank, there rose up cries of joy. Maliu had killed the giant eel and the people could once again swim without being afraid.

Unfortunately, this was not the case. After waiting for several agonizing hours, the villagers began to give up hope. It was not the man that had won but the eel. Old Maliu had been swallowed by the eel. Since this day, the river at the foot of Tabwemasana has been considered tabu. Indeed, foolish would be the diver that, like old Maliu, wanted to disturb the eel under its rock!

Broadcast "Alors...Raconte!" Radio Port-Vila

The legend of the namarae from Santo
(Santo)

A long time ago, on Santo at the foot of Tabwemasana, the highest summit of the island, there was a village just like any of the other numerous villages across the archipelago. However, life in this village depended upon a little spring that came from a rock and then disappeared a little further on into the stony ground. It was in this little stream that a *namarae,* or eel if you prefer, had chosen to live. This *namarae* was enormous. Each time a person crossed the stream on foot, they walked on its body thinking that it was the trunk of a palm tree. The *namarae's* body was so big that this mistake was easy to make, especially because algae had started to grow on its back, making the eel completely unrecognisable.

One day, however, a keen observer from the village realized that this trunk was actually a *namarae.* A little frightened by this discovery, the man ran back to his village to announce his findings. The other villagers were stupefied when they heard what this man had to say. Just to be sure, everyone went to the edge of the stream. Each person in their turn was able to identify the *namarae.*

Their discussion went like this:

"We should kill this *namarae,*" some said very enthusiastically.

The man who had first discovered the *namarae* was a little more reserved. "No, we shouldn't kill it. If we do that, it will bring us bad luck."

The discussion took a different turn.

"And why, pray tell, do you think that we would have bad luck by killing this eel when we have eaten many others without so much as a worry?"

Each person gave his opinion, but almost everyone wanted to kill the beast. The biggest challenge was to convince he who had been the keenest observer among them. The discussion continued for a long time, but finally the majority won. They decided to kill the *namarae* and then eat it. A villager got a spear and put the animal to death.

Once the *namarae* was dead, the village became very active. Some people were put in charge of finding the leaves for the *laplap* while others went to find food to accompany the meat. However, all this activity did not reassure the man who had first discovered the *namarae.* He went looking for his wife and son.

"Listen to me. If someone brings you something to eat later on, do not accept it! As for me, I have to go and keep the others company, but I will only be acting. In reality, I refuse to eat this gigantic eel."

After having said this, the man returned to his friends. The *laplap* was already in the oven, and it was barely eleven o'clock when they took it out. To everyone's big surprise, the leaves had stayed just as green as they would have been had they not been put in the oven. Once again, the discussions began.

"We were in too much of a hurry. We shouldn't have taken it out of the oven right away."

Each person gave their own opinion with even more force this time because of the worry that had started to nag them.

"It's not normal, though, that nothing has been cooked. The fire was at its hottest. We're not crazy; the stones were good and hot!"

Another man spoke up. "Maybe we put on too many leaves. We should put the *laplap* back in the oven, but this time we'll take off some of the leaves."

Everyone thought that this was a wise solution, and so it was done. The moment the *laplap* was put back in the oven, a kingfisher started to swoop around the man that had found the *namarae*. This man was now utterly convinced that bad luck was on its way. In haste, he went to find his wife and son.

"I don't think that we should stay here," he said. "When we start to eat in a little while, you should leave. Don't worry about me, I'll come and join you. You have only to wait."

This new advice given, the man left to find his companions. He found them once again in deep discussion. Their problem was deciding what to do if they found that the *laplap* was once again uncooked. A little later, the villagers apprehensively took the *laplap* from the oven. Again, the leaves had retained their original appearance. The mystery, though, became even bigger when they realised that the pieces of *namarae* inside were done to perfection.

Everyone decided to eat anyway. The men sat down in a circle. One of them started to taste the *laplap*. Everyone hung on his movements, waiting for the verdict.

"Is it good or not?"

The man tasted it, smacking his lips to be sure.

"It's absolutely fantastic!"

Everyone felt very relieved. They all set to with sharpened appetites. The men seemed to be enjoying themselves so much that some of the women started to taste it as well. After a while, though, the first man to have tasted the eel started to feel ill.

"You probably ate too much! Me, in any case, I love it!"

Nobody paid any attention to his illness, but the man started to feel more and more uncomfortable. Suddenly, he looked down at his legs. How awful! He realised with disbelief that they had become one big block of flesh. His shock grew even more when, before his very eyes, this mass of skin turned into a magnificent *namarae* tail. To hide what the others hadn't seen, the man covered the bottom half of his body with some *laplap* leaves.

However, it didn't take long for the others to start having the same symptoms. Everyone felt ill, and everyone realised with horror that their legs had turned into magnificent *namarae* tails. Nobody dared say anything. Each person wanted to hide their handicap from their neighbour. Soon, nobody was moving; the villagers looked at each other without saying anything. Without understanding exactly what was happening, the man that had discovered the *namarae* realised that the atmosphere had become heavy and something strange was happening. Quickly, he got up and ran towards the mountains to join his wife and son.

Arriving at Tabwemasana, he turned back to look at his friends and was shocked by what he saw. The first man that had tasted the *laplap* wanted to get up, but was unable to do so. Not to be undone, he tried to pull himself up on all fours, but his arms started to shrink and then disappeared all together. Presently, he looked like an eel. Of his human form, only his head remained. Soon, this mutation happened to everyone in the village who had tasted the eel.

On the mountain, the man was shaken by witnessing such an event, but he didn't have much time to think about it. Suddenly, he heard a loud noise coming from the coast. A huge torrent rushed towards the village and swallowed it up along with all the eel-men. When the man had heard the noise, he had run towards higher ground to join his wife and son. He hugged them tightly in his arms and looked down at a stretch of water that can still be seen today at the foot of Tabwemasana.

Some say that one can still find enormous eels, but nobody dares to fish for them: the water is taboo!

Nabanga n°18 (20/12/75)

The legend of Taribowe
(Santo)

At this time, at the foot of Tabwemasana, the highest summit on the island of Santo, there was a village. It was in this little village that the flute was played, the flute of all men from Santo. This little village in the middle of the big island was called Boesisil. The village, clinging to rocky slopes, was located just a little under Nokobula, which was the highest village of Tabwemasana. At Boesisil, there was a simple *nakamal* constructed like all *nakamal* in Santo. One entered into the building by a little door and inside one would find beds made of bamboo. Next to each of these beds was a fire that burnt day and night. It was cold indeed on top of that giant peak. Taribowe was the chief of the village. He was a mountain man, very strong but little, just like the majority of the men from his region. He was a very short man that walked very quickly on strong legs. Taribowe had ten wives, wives who tended his pigs and his gardens. He was a chief and the women lived next to him in the village, but not with him. They lived in huts with the pigs, near him.

One day, one of the wives became pregnant. And what happened then? Well, it was very curious and unexplainable. The other women were jealous and a dispute between the wives ensued. The pregnant woman took the coals from her fire and threw them into the bush. Then she took her mat and burned it. Finally, she packed the few pieces of jewellery that she had, bracelets made from *troca* shell, little sticks of seashell that she put in her nose, and she started to cry. She cried and cried because her heart was broken. She cried and she sang, she sang for her sadness. Then, she ran away down the mountains, through streams and rivers, crossing the great Jordan, and finally arriving at Big Bay in the village of Malao.

That evening the men of the village spoke to her and said, "You should stay here with us."

"No, I must continue on my way."

She left Malao and continued to follow the coast. She walked. She, the woman from the mountains, followed the sea. She was not used to the beach and finally arrived at Malotsitsiriki.

Again, the men of this village spoke to her saying, "Stay with us. We are in need of women in our village."

"No, you see, I want to go far, far away. Very far. I must leave."

And the woman took up her path once again. She left the Big Bay area and arrived at Nagogu. However, this village did not please her and she continued on until she reached Tasmate on the west coast. There, she felt at home and she built herself a house. Time passed and, one day, the woman gave birth to a child. It was a boy.

He grew and grew until he was able to say to his mother, "Mother, I want you to make me a bow and some arrows."

His mother made him his bow and his arrows. The young boy went into the woods with them to kill birds. He saw one on the edge of a branch. He pulled back his bow and sighted his target, but the bird had disappeared. He saw the bird alight further away, so he pulled back his bow and shot but the bird had once again flown off. Little by little the boy was drawn further into the woods by the bird, until he found himself in front of a white substance called 'salt' by men. The bird had intended for the boy to find the salt. It was a discovery that would serve him later; the mountain men come to find salt on the seashore because it does not usually exist in the bush.

The bird alighted on the big white pile and disappeared. The boy could no longer see his prey. The young boy could only see the salt. Then, he picked some *burao* leaves and by sewing them together he made a basket. He filled this basket with the salt and closed it by using the supple bark of the same *burao*. He took the basket back and hung it near the fire in his hut.

In Tasmate, the villagers needed to buy pigs. However, they had a problem because none of them had any.

One of them said, "At Boesisil, in the mountains, there is a big chief who has many pigs. We have often heard tell of him, but we do not know the path to his village."

"I know the road! I can show it to you! Taribowe is my father."

"Kindly shut up, young boy, you were born here and don't know anything."

"Yes, I do! I know that man and I know the path through the mountains. Come and I'll show you."

"Alright, if you're telling us the truth, you go on ahead and show us the path."

The young boy took up his basket of salt and marched into the forest, the men following him. They went through the thick woods of Santo and walked between the mountains. They walked through big rivers, little mountains, and little streams. They walked up and they walked down. That's Santo for you. Finally, they arrived at the source of the river Apuna. From on top of this mountain, one may see the vast horizon stretching out from Santo.

"Do you see that big banyan on the last mountain? At the foot of this banyan is my father's village."

And with this, they took off again. They crossed the Apuna River, climbed the flanks of Tabwemasana and arrived in the village of Boesisil.

"This is my father!"

However, because Taribowe was not expecting them and thus had not changed into his chiefly regalia, the men from Tasmate did not recognise him.

"This man is not Taribowe."

"Wait just a little. He will first go to the garden and then he will come back."

Taribowe went to the garden, dug up some yams, and then sent one of his wives to get a basket that she filled with pigs' tusks and brought to him. Taribowe took out the pigs' tusks and replaced them with yams. The woman slung the basket around her forehead just like all women from Santo do when they're carrying baskets. Then, she returned to the village. In the garden, Taribowe put the tusks on his arms one after the other and then tied a *namele* leaf above his buttocks. When he arrived in the *nasara,* the men were surprised.

"This is my father."

"Yes! That is Taribowe!"

"And you thought that I was lying! Taribowe really is my father. Look at him!"

While the women were preparing the yams, the men started to dance. In the centre of the *nasara,* the old men hit the floor with bamboo poles while, around them, the guests danced. Taribowe danced with them as a sign of welcome. The dances lasted for two days and at the end, the guests bought nine pigs from Taribowe.

The chief then told his son, "I want some salt. What price do you ask? Choose from among my pigs. Do you want this one?"

The young boy did not look happy.

"How about this one?"

No, he was not interested.

"And the one that has the tusks that turn twice?"

But his son still did not agree. Then, Taribowe showed him a female, a pregnant female. He crushed her belly and she immediately gave birth to a piglet.

"This one? Do you want it?"

"Yes! That's the one that I want!"

The men were satisfied and took their leave of Taribowe to start on the long trek home. Once they had arrived at the Apuna River, the whole group stopped to rest. When the young boy let his piglet walk alongside the other pigs bought from Taribowe, one of the pigs died. The men then started walking again. As they climbed the Tavol Mountain another pig died, and the young boy's piglet doubled in size. The group continued on and went down into the River Tavol. Another pig died suddenly and young Taribowe's piglet grew again. They then arrived at the hill called Nokobula. They passed between two mountains and yet another pig died. Young Taribowe's pig had now become enormous. It even had tusks that looped twice around themselves. The group continued its walk. They arrived at the summit of the mountain that overlooked Tasmate village and the last pig died. Finally, the men from Tasmate became angry.

"He's to blame! Let's kill him!"

The young Taribowe turned to one of his friends and said, "If they kill me, take care of my pig. I'm giving it to you."

The men then killed the young boy. They started to fight about who would get ownership of the pig. However, Taribowe's friend intervened.

"This pig is mine. He gave it to me."

The group once again got under way. They crossed the fields of white grass and the sea winds blew around them. Suddenly, one of the men saw something.

"Oh! Look over there at that black dot on the pile of salt. Over there on the shore! It's him! It's the young Taribowe! Don't forget that that pig is his! Let's go!"

When they came close to the young Taribowe, he proudly approached them. His pig rolled itself at his feet in pleasure. The men from Tasmate decided then and there to choose the young man as their chief.

"Thank you for having the confidence in me," said Taribowe. "I am your chief, so let's dance!"

And the dances began...

This legend was given by Chief Tinol from Matantas on Santo.

*This legend appeared originally in French
on the radio and in Bislama in Nabanga.*

The life and death of Mol Malamala
(Malo)

Once upon a time, on the hills of Malo Island, there was a very famous man. His name was Mol Malamala. This man owned much land and had many riches such as a *nakamal*, yam fields, taro, banana trees, and a host of chicken and pigs. He had worked hard since a young age to gain all of these riches. He was very respected by those around him because he contributed greatly to trade within his village and with other islands.

At this time, the people of Malo were especially keen on trading ceremonial pigs for mats from Ambae, Maewo, and Pentecost. They even traded with the islets at the northeast of Malekula, Santo, and other neighbouring islands. However, despite all of this hard work, our friend Mol Malamala was bored to death because he lived alone.

"Who will inherit all these riches when I am no longer of this world? One day, my fellow, you'll have to end this lonely life and ensure that you have some descendants so that they will be able to take over the inheritance," he often said to himself while sitting alone next to a fire after a long day of working, hunting or fishing.

One day, Mol Malamala married a woman named Ahae who came from a neighbouring village. He paid for her in yams and ceremonial pigs with rounded tusks. During the first days of their married life, the man did all the domestic chores so that his wife could take full advantage of their honeymoon.

However, when Mol Malamala was ready to go to work again, he wanted to turn the domestic chores over to Ahae.

He called to her and said, "Darling, would you go and get us a little dry wood, please? While you do that, I'll go into the fields and get us some food."
"No, I don't want to. Do it yourself, just like you've always done!"
"In that case, will you go find some germinating coconuts to feed the pigs?"
"No, I didn't come here to take care of your pigs!"
"Alright, you can sweep the *nakamal...*"
"No way! I'm neither your slave nor your servant."

Mol Malamala, terribly disappointed, felt like committing suicide. He went into his *nakamal* and took all the curved ceremonial pigs' tusks, called *ase mansa* in the language of Malo, that he owned. These tusks were bound together by a rope made of coconut fibre. He then climbed up to the top of the hill behind his home. Once he had arrived at the top, he started to sing. He sang loudly so that his wife could hear him from the house. He sang this way for a long time.

His wife who was sleeping lazily in their hut thought she heard a song coming from far, far away.

"I think that I'm imagining things... there's nobody around for miles. Perhaps it's the wind that's rustling the iron tree leaves on the shore."

As for Mol Malamala, he descended into the plains and started to sing a second time before heading towards the sea. This time, the ever-listening wife recognised the voice of her husband. Mol Malamala was determined to go and drown himself in the ocean. He had already reached the beach and started into the water. He was on the reef with water up to his navel. Ahae, having understood what her husband was doing, ran to the beach. She saw him standing on the reef in full tide. At the same time, Mol Malamala started singing again. He then turned towards the beach and saw that his wife was calling to him.

"Come back! Come back to the house! I'll do whatever you want from now on!"

"Look! Look up to the top of the hill! The chickens are loose. They are flying away! Look well, I tell you! Our house is burning!"

Mol Malamala's wife looked up to the hills and at the same time, decorated with all his ceremonial pig's tusks, the man tragically drowned himself in the sea.

This legend was told by Titus Vatu from the village of Atarboi on the island of Malo

The legend was originally published in Bislama,
and translated into English by Kendra Gates.

Nabanga n°28 (08/05/76)

The legend of the new moon
(Malo)

A long time ago, on Malo, men lived simply and made their homes in the middle of the bush. To tell the truth, their lives would have been rather boring had it not been for one of their customs. At each new moon, they came out of the bush and went down towards the sea. There, they walked towards the mouth of a river, a very small river, to a place called Nangarai. They carried taro and yams to roast over a bonfire. They made their fire on the bank of the river and while their food was cooking, they talked softly and told stories about their adventures and always during these evenings, they were waiting for a visit... a visit from the moon!

It should be said that at this time the moon was not wild. When the moon was new, it would slide slowly down the sky and approach the island. When it arrived at the mouth of the small river, it would dip itself halfway into the cold, clear water. It was said that the moon came there to wash and freshen up. The moon stayed there for quite a while before it would gently start to rise into the sky once more. However, before it regained its rightful place, the moon would hover a few metres above the ground shining down on the small river of Nangarai. This was its way of saying good-bye before the next new moon. The same thing happened each time and the men looked upon the moon with a sort of veneration.

One of the men, however, only wanted one thing: to catch the moon! That was the wish dearest to his heart; he had never spoken of it but guarded the secret jealously. One day, though, he did tell his secret to some friends in whom he had complete and utter confidence. The friends were dismayed and tried to dissuade their friend by whatever means possible. The man was convinced by their pleadings... or at least he seemed to be convinced. In reality, his friends' protests had only sharpened his desire to catch the moon. He swore to himself that he would catch it the next time it came.

The man waited impatiently. Finally, his big night arrived. He came out of the bush and walked towards the sea with all the other villagers. He acted naturally, speaking with everyone and carrying his share of taro and yams to roast. Once they had arrived at Nangarai, everyone went in search of wood and kindling to use in the traditional fire. The flames lit up the faces of those sitting near the fire in order to cook the food. Everyone was there, happily busy. Everyone? No! No one had seen one of the men sneak off and hide himself behind a large rock to the right of the river. Thus hidden, he waited for the moon. It finally made its appearance, slowly easing itself down from the sky. The man was ready. As usual, the moon came to the mouth of the small river and dipped itself halfway into the cold water. It was time! The man jumped from his hiding place and threw himself at the moon. He was able to grab onto it with one hand, however, the moon was quite lively and it quickly slipped from between the man's fingers. The moon was soon high in the sky, taking its rightful place.

Alas, the moon had changed! The man had carried taro and yams, fetched wood and helped to light the fire; his hands were dirty and when he grabbed the moon, he stained it. The moon would never be the same again. Since this fateful day, the moon has never returned to shine on the Nanagarai. You can also see why the moon is now wild! And if you look at the moon very, very closely, you can see the that it has black stains on it... the handprints of a man that lived a long time ago on the island of Malo.

Nabanga n°11 (13/09/75)

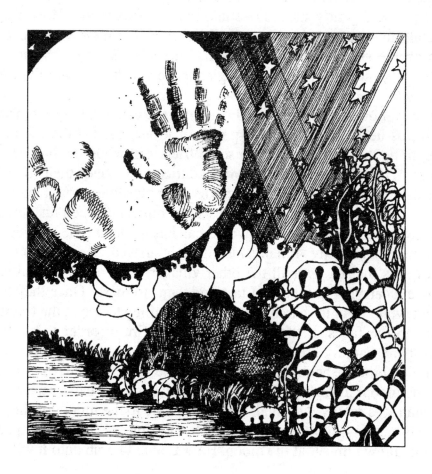

The legend of the fisherman and his five children

(Malo)

Long ago, on the island of Malo, lived a poor, unhappy fisherman. One day, destiny smiled on him because it allowed him to meet a charming young woman that he eventually fell in love with. The woman was also taken with this gentle and kind man. However, their love did not make them richer. They continued to live in extreme poverty, happy but poor. Their hardships got worse when their children were born: a first, a second, a third, a fourth, and finally, a fifth son. Yes, they were all boys. The parents didn't know how they could raise this large family. The poor wife had to stay in the village to look after the children while the father left to go fishing each morning. He either went to the sea or he tried to catch a few fish in the river. It was a difficult life, full of deprivation. This poverty, though, united them and they all adored each other. The years passed. The five sons grew up. However, the raising of her children had drained all the energy from the mother. She did not go out much anymore. She was contented to watch her husband and her sons leave to go fishing. Very quickly, the boys wanted to go with their father. Their father was too proud of them to refuse, and so catching fish became almost like a game. He who caught the most fish in his net won. However, the boys often saw their father smiling sadly. Life had aged him prematurely. The children felt this and it made them sad. Every morning, they looked at their father closely. If they felt that he was too tired to go fishing, they told him to stay at the house.

"Relax! We're going alone to bring home the fish today!"

The parents were happy to see so much affection and attention from their boys. They watched them leave, emotional and proud.

One day, they boys woke up and looked at the sky. It was clouded over but did not seem to be threatening rain. This was good news because it had not stopped raining for a week. The father was ready to leave with his sons, but the eldest stopped him.

"No! Stay with mother! The paths must be muddy... it has rained too much lately. You'll be better off at home."

The children left alone. The hours flew by and noon came, but the boys still hadn't come back. The mother and father started to become impatient. Soon, impatience became worry.

"I'm going to look for them. What could have happened?"

The father started off and it didn't take long for him to find out what had happened.

Swollen by the rains, the river was a raging torrent. The rapids swept away everything in their path: coconut palms, plants, and rubbish. The children had probably been taken by surprise by the force of the current. The man and the woman cried for a long time, mourning the disappearance of their children. They lamented the life that had brought them only unhappiness and grief. But because they were used to bad luck, it didn't take long for them to get back on their feet. The next day, seeing that his wife was still beaten down by grief, the man had only one thought in his head: his wife would not die mourning.

"I'm going to go fishing. You are pale and sad. Besides, you haven't eaten for eight days because of this awful rain that took away our children. I'm going fishing and I'll bring back some food for us. You'll see, things will get better and life will be like it was before our children were born."

The mother didn't say a thing, but let her husband leave alone.

As was his habit, the man cast his net into the river. This time, he chose the mouth of the river near the entrance to the sea, and he waited. You cannot imagine his surprise when he pulled in his net and discovered five goldfish. He had never seen any so beautiful. He was so enraptured by them that he didn't even lament the small size of his catch. Suddenly, the five goldfish were transformed into five boys. The man thought he would die of surprise! He had found his children! He couldn't believe his eyes! He had found his beloved, lost children. He imagined his wife's joy upon seeing them again.

Their triumphant return was so joyous that no one thought to bring anything to eat. Their happiness was too great. The rapids had given back what they had taken the day before; justice was served for the poor parents.

Radio Broadcast "Alors... Raconte !"

PENAMA Province

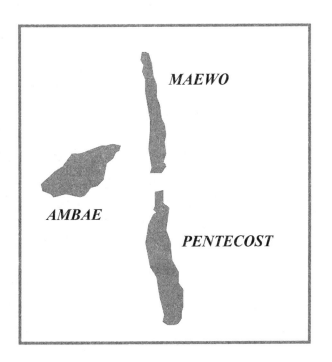

Ulunwel and the devils
(Pentecost)

Once upon a time, there was a young man by the name of Ulunwel who lived in a little village surrounded by woods on the island of Pentecost. He lived there with his widowed mother. He often went to Bantore to fish.

One beautiful day, he said to his mother, "Mother, cut me down a bunch of bananas."

He took the bunch and went to the shore to fish. When he had arrived at the beach in Bantore, he saw that the tide was moving out to sea. Ulunwel was very shy and never dared show himself to the girls that came to this place to fish. So, he hid himself and waited for low tide.

One day, he went to fish with his bow and arrows on the flat reef, as was the custom of this time. Suddenly, Ulunwel thought he heard the sound of a *tamtam* coming from the hills that crowned his village. It was the rolling of the devils' *tamtam,* those spirits of long-dead ancestors that roamed Pentecost during this time. As the tide got higher, Ulunwel was attracted by the sound of this devilish *tamtam* that was getting louder and louder. The curious young man, obsessed by the sound of this mysterious drum, left the reef and ran towards the hill where he heard guttural voices that attracted him like magnets.

Once he had reached to the place where the devils were dancing, the chief of the ancestors invited him to join them. Ulunwel threw himself into the middle of the shouting and singing devils who were undulating to the rhythm of the *tamtam.* He tried his best to follow the rhythm of the devils' dance and soon knew it by heart.

At the end of the dance, the chief of the devils stopped him and said, "Alright! Dear friend from the land of the living, I am very pleased with your performance among us today. From now on, you are in charge of teaching this dance to your people. You shall be charged with the task of making sure that this dance is performed in the *nasara* of the living. If you refuse to obey me, I'll put a curse on you."

"I have no problem taking this mission and accepting your challenge, oh Great Chief of the Netherworld!"

Once he had returned home, Ulunwel asked his mother to make him a belt of bark and a 'bacon.' His mother immediately started making him these dancing ornaments.

One day, a little after the devils' dance on the wooded hills of Melsisi, the young man, wearing his dancing accoutrements, announced to his mother, "Mother, I am going to dance."

"Where will you dance?"

"With the devils!"

"Go ahead! But be sure not to repeat your father's error!"

"Don't worry, Mother. I will be careful. I can take care of myself."

With this, Ulunwel went to dance with the devils. After the dance, on his way home, two girls who had been admiring him from afar started to follow him.

Worried, he turned around and asked them, "May I ask you where you are going?"

"We're following you! We are coming with you!"

"No! That's not possible. Go back to your own homes. Your father will be angry with me."

Then, he took off his belt and gave it to them.

"Take this, I am giving it to you. Now, go back to your home, please!"

The two girls replied, "This is your belt. We'll hold on to it and we shall all go together to your house."

Ulunwel took off his *bacon* and gave it to them, saying, "Take this as a souvenir and go back to your house, in the name of the gods!"

The two girls replied again, "No! This *bacon* is yours and we shall all go to your house."

The young man tried to make the girls go back to their house but his efforts were in vain. He couldn't understand what had got into them to make them such pests. Lost in his thoughts, he hadn't realised that they had come within sight of his village. So, with the help of some large *laplap* leaves, he hid the girls and directed them to his house.

Once they had arrived in Ulunwel's village, the two girls didn't want to go back to their parents' house. They were taken with the young man, and so it was left up to Ulunwel to find them a secure hiding place so that he would not be in trouble with his mother and especially the girls' parents.

After having hidden the obstinate girls, the young man went to his mother and said, "Mother, I think that we need to double our food rations."

"What do you mean by that, my son?"

"I think that from now on, we need to feed our pigs better so that they will be nice and fat. Our ceremonial pigs will quickly grow rounded tusks."

"Why?"

"Look mother, you know that our ceremonial pigs are our only resource. If I want to rise in the chiefly ranks, what would I do without pigs?"

62

"Alright. I understand better now. I agree with you because I have a premonition that you will soon be married. Let's raise the rations."

In the following days, Ulunwel's meals doubled and even tripled in size so that he was able to feed his two protégés in hiding. However, one afternoon while coming back from her garden, the mother heard voices coming from a giant, leafy *nakatambol* tree near her son's pig enclosure. She went to see who was talking and was surprised to discover her son talking with two girls who were, up to this point, unknown to her. By eavesdropping, she learned that the trio got along impeccably. This discovery disappointed her immensely. She thought that her son was someone responsible, frank and loyal, in whom she could confide all her worldly possessions. She went into a rage and jumped out into the midst of the young people.

"Aha! You have at last found what you were looking for! I warned you. I warned you not to commit the fatal error that your father had. That man was without a heart; he got me pregnant and then threw me away like a used handkerchief. You are so much like your father."

While the old woman was divesting herself of her anger against Ulunwel, one of the young women started to find the situation particularly unpleasant and provocative. She grabbed a heavy piece of wood and brought it down on the head of Ulunwel's mother, killing her instantly. Full of remorse, the girl who had killed the mother ran away.

Thus, Ulunwel was free to marry the other girl according to the customs of Pentecost. After their marriage, Ulunwel summoned the men in his village and taught them *dong,* the devils' dance. After countless rehearsals, Ulunwel and his friends performed the devils' dance in public at the *nasara,* just as the Chief of the Netherworld had commanded. Invisible, all of the devils present in Melsisi participated in the dance. Finally, the ancestors' spirits could rest in peace. Even Ulunwel's mother found some peace because she knew that her death had served to create a link between the living and the spirits of the ancestors.

This is how certain traditional dances, passed down from generation to generation, originated.

This legend was given by Vincent Tabigerian.
It was translated from Bislama into French by Patrick Rory,
and then adapted into English by Kendra Gates.

Nabanga n°10 (30/08/75)

The legend of the moon and the sun
(Pentecost)

A long time ago, the sun and the moon lived together, happy to be linked by that noble sentiment: friendship. The two friends lived under the same roof and their lives were free of problems. They spent a good part of each day walking next to each other, savouring the sweetness of nature. This carefree life lasted a long time, a very long time.

One day, as was their habit, the sun and the moon went for a walk. They had no particular goal in mind. They were just going for a stroll. Suddenly, the sky clouded over and it started to rain, a terribly violent rain known only during the rainy season. It was so strong that the two friends decided to take cover. They found a house located conveniently next to them. Quickly, they went inside. Because the rain had cooled the air, they decided to build a fire. As if by chance, some sticks of wood were lying on the ground. The sun started to light the fire. The fire was soon crackling merrily, nourished by the wood.

"I'm hungry," the sun said suddenly.

"Me too! I'm hungry," echoed the moon.

While searching for their shelter, the two friends had found a couple yams. They decided to cook them. It was then that the unforgivable happened.

"I'm going to eat first because I'm very hungry," said the sun crossly.

"Oh no, you won't. I'm going to eat first because I'm hungrier than you," replied the moon.

The fight was terrible. It could even have been called war. The sun caught the moon and threw it into some cold water. The moon got back up and threw the sun into the fire. The battle lasted a long time. Since that fateful day, the two friends have become enemies.

When the sun rises in the morning, the moon disappears. When the moon rises in the evening, the sun disappears. The two old friends can no longer be in the same place at the same time. You will never see them together. It is said that the sun is very hot because the moon threw it in the fire. The moon, of course, is very cold because the sun threw it in freezing water.

This legend was collected and transcribed by Father Tattevin in 1931.   *Nabanga n°16 (22/11/75)*

The story of Tabi and Bule
(Pentecost)

Today, I will tell you the story of Tabi and Bule. On the entire island of Pentecost, first names are given by either the Tabis or the Bules. A long time ago, when there was tribal warfare, the Bules and the Tabis were fierce warriors. Matan was Bule's sister and Mabon that of Tabi. Following custom law, Bule had to marry Mabon, and Tabi with Matan. This is where everything started.

One beautiful morning, on the island of Maewo, a man was walking happily on the beach. This man's name was Tabi. Suddenly, he found a cooked *laplap* leaf on the sand.

"Hey! Where did this leaf come from? There is a man somewhere. This leaf must have come from that island, the island of Raga. I must see this man."

Tabi paddled his canoe in the sea and glided towards Raga. Arriving at Laone, he found other *laplap* leaves floating in the water. Arriving at Loltong, he found even more leaves. Finally, in Bwatnapni Bay, he saw smoke rising from the top of a high hill. He pulled his canoe onto the sand and climbed in the direction of the smoke. In a clearing, he saw a big *nakamal* and pigs tied beneath trees.

He went into the *nakamal*. A woman was busy making *laplap*.

Tabi asked, "What is your name?"

"My name is Matan."
"You have a beautiful name. Are you alone here?"
"No, I live with my husband."
"And where is your husband?"
"He went to the garden."
"What's that?"
"It is a *laplap* made with yams."
"Do you eat it raw or cooked?"
"It is eaten cooked."

The woman pointed to a fire. Tabi walked around the *nakamal,* admiring the workmanship. On his island, there were no *nakamal*. He slept alone under a hut made of reeds.

He thought, "This man is stronger and more intelligent that I am."

Bule, returning from the garden with some kava slung over his shoulder, found his wife sitting outside. He asked her, "Is the *laplap* ready?"

"Yes, but there is a man waiting for you in the *nakamal.*"

"Renmamak kari (Hello, my friend)," said Bule.

However, Tabi did not answer. He looked at Bule, a strapping young man, up and down. He himself was a small, frail man. He thought, "If there are any problems, this fellow could kill me with one punch."

"Where are you from?" asked Bule.

"I come from Maewo."

"Did you come to see me?"

"Yes, I have known for a long time that you live here."

"How did you know that?" asked Bule.

"Your wife often sends messages to me."

"What? Messages!" exclaimed Bule.

"Yes, each time that you eat *laplap.*"

Tabi had just lied to see if Bule was cleverer than he. Bule, vexed and jealous, said to Tabi, "Well, seeing as you have known about me for a long time, let's go and drink kava."

However, Bule was thinking something completely different. "I must kill this weak man. He is beginning to bother me."

To make Bule angry, Tabi boasted, "You know that I am more intelligent than you."

"No, I am more intelligent than you. I have a *nakamal,* pigs, big gardens, a wife, and I always eat *laplap.* You, though, you must come like a fish and eat the leftover *laplap* that my wife leaves on the beach so that you do not die of hunger," responded Bule.

"Listen to me. So that we don't have to fight, because I know that you are stronger than I am and you could easily kill me, I will make you a proposition. I will return to my island. In three days, you will come to my house and you will see that I am more intelligent than you."

"Alright, I accept your proposition."

"On the third day, I will light a fire. You shall see the smoke and leave your island. I will be waiting for you in my *nakamal.*"

Thus, Tabi returned to his island. In great haste, he built his *nakamal* just as Bule had built his. When he had finished, he caught some turtles and attached them around his *nakamal.* Then, he went into the bush to gather bunches of *navele,* those nuts which are eaten by cutting them in half and prying out the flesh. He hung these bunches from his *nakamal.* When the last day came, he lit a big fire and waited.

Bule pushed his canoe over the sand and pointed the prow in the direction of the smoke. He saw Tabi's *nakamal,* the turtles tied to the surrounding trees, and finally, in the *nakamal* itself, the bunches of *navele.* Bule started to laugh and laugh. When he saw a big hole that Tabi had dug in the middle of the floor, he asked, "What is that?"

"It's a hole. That's where I do my duties when the weather is bad."

Bule laughed once again. "I have never seen a man as stupid as you. You have built your *nakamal* exactly like mine, you have replaced pigs with turtles, and you only eat nuts. Truly, you make me laugh!"

Angry, Tabi said, "Alright, you see this *nakamal?* I will remain inside and you will set it on fire. If I burn with the *nakamal,* you are more intelligent than me. If I live, on the contrary, I am more intelligent than you."
"Ok!" and Bule lit a big fire.

The *nakamal* burnt and burnt. When the smoke had finally cleared, Tabi was still there, alive!

How had Tabi managed to survive and not be burnt with the *nakamal?* It was very simple. He had climbed into the hole that he had dug, and with a piece of wet wood, he blocked the entrance. When the *nakamal* had finished burning, he lifted the piece of wood and came out of his hole.

"That was easy," said Bule. "I could do that."

"Try it then," responded Tabi. "If you can do it, you are truly more intelligent than I."

"Alright, let's do it. We'll go to my island and you will see."

The two men pulled their canoes across the sand and pointed their prows towards the hill that led to Bule's *nakamal.* Once there, Bule went inside and sat down right in the middle of his *nakamal.* It burned. Amidst the roaring of the flames, Tabi heard an agonizing cry. Bule had just burnt with his *nakamal.* When the smoke finally cleared, there was nothing left but the charred body of Bule, lying in the middle of the *nakamal.*

Bule had been intelligent, but not clever. This was the cause of his death.

Tabi never returned to the island of Maewo, but took Bule's widow, named Matan, as his wife. She gave birth to a girl named Mabon and a boy named Bule. When their children had grown, Bule married his sister Mabon and from them were born two children, Tabi and Matan, who would later marry, and so on and so forth.

This legend was told by Donato from Lebukuvini and written by M. Tabi Marcel from the village of Kulbaga on Pentecost

Le Mélanésien n°11-13 (04/05/81)

Barkulkul the God

(Pentecost)

It is written in the Bible that in the beginning God created the heavens and the Earth. At this time, the Earth was empty and covered in darkness. God's spirit hovered above the waters.

"Let there be light," and there was light.

God saw that the light was good and He separated light from dark. God called the light 'day' and the dark 'night.' There was evening and there was morning. This was the first day. God deemed that there should be land amidst the waters and thus separate ocean from ocean. And he did so.

At the same moment, in the south of the island of Pentecost, there was a beginning. In the beginning, land alone existed. Trees also existed but there were no men. On this land, there was a coconut palm, only one. There was only one coconut palm on the Earth; only one located in the place called Rebreone. One day, the coconut palm bloomed. The bud enveloping the flower was of a prodigious size. Once the bud had completely opened, eight men could be seen inside. The first was Barkulkul. The eight men climbed out of the bud and stretched out on a banana leaf that was lying at the foot of this famous coconut palm. A young coconut, barely formed, was also hanging from the tree. The juice, which ran from a wound in the nut, was gathered by the men and used as milk. This coconut palm thus became their wet nurse. The men grew. They constructed a communal house called a *nakamal*. This was used as a place to come together in times of crisis. Then, they built their own houses. Their intention, however, was to stay together in the *nakamal*.

He who was called Barkulkul said, "We will all die and disappear from this land if we don't create another being. That way, we can stay on Earth."

Because Barkulkul was their chief, he again said, "Do you see that tree over there that bears fruit like chestnuts? It's a *namambe*. Go and pick some."

The men went down the hill into a valley, climbed the *namambe* tree, picked the fruit, and went back to the communal house with their spoils. Then, they rubbed two different kinds of wood together, built a roaring fire, and let it die down a little. On the coals, they roasted the chestnuts.

Because Barkulkul was their chief, he said, "Let's eat them!"

And he ate the *namambe* and found them very grainy. Thus, Barkulkul took a chestnut and threw it at the seventh brother. The chestnut stuck to his genitals. The man started to cry and tried to pull the chestnut off. At first it resisted, but then it came off, pulling his genitals with it. The man cried again. He had become a woman.

68

When the other men realised that he had become different from them, they cried, "Go away! Go away to another house! You can't stay with us!"

The new woman did what she was told and set up house for herself.

The men that ordered her around said, "Take this banana leaf. It's yours."

The woman realised that she had to use it wisely, so after some thinking, she tore the leaf into fringe. Then, by using the spine of a *natangura* leaf, she made a belt and a short skirt. This skirt hid the place that had caused her so much trouble.

The men lived in the *nakamal* and the woman in her own house at a small distance from them.

Barkulkul, who had become the chief of this little society, said, "We should try to eat something else and diversify our food. Let's go in search of something tasty!"

He sent the sixth brother to get some fire from the woman so that they might cook.

The sixth man went to the woman and said, "Sermop, I need a little fire..."

Sermop, in the language of southern Pentecost, means "the split chestnut."

The woman responded, "Of course, my brother. Take some fire!"

He took the fire and went back to the communal house. When he entered the *nakamal,* the other four men asked, "Did you go? What did she say? What did she say to you?"

The man, very happy, replied, "She called me her brother!"

The men, surprised at this new word, but used to new creations, started to cook. Barkulkul now sent the fifth brother to the woman.

"Go and get some seashells."

The man, used to his brother's commands, went to the woman and said, "Woman, I have come to get some seashells."

Sermop looked at him with kindness and said, "Of course, my father, take some seashells."

The man took the shells and went back to the *nakamal.* The men, who had been waiting anxiously for him, said, "Did you go see her? What did she say?"

"She called me her father."

Barkulkul thought a bit and sent the fourth brother to go get some vegetables from Sermop. The man followed Barkulkul's orders.

Sermop saw him arrive and said, "My cousin, what do you need?"

"I have come looking for vegetables."

Sermop went to get some vegetables from her garden and gave them to him. When the man returned to the *nakamal,* the others questioned him as usual.

"What did Sermop say when you went to get vegetables at her house?"

"I went to see the woman and she called me cousin."

Barkulkul looked at the third man and said, "Go find a bamboo to carry water!"

Once he arrived at Sermop's, he said, "Woman! I want a bamboo in which to carry water."

"Of course, my grandfather. Take some bamboo. It will keep your water cool for several days."

Arriving at the *nakamal,* he felt older and said, "She called me grandfather. She is a very kind girl."

When the vegetables were thoroughly cooked, he sent the second brother to get some seawater.

Sermop, seeing him coming, said, "My son! You have grown and are strong now! What do you want?"

"I would like some sea water."

"My son, take the sea water and come back to see me often."

When he returned to the *nakamal,* the others questioned him.

"She called me her son!"

When they had eaten, Barkulkul went to Sermop and stood in front of her.

"I would like some water."

The woman looked at him tenderly and said, "Friend, take some water. But what kind of water would you like, you whom I love?"

Barkulkul started to smile, took the water, and returned to the *nakamal.* Seeing him coming, the brothers ran towards him.

Barkulkul, still choked up, looked at them and said, "She called me her friend and told me that she loved me!"

The others, understanding immediately what was happening, said, "This is good! It is you whom she will marry."

The evening came and, at the moment when the sun set behind the Ambrym volcano and the night-noises became loud, Barkulkul went to the woman's house. The two united in love. Nine months later, the woman gave birth to a little Barkulkul. This is how men came to live on the Earth and multiplied in the south of Pentecost.

The myth that you have just read was given to Paul Gardissat in Bislama
by the elder Fabiano Owa of Rentas, a little village next to Barrier Bay in South Pentecost.

Radio New-Hebrides

The legend of old Wakos
(Pentecost)

Geologists think that the island of Pentecost is the oldest in Vanuatu. That's what they think. Indeed, they're very sure about it. Those who actually live on Pentecost are more or less divided on this subject, but most do believe that it is the oldest island. The inhabitants in the north of the island think that Tagaro, who has always been the strongest and the biggest, was born in the Gumbio territory on the east coast of the neighbouring island of Maewo. Indeed, for these inhabitants of northern Pentecost, a people better known as Raga, Tagaro was born on Maewo. It is strange, but the Raga do not think that their island is the oldest. The Raga do not think that creation started on their island. However, the men from the centre of Pentecost, those who live in the middle of that land thought by geologists to be the oldest island of Vanuatu, those men, the Gihare, the mountain men, have no doubts that this world started on their island. The men from southern Pentecost, those from Bunlap and Barrier Bay, think that Barkulkul, the strongest of all men, was born in the south of this island which, you must know, is the oldest in the archipelago. They, the Gihare, the men who live up high, the mountain men, those who live around Melsisi, think that everything started on their land. They believe that the beginning of the world came from the strength of Tagaro and Barkulkul who, in reality, are only one person. Oh, yes! In the grand tornado of history, everything started there. The Tabis and the Bules, those two big Pentecost families, would certainly tell you no different. Tabi Marcel is from Wanmel, a little village in the centre of Pentecost, and he's the one that is going to tell us this story.

Built up against the hills and the cliffs, dug into the rock, there existed long ago many villages. In the confines of these hills, between a stream, a ravine, a cascade and another hill, there was a village named Wanmel. The people that lived there were happy as only they could be during those simple times. There were, of course, wars, but people had gotten used to them and besides, they never lasted long because people were obliged to raise pigs! During this time, when one spoke of custom, one spoke of pigs. When one spoke of pigs, one spoke of grade taking and rising in the ranks of Melanesian society. The little people from the centre of Pentecost thus raised pigs.

The men often spoke to their pigs. "Don't make all that noise! There will be enough to eat for everyone. Have I ever forgotten you? Grow fat and big! You will be my wealth and thanks to you I will be the most important of all."

The people of this region raised pigs happily, but from their hills they looked to the east and were afraid. They were scared of this area because this was where the dead met with their spirits. It was an unexplored place and the name alone made people tremble in fear. The east coast was the land of the dead.

Wakos was an old man that, all of his life, had heard tell of the land of the dead on the east coast. He had heard so many things, so many extraordinary things, about this place that one day he decided to go there.

So, he said to his pigs, "Come, my little ones. We are going on a great journey."

Thus, Wakos left with his pigs in tow. He went down to the east coast for the first time in his life. The whole village of Wanmel watched him leave, anxious and surprised.

"Where are you going, Wakos?"

"I'm leaving for the east coast."

"You're crazy! You'll never come back alive. Wakos, that's the land of the dead. You won't come back. Stay with us."

The old man didn't listen to them and went on his way. Once he had reached to the east coast, he started to chop down branches. He made a pen and enclosed his two pigs. Once the fear of having his garden wrecked by his swine had been overcome, Wakos took one of his branches and started to plant yams. The garden got bigger by the day. Because he did not have enough plant variety, he left once again for Wanmel. When he got to his house, everyone was surprised to see him and gathered around him.

"Wakos! We are so happy to see you!"

"We thought you were dead! We haven't seen you for two weeks."

"Tell us of your adventures, old man. Tell us!"

"What do you want me to tell you? My pigs are in their pen and getting fat. My sow is pregnant, my garden had been weeded, and I have come to get some yams to plant."

"But Wakos, have you seen our long dead ancestors? Did you see their spirits?"

"No, my friends, I haven't seen anyone."

The next day, Wakos left once again for the east coast and started to work on his new garden.

"What does that *notou* want?"

He took a stone and threw it at the bird.

"You're bothering me. Go away."

The *notou* flew away to another branch but soon returned to bother Wakos again."You're bothering me, *notou.* Go away! I have work to do," and he threw another stone at the bird.

"Why are you throwing stones at me? You, a living man, don't you recognise me? I am the chief of the dead and this is my country."

Wakos felt a feverish heat run through his body. He started to get dizzy and everything around him became hazy. Eventually, he lost consciousness. The bird's voice hypnotised him.

"Wakos, take the leaf that is before you and eat it. When you have eaten it, you will close your eyes and only open them when I say to. We are going to see the dead."

Wakos took up the leaf, ate it, closed his eyes, and felt his body lift up from the ground. Wakos felt nothing more; his body had become light as air. He started to dream, a dream that lasted and lasted until he heard the voice once again.

"Wakos, open your eyes."

Wakos opened his eyes and found himself before a big stone in a place that he did not recognise. This big stone was called the moonstone. The stone spun around and a gaping hole opened. It was the entrance to a cave.

"Enter, Wakos, enter."

Wakos entered and the moonstone behind him rotated back into place, closing the hole. This is when Wakos noticed the strange land before him. There were three very straight lines of men. Their feet did not touch the ground. It was as if they were suspended in the air. Each individual was enveloped in a foggy cloud. The heads of these petrified men were turned towards the sky. They seemed to be waiting for something that would come from the heavens. Wakos, holding his breath, advanced and walked between these statue men. He went into the land of the dead and seemed to bump into a spirit at each step. All of a sudden, Wakos recognised his son who had been dead for four years.

"Wakal! My son! I can't touch you. I hold only air in my hands!"

Wakal did not move. Wakal couldn't hear. He couldn't hear anything. He was dead.

He went towards another statue and recognised his father.

"My father! It's you!"

He went towards another and now recognised his mother.

"And you, mother!"

He advanced towards a group of statues and recognised those from his village.

"And all of you from my village! You who are dead and that I knew so long ago! Answer me! You hear me. Answer me."

At the same time, in the village of Wanmel, people started to worry.

"It has been a whole month since Wakos left for the east coast and we haven't had any news of him."

"We told him not to leave. We warned him. What if we went to see him? But, we've only heard tell of the east coast. Our fathers never went."

"Let's try anyway."

"Look! It's his garden! His pigs have starved to death, his basket is there with his axe next to it."

"Let's get out of here right now! I'm scared... let's go see our chief."

"Like we told you, Wakos has disappeared. We found his basket and his axe. His pigs have both starved to death."

"Let's wait a little while longer. If he doesn't come back, we'll organise his death feast. But let's wait just a little while longer..."

Wakos was living among the dead. He felt neither hunger nor thirst. However, he felt cold; he felt the chill of the cave, the chill of death penetrated his bones.

"You, chief of the dead, I am begging you! Take me back to my village! I can't take living with these people that don't speak, don't move, and this never ending cold... Chief of the dead, I want to go home."

"Wakos, you will go home, home to the living, home to your people. I will give you one more chance of survival, one more chance to live at home again. Then, you will die and your spirit will belong to me. Close your eyes. Only open them when I tell you."

Wakos closed his eyes and felt his body lifting from the ground. Then, he didn't hear anything more.

"Open your eyes. You are home."

Wakos slowly came to and heard people talking at a distance from him.

"Look who's coming! It's Wakos!"

"Wakos, we are so happy to see you! We thought you were dead. What happened?"

Wakos started to tell his story.

"I was in my garden planting my yams when I heard a *notou* chirp. Like we all do, I threw a stone at him. Then, the *notou...*"

The people of Wanmel listened and thought that he was crazy.

One of the villagers spoke up, saying, "He might be crazy, but he can heal our sicknesses."

"Look! I couldn't bend my arm at all! Since he touched me, I can bend it normally!"

"Wakos, if your story is true, can you take me there? I so desperately want to see my son again! You know that he has just died. I miss him so much and I am so old now."

"Alright, come with me."

"Wakos, wait for me! I'm going to bring some sugar cane for him. He always loved sugar cane when he was little."

The two men left for the east coast. The old man ate the required leaf and both of them felt light. Wakos opened his eyes. The same strange scene was in front of the two men. It was exactly as Wakos had seen the first time.

"There is your son. Put the sugar cane at his feet. Don't try to touch him, and close your eyes."

The next day, the old man died and Wakos himself felt death encroaching.

He called the village together and said to them, "I am going to die soon. As soon as I am dead, put my body in an isolated house. Don't cover my body with mats like you normally do. You must also leave the door of the house open."

Three days later, Wakos died and his body, devoid of mats, was placed in an isolated house. Only his wife stayed close to him, mourning. The day after the evening of his death, the villagers arrived to bury Wakos' body.

"His body isn't here anymore! Look! Footprints! Let's follow them!"

"Look! The prints stop before this big stone."

The old men call this stone the moonstone. It is since this day that the people of Wanmel believe Wakos' story.

This legend was given in French to Paul Gardissat by Marcel Tabi who is a descendent from the tribe of Wanmel. Wako's daughter is still alive today and is married to a man from Bunlap. They have six children.

Radio New Hebrides

The story of two brothers Taisamul and Fassel
(Pentecost)

In the South of the Island of Pentecost, between Barrier Bay and Rentas near the village of Bunlap, there lived two brothers: Taisamul and Fassel. These two brothers had always lived happily together. One day, Taisamul saw that the sea was calm, the winds had fallen and there was only a gentle breeze. In the distance was the Island of Ambrym and the northern tip of this Island seemed to be coming closer. The volcano Marum was smoking a little. Taismul thus decided to go and see his parents on Ambrym. So, he set off for the Island of Ambrym. It had been a long time since he had seen his family on Ambrym Island. However, before leaving Pentecost, Taisamul had taken all the necessary precautions. He knew his wife well... so, he created a *fela* A *fela*, in the language of southern Pentecost, is a sort of picture created by taking a soft piece of rope and attaching it to one finger on the left hand and then pushing your right finger through it. In this way, one can create geometrical drawings much like those that the old men in southern Pentecost scratch into the sand with their fingers. Taisamul thus created an enormous *fela* with a long supple vine and he encircled his wife's house with it.

"You will stay here while I go to see my family on Ambyrm," Taisamul said.

The *fela* became his wife's guardian. His obedient wife was obliged to stay closed up in her house during her husband's entire absence. On Ambrym, those who lived on the shore saw the canoe arrive. At first, it was only a little black dot on the horizon but then it got bigger and bigger. Finally, Taisamul could be recognised. His family opened their arms in reception of this brother from another island. Taisamul bathed himself to wash off the day's heat. Kava was drunk and the men danced in honor of their guest. As for Taisamul, tired out from the day's journey and knocked out by the welcome kava, he slept the hard sleep given to those who partake of the root, kava.

On Pentecost, Taisamul's wife was a prisoner. After having closed the door to the house, and after having created a veritable spider's web of a *fela* in guise of protection, Taisamul had spoken to his wife.

"I am going to Ambrym, but I will come back. If this drawing has been bothered or moved, I will know that someone has been to see you."

Persuaded that no one would have the audacity to break the taboo, he left, sure of himself and the *fela* that guarded his wife.

Fassel, Taisamul's brother, had gone hunting. He took his bow and his arrows. He was looking for birds in the forest. He saw one on a branch, shot at it, missed, and the arrow fell onto the *natangora* of his brother's roof. Taisamul's wife quickly hid the arrow and left Fassel to keep looking for it. Then, she put her lips to a crack in the door and spoke to him.

"Are you looking for something?"

"I was hunting some birds and I lost my arrow near your house," Fassel said.

"Oh! The arrow is here. It came into my house."

"Give it to me!" he said.

"I can't move because I'm in the middle of weaving a mat. The mat is too long and I have attached a part of it to my foot. I cannot bring you your arrow, so you will have to come and get it."

Fassel went into the house to get the arrow, and the woman gave herself to him. Then, he left, looking around to see that no one had seen him, and forgot to put the *fela*, that spider web guardian, back into place.

After having danced to his heart's content on Ambrym, and after having drunk cup after cup of kava as strong as the volcano Marum, Taisamul went back to Pentecost.

"Who has bothered the *fela?* Who came into this house?" Taisamul asked his wife.

"No one came here while you were on Ambrym," his wife said.

"Yes! Someone has been here! The *fela,* the spider web protector that I put around the house before I left, has been displaced."

His wife wouldn't admit anything and so Taisamul gathered all the men in the *nakamal*.

"Friends, friends, friends, wait a little because I have to talk to you. My friends, let us draw in the ash, you know, those drawings that look like large spider webs and that the old men know how to start and finish without ever lifting their finger from the ground."

The men slid their fingers around in the ash, some drawing canoes, others turtles, and still others flying foxes munching on papaya. Taisamul examined each one. When he got to his brother's drawing, he recognised the *fela* that had surrounded his house. His anger was great.

Fassel! My own brother went into my house! Taisamul thought.

But he said nothing aloud except, "Friends, tomorrow we will go hunting. We will go two by two. Fassel and I will be together."

The next day, Taisamul sang to the heavens and a heavy rain started to fall. The men of the village left to go hunting in pairs just as Taisamul had ordered. As for Taisamul himself, he was accompanied by Fassel, his brother. Each man had his bow, arrows, and club slung across his shoulder. One never knows when one might be attacked by a neighbouring village!

While they were walking, Taisamul said to his brother, "Cut down those *suf-suf* bananas and bring them along."

When they had arrived in a yam field, he said, "Unearth this long yam and don't break it!"

Fassel did what his brother told him to do. He took a large stick and dug up the yam. To do this, he was obliged to dig a big hole around the tuber and then lift out the dirt.

"The hole isn't big enough yet! Keep digging!" Taisamul said.

And Fassel started digging again. He then climbed down into the hole and lifted out the long yam.

"Help me to get back up," he said to his brother.

Taisamul took his club and in one foul stroke, cracked his own brother's head open. Fassel slumped into the bottom of the hole. Then, Taisamul threw in the bunch of *suf-suf* bananas, filled in the hole, and went back to the village as if nothing had happened. When he got back to the village, his old mother spoke to him.

"You weren't with your brother?"

"Yes, but on the way we got lost. We were together hunting but I don't know where he has got to now. He went in one direction and I went in another. He'll come back."

Taisamul had taken a few of the bananas that he had buried with his brother. On the fourth day, the bananas were ripe.

"Tomorrow, we'll go and dig up the bunch."

The next day, Taisamul said to his wife, "We are going to get a bunch of *suf-suf* bananas that I buried in the garden. Come with me!"

They took off for the garden. Once they got there, Taisamul spoke to his wife.

"Dig a little and bring up the bunch of bananas."

The woman did as her husband told her, but while she was digging she started to notice a horrible odour emanating from the hole. Then, flies started to arrive. The smell of decomposing flesh became stronger and stronger until the wife finally saw the body. "A man is buried here! It's a man!"

"Yes, it's a man! Do you recognise him? Now, you're going to eat him."

"But I cannot eat a decomposing man!"

"This man came to see you! You slept with him, hid it, and lied to me. Now, you are going to eat all of him. Do you hear me? All of him! You will only leave his bones, and if not..."

It was this woman's fate to eat the man with whom she had slept and whose pestilential odour was now attracting flies.

"Take pity on me, Taimasul. Pity!"

"Eat!"

And the woman ate, leaving nothing but a pile of bones in the end. Then, the two of them returned to the house. During this time, Fassel's bones had come together and formed a complete skeleton.

Fassel's skeleton slowly started to make its way to the village.

When Taisamul and his wife had arrived at their house, Taimasul said, "Woman, our fire is dead. Go and get some at my mother's house."

When she got to her mother-in-law's, the old woman said, "Woman, you smell like decay. I know that Fassel is dead and that you have just eaten him."

"Yes, it was Taisamul that killed him and forced me to eat him."

The old woman ran to her son's house and said, "Son, why did you kill your brother? Your own brother?"

"He came into my house and neither he nor my wife would admit it. In five days, he will rise again. I told him so."

That evening, the old woman heard the noise of bones scraping against each other.

"Is that you, Fassel?

"As you can see, I am living. Taisamul killed me and I have come back. However, I think that if Taisamul were to die, he would be dead forever. Mother, take everything that is in this house. As for me, I will take this pebble and go to see Taisamul."

Fassel went to the *nakamal* and called his brother.

"Come here!"

"Why are you calling me? What do you want?"

"I only want to speak to you."

Taisamul came closer to his brother.

Fassel said, "You cannot come back to life. Do you see this pebble? I am going to plant it far from here and then set up house for our mother next to it. The day after tomorrow, you will die."

"How am I going to die? You are dead! I am living and in good health!"

"If you find this pebble and take it far away, you will live. If not, you will die! Oh yes, you will die! At any rate, we shall see..."

Fassel called to his mother and pulled the pebble along behind him on a string. Then, he sang. Fassel had attached the pebble to a little vine and, always singing, dragged it along behind him. Fassel and his mother walked a little further and sang some more. Fassel pulled his pebble behind him as the two of them walked through a stream.

Then, Fassel said to his mother, "Climb up on that hill and tell me if you see the village of Sile in the distance."

"Oh, yes! It's still very far off."

And Fassel pulled some more. By pulling the pebble up the hill, it had become a stone.

Fassel then said to his mother, "Mother, do you see Sile? Is it still far off?"

"Yes, my son. It is still far off."

And Fassel pulled some more. Now, the stone had become a boulder and the vine was too small for it.

Fassel spoke to his mother again, saying, "Can you still see the place where we are going?"

"Yes, my son."

"And Sile, is it still far away?"

"Yes, son. Pull, son! Pull! Pull!"

And Fassel continued to pull his boulder. Once they had arrived above the village of Yep, a piece of the boulder crumbled off and fell into the bottom of a ravine. However, Fassel continued to pull.

He then said to his mother, "Mother, are we still far off?"

"Son, I cannot see that place anymore."

"Then, this boulder will stay here at Gusnone. You will stay here as well. In five days, Taisamul will die and when he is dead, he will come to see you. After he has seen you, I will come back to see you."

Five days later, Taisamul died and went to see his mother at Gusnone. He recognised his brother and went towards him.

"So, you're dead?" questioned Fassel.

"Yes, I am dead."

"But you told me that you couldn't die!"

"I'm so sorry, my brother, but I am dead."

"Well, my brother. Remember the old days when we would dance in the nasara and the ground would shake under our feet. We were happy then, my brother. Everything is your fault. Remember those good days..."

This legend was given in Bislama by Claude Asal from Rentas in Southern Pentecost.

Radio New Hebrides

81

The legend of the namarae from Pentecost
(Pentecost)

This story took place a very long time ago, even before Captain Bougainville first set foot in the New Hebrides. At this time, the island of Pentecost was known by the name of Raga. In the north of Raga, there were villages and the inhabitants of these villages occasionally took their canoes and visited the south of Maewo island or the northwest of Omba island. The inhabitants of north Raga liked to exchange mats and women in the country of Tagaro. In the south of the island of Raga, people lived differently and relationships were built with the north of the island of Ambrym. In the centre of Raga, men, smaller than other men, built relationships with the north and the south of their island. These men in the centre were mountain men and hard workers with large gardens.

This story took place in one of the villages in central Raga, next to Melsisi in a village called Lehoah. Everything was fine in Lehoah. Life was calm and the chiefs in neighbouring villages had powerful authority. They were respected and heeded. Their people worked hard without being forced to. Gardening was the principle occupation of these little people who put their whole heart into cultivating their yams and taro. As there were many rivers on Raga, their water taro was reputed to be the finest. Their yams were beautiful and enormous, the many different varieties were famous around the island. The villagers of Lehoah also had pigs, thousands of pigs, that were killed either to eat or to sacrifice during grade-taking ceremonies. These pigs were raised in enclosures and some had tusks that encircled themselves several times. These pigs were raised with particular care. The man that owned one of these was considered rich: an important chief! In order to protect their gardens from wild pigs, the men from Lehoah, always hard at work, had built stone walls around their plots. The village was well protected from intruders and thieves; that is wild pigs in search of well cleaned gardens or freshly dug earth. And so, life was good. The men in their gardens cultivated their taro and yams, and the wild pigs looked on from the other side of the stone barriers. However, one day, a catastrophe occurred.

All the gardens were ruined! The fences were toppled, the ground churned up, yams and taro unearthed, and banana trees felled. It was utter devastation.

"There are no hoof prints!"

"It wasn't the pigs?"

The men from Lehoah looked all around them and couldn't find any traces of feet or hooves, not even one mark that would allow them to explain the destruction and identify the vandals. Finally, all the men came together in the *nakamal* to listen to the chief, Tanmonok. However, the chief was quite bewildered and could only say, "My friends, I don't know what has happened. Like you, I have seen our gardens. There is nothing left. What will become of us? We must find the guilty parties; there must be many of them to have wreaked the havoc that we have seen. Tomorrow evening, two of us will spend the night in the big garden to keep watch. Then we will see! Who would like to volunteer?"

There were several volunteers. The chief chose two.

"Temadilol and Wengo, you are brothers. You look strong enough and especially angry enough! Tomorrow night, you will keep watch in our gardens. If you are frightened and if you run away, you will be killed."

The next evening at dusk, the two brothers walked towards the garden. As the chief of Lehoah had asked them, they set up camp under a big tree. Everything was calm. Only the crickets could be heard. Suddenly, an enormous noise came from the river. It approached the garden. The two men were stricken with fear. They saw an enormous eel, or *namarae,* rise from the river and crush everything in its passage, breaking the walls and eating the taro and yams. When it had its fill, the *namarae* returned to the river in sight of the hidden Temadilol and Wengo.

At daybreak, the brothers hurried to the chief's house. Temadilol told him, "Chief, we saw it. It is an enormous *namarae*. It came from the river, destroyed everything, even the fences, and it ate the taro and yams. We must kill it."

"I find it difficult to believe you," responded the chief. "We have never heard tell of a giant *namarae* capable of destroying gardens. I will gather the village," and the chief struck the great *tamtam*.

The crowd did not believe the two men and thought that they were making it up. Then, the chief spoke up. "My friends, we should listen to them. We don't have any other option. As for you two, if we don't find this *namarae,* we will attach you to this *namele* tree and burn you. Have you heard? If you are lying, you will die. So, take up your axes and knives, your sharp bamboo lances and your longest spears. We shall empty the river."

The whole village went towards the river. While some were busy blocking its original path, others emptied deep pools in the river with bamboo and gourds. All of a sudden, a man found a *namarae* and said, "That's it, I see it, it's under the rock!"

"No," said Wengo, "that's much too small."

At the same time, high in the mountains, a large black cloud tangled itself in the branches of the banyan trees. Thunder boomed and rain began to fall. Even in the rain, the men continued to empty the river with great zeal. Unexpectedly, the ground began to shake and under the cover of thunder the *namarae* arrived. The men started to throw their weapons: axes, knives, lances, and stones. With a great stone, a man crushed the head of the *namarae* which then wound itself around a rock like a snake. At the same time, the thunder shook the earth and the rocks from the river fell on the *namarae* and finished it off.

The *namarae* was dead. The men wound its body around a tree trunk and took it back to the village. Then, they went to find wood in the forest so that they could cook the beast. Everyone, giddy with victory, danced in the *nasara*. Temadilol alone had stayed in the *nakamal* to guard the giant eel. While he was alone, he heard someone calling to him. It was the *namarae* who was in an upright position as if it were alive.

"Don't be afraid. I only want to warn you. If your brother arrives when the men start to burn me, neither of you should stay in the *nakamal.*"

Temadilol would have liked an explanation, but the *namarae* wouldn't speak anymore. Alas, when the men returned with enough wood and were in the process of preparing the fire, Wengo did not want to follow his brother out of the *nakamal.*

"Leave me alone! I want to stay with the others," he said.

At that moment, the *nakamal* filled with smoke. The earth shook and the *nakamal* rocked back and forth. The men inside were frightened and wanted to get out but the smoke blinded them. The *namarae* then picked up the *nakamal* on its back and went into the river. When they arrived at the place where the men had killed the *namarae,* it submerged the *nakamal* and all the men inside it. The building and its occupants sank into a deep hole. Then, the *namarae* curled its long body in front of the *nakamal* door. The men turned into stone and the *nakamal* into one large block.

Today, you can still see the petrified men and *nakamal* of Lehoah. You can also see the *namarae* and the traces that he left in their gardens. No grass will grow in these places. While visiting the village, you can see the oven and the stones that were to be used to cook the giant eel. The river in which the *nakamal* and the men from Lehoah were drowned still flows today between the hills of Pentecost before it throws itself into the sea at Batnavne.

This legend was written in Bislama by Johnson Tabisu from Melsisi.

Nabanga n°96 (13/01/79)

Muehu Katekale, the unsatisfied
(Ambae)

On Ambae volcanoes spewed forth, lava ran and covered a virgin land on which nobody had set foot.

Finally, the volcanoes calmed down and Tagaro, the all powerful, took Omba's fire and threw it on to Ambrym Island. Then it rained and the water arrived in big quantities, enormous quantities. It was a war between fire and water. Tagaro, the god of Ambae, chanted so much, that water was able to beat fire and took its place.

Little by little, the fire went out. Water filled the fire's eyes. These two eyes are called "Manaro." One is the Manaro Kesse and the other is the Manaro Lakuha Vui. Ambae does not have a man's eyes and that is why there is a third eye which has always refused to receive any water. This we call Manaro Ngoru: the dry lake.

Men arrived. They were short, very short, and nasty, very nasty. They knew how to make pottery and understood everything backwards. The old men said that they were stupid. They were called "Talu Tuei." They left just as they had come.

During this time, a long, long time ago, there lived a man, Muehu Katekale, between the villages of Lolopuepue, Ambanga, and Lolosori. He was tall and strong, with lots of hair and a big beard. His wrists were encircled by pigs' tusks because Muehu Katekale was a rich man whose herd of pigs demonstrated his wealth.

Under his belt of bark was tucked a finely woven mat named 'Singwotamarino.' On this mat it was written that he was a great chief. In his garden, Muehu Katekale was hard at work with a spade, digging holes in which to plant his yams, long yams that also attested to the fact that he was a big chief. He worked and little by little the hole got bigger, the earth was stirred up and the work was finished. The next day, he came back and his anger was enormous.

"Who dared to come in to my garden? There! Someone has walked all around my yams!"

Furious, he followed in the footsteps of the intruder which eventually led him to the beach. He heard a noise, the noise of people amusing themselves by splashing in the water. Then, he hid himself behind a tree and watched.

A dozen men were there swimming. With them, there was a woman carrying her child on her back. Muehu Katekale watched them; they came close to the coast, gathered their wings, hooked them onto their backs and flew into the sky.

The woman was left alone with her child. It was time for their baths. Muehu Katekale scratched his head and decided to hide the wings of the woman and the child.

The woman, who had not yet seen Muehu Katekale, said to her son, "You are clean now, and you feel good. Let's go dry ourselves in the sun."

After drying themselves, the woman went to find her wings.

"My wings, my child! My wings, where are my wings? I have lost my wings! How will we get back up to heaven?" and she started to cry.

Muehu Katekale felt that the moment had come to show himself.

"Woman why are you crying?"

"We have lost our wings. How can we get back to our home?"

"But where did you put them? We will try and find them" said Muehu Katekale.

Muehu Katekale and the woman searched and searched until finally, they found the wings. The woman and her son thanked him, fastened their wings onto their back and flew up into the sky.

Alone again and despairing, Muehu Katekale sang his hopelessness in the *nakamal*. The next day, he went to his garden to cut some reeds. He cut one hundred reeds, pulled off their leaves, and cleaned them well. Then he took up his bow, adjusting the big wooden bracelet that all men from Ambae wear on their wrists. It prevents them from being hurt by the tendon of the bow during the backlash after the arrow has flown. Thus, he concentrated and shot his first arrow towards the sky.

The arrow buried itself in the heavens and Muehu Katekale shot the second arrow that buried itself into the first, then a third that buried itself in the second and so on and so on. Muehu Katekale sweated and his arm hurt him. Little by little as he shot his arrows, he saw them coming closer and closer to him, until the last one touched the ground.

Then he called the wind to test this sort of rope that he had just made with all of his arrows buried one into the other. The wind arrived softly at first and then stronger and stronger. Muehu Katekale yelled into the storm, "Come, bend them, but don't break them. I want to climb into the heavens!"

And the wind bent the reeds but it did not break them.

Muehu Katekale grabbed on to the reeds and climbed, climbed into the clouds. When he arrived in heaven, everything was different. There were a lot of people talking, but he couldn't understand their language. Nobody walked, everyone flew. Muehu Katekale hid behind a cloud and watched.

"Look! The men that I saw swimming in the sea! Oh! They've disappeared! And the woman, she doesn't walk but flies!" said Muehu Katekale.

Muehu Katekala ran after the woman and cried, "Woman, woman, listen... listen..."

The woman didn't hear him, she spoke and everyone went down on their knees in front of her. She was tall. Muehu Katekale was scared of everyone there. He climbed a *navele,* those trees that bear fruit like almonds, and stayed there all night.

The next day, the woman appeared again. She talked and she talked. Muehu Katekale plucked a green almond and on the pulp, with his nail, he drew his face, his face that he had often seen in the clear waters of the rivers. He then threw the almond at the woman's feet. The woman didn't see it and continued to speak. Muehu Katekale plucked a second almond and drew his face once again on the pulp and then threw it again at her feet. The woman didn't see it. A third time, he drew his face on an almond and threw it at the feet of the woman who was still speaking.

The child picked up the almond and said to his mother, "Mother, look! My father's face is drawn on the pulp of this *navele!"*

The woman looked at the almond.

"You are right, my son, but..."

Lifting her head, she saw above her Muehu Katekale in the *navele.*

"What are you doing here and how did you get here?"

"I love you, woman, and I wanted to find you again. I shot arrows into the sky and then I used them like a rope to climb up here."

"You love me, man? That's strange. I'm not from your home. Look..." said the woman.

The woman then took a fan, the kind of fan that we call *"Iri"* in the language of Longana, and waved it so that the winds of heaven swept away all bad thoughts and dirty things; not one was left there.

Raising herself up on a cloud, she said, "Go back to where you came from! You are in a sacred, sacred place here! In our language we say that you are in a *"Outekokona."* Go back to your home. Climb back down your rope of arrows, and when you have arrived on your Earth you will shake your rope of arrows. My son will free them and they will fall back into your garden."

Muehu Katekale, weakened, climbed back down to earth. He called out to his friends and started to dance in an effort to forget. After the dance, he felt strong once again. He was the powerful Muehu Katekale. Not heeding the words of the woman, he took up his bow and shot an arrow into the heavens. The arrow touched the sky and fell back to earth. He then supplicated his god, "Tagaro, help me!"

He shot another arrow and then another but both of them fell at his feet. The doors of heaven were forever closed to him and Muehu Katekale was left alone with his sorrow.

This legend from Longana was given to us in Bislama by Marsden Lolo.
Adapted by Paul Gardissat.   Nabanga n° 52-53 (1977)

The legend of Tagaro
(Maewo)

Before Man

A long time ago, the island of Maewo was joined to Ambae and Pentecost. However, a horrible woman started peeing and peeing without realising that she was changing life as it was known then. The sea started to encroach upon the lower parts of Maewo and separated the lands. Good to drink in times past, the water took on a very salty taste. Then, the rocks started to explode. The island of Ambae was born, spitting fire and throwing red stones into the salted sea.

It rained for months, unleashing the battle of water and fire. Little by little, the water won. The volcanoes were dampened and its craters became lakes that still exist today: Manaro Ngoru (the dry lake), Manaro Lakuha (the big lake), and Lanaro Lakuha Vui (the big lake of spirits).

Finally, the rained stopped and strange beings began to arrive from no one knows where. They were the *Talu Tuei*, crazy and ignorant beings. They ate the pips of the fruits from which the pulp is eaten, and the pulp of the fruits from which the pips are eaten. They lived in caves and under trees, and they never built houses. When they encountered rocks in their path, they hacked at them with stone axes instead of going around them. They did not cultivate yams, but ate instead the bitter, wild yams. When the sea was wild, they fed it *laplap* to calm it. They showily committed suicide. To do this, they would thrust a sharp wooden stake into the ground under a tree and then throw themselves on it. Those who did not impale themselves were ridiculed. On the contrary, those that died were given innumerable honours. It has been said that they walked backwards and did everything in reverse. From time to time, pieces of their pottery can still be found while working the land for gardens. Next, others, the *Ragmuehu,* arrived, but nothing is known of them.

Tagaro creates man

Before the creation of man as we know him today, these beings were governed by two principle entities of which the nature is not well-known. It is sometimes said that they were men, but others say that they were spirits. The first of these man-spirits was Tagaro who was industrious and able. He was not very strong, but he was the epitome of well-being. The second, Mueragbuto, was very ignorant, stupid, and ugly. He exemplified disaster and war. In an effort to seem as intelligent as Tagaro, he imitated him in everything. Tagaro, tired of his antics, burnt him alive.

Tagaro then found himself alone on the sodden island, and so he took some mud and fashioned an image of himself.

"Here is a head," he said, "and these two holes will be eyes." Next, he sculpted a nose, ears, a mouth, and thought, "From here will issue forth the most beautiful speeches and sometimes the ugliest too."

He made hands, a sex, and legs. When Tagaro had finished this first person, it looked like him. He was so pleased, that he made ten additional figures. He thought, "This way, the first will not be alone. He would have been lonely in his solitude. To whom would he have spoken, for whom would he have created beautiful things?"

Once the ten figures were finished, Tagaro blew into the mouth of the first and out of it came a cry. He then blew on the ears and the new man heard. Tagaro blew on the feet, the hands, the sex, the eyes, and the man started to live.

Tagaro took the second and repeated his actions. He continued with the third and the fourth when he exclaimed, "This is marvellous! I have created beings. They can move, think, and they came from my fingers!"

When he beheld his creations, Tagaro was perplexed. He turned them around and around, and realised that he had made only males. "You all have the same sex. I haven't made any women!"

Tagaro creates woman

Tagaro told his men to form a line. He took an orange and threw it at the testicles of one of the males. They broke off and fell to the ground. The man twisted in pain and began to cry. He had become a woman. Then, Tagaro took the leaves from a vine called *Tupe* and made a belt. He placed it round the kidneys of the woman and told her, "You are a woman. You may no longer stay with us. Leave."

The woman left, disappointed, and went into her house alone. Tagaro then told one of the men to go and visit the woman. "You will listen well to what she says," he ordered.

The woman welcomed the man sent by the creator. "My older brother, I am pleased to see you. But what do you want from me?"

Tagaro explained to the man that she considered herself as his younger sister. He sent a second man.

The woman said to him, "Hello, my little brother."

Finally, Tagaro sent the last man.

The woman said to him, "My husband, why do you come to see me?"

The man went back to Tagaro and told him, "The woman called me her husband."

Tagaro responded, "Then she is your wife. You will live together. However, you should have no sexual relations until I come to show you how it's done."

Alas, the husband disobeyed the creator and the same evening, deflowered his spouse. She cried out, and blood ran onto the mat. Attracted by the cries, Tagaro came running. He scolded the man.

"You didn't wait for me. You have hurt her. Now, we will have war."

The woman gave birth to two boys. From her left breast, she nursed Mueragbuto and from her right breast, Tagaro. It was in this way that men were separated into two clans and in this way that men are now obliged to choose their wives from the opposing clan.

The legend that you have just read was taken from a collection of books written in Ambae language by Father Jean-Baptiste Suas in 1911, while he was missionary at Lolopuepue.
It was orginally told in Ambae language by Tai and translated into bislama by Marsden Lolo. Paul Gardissat wrote the French adaptation.

Nabanga n°90 (21 Oct. 1978)

How Tagaro beat Mweragbuto the traitor
(Ambae)

Once upon a time, at Lolovenue on the island of Ambae, there was a venerable chief by the name of Tagaro. This man was known for his war strategies, his courage, and his generosity to his people. In fact, during this time, Tagaro and his men did a lot for the prosperity of their clan. It was at this time that they possessed immense wealth. This made other neighbouring chiefs jealous, but they did not dare confront the redoubtable and prestigious chief of Lolovenue. It was even said that the objects that he owned made him invincible in battle.

Mweragbuto, the chief of one of Tagaro's allied villages, secretly coveted his riches and his fertile lands. He was planning to overthrow Tagaro and to take his place as the head chief of Ambae. Tagaro, however, suspected that Mweragbuto wanted to get rid of him. One day, the chief Mweragbuto appeared in Lolovenue loaded with gifts. According to custom from time immemorial, the two chiefs proceeded to give and receive gifts. They discussed at length the institution of a new law that would favour commerce and exchange throughout the Island. Night was falling when the two chiefs finally finished their discussion, satisfied that peace had once again been restored. Tagaro, far from understanding the evil designs of Mweragbuto, offered proper hospitality to his guest who then spent the night in a hut reserved for visitors. The next morning, while Tagaro was bathing in the sea, Mweragbuto went down to the shore. Seeing Tagaro's clothing, he wanted to take off with them in order to acquire their magic powers.

"Mission accomplished! I'll put on Tagaro's clothes and that imbecile's power and glory shall be mine!"

So, the spy went into action. To distract Tagaro, Mweragbuto questioned his host while discreetly putting on the clothing lying on the sand.

"What is this pile of accessories?"

"They are my clothes, my friend. Leave them alone."

However, Mweragbuto, still teasing Tagaro, continued to put on the accessories that constituted Tagaro's clothing.

"Do you find my accessories nice?" asked Tagaro.

"Of course, my friend. They become you!"

93

"Thank you for your compliments, dear friend. Now, all you have to do is find yourself new clothes. As for me, it's not that I haven't appreciated your hospitality, but I have some work to do."

"Hey! Mweragbuto! Thief! Give me back my clothing!"

Tagaro yelled and yelled at his guest to bring back his clothes, but Mweragbuto was already deep in the bush. The chief's guards ran after the thief, but he was gone. The big chief Tagaro sent a messenger to Mweragbuto's clan that same day to get his clothing back. The thieving chief threatened to kill the messenger, but decided instead to send the following message.

"Tell your chief that his clothes are now mine and that he will never get them back."

Having received this message the next day, Tagaro started to worry about his stolen clothes.

"I must get my things back or else Mweragbuto will use their magic powers against me and my reign will be finished" Tagaro said.

Thus, he bade his fastest warrior to come to him and he gave him a message to pass.

"Run quickly and tell that dirty thief that he must give me back my things. If he does not, he will be severely punished for his crimes."

When the second messenger from the chief of Lolovenue had given this news to Mweragbuto, the latter declared, "Tell your chief that if he wants war, he will have it!"

So, without waiting, the warrior took this message to his chief who immediately convened his war council. Once the war had been unanimously approved, Tagaro mobilised his entire force against Mweragbuto whose men were only three hundred strong. At dawn the next day, Mweragbuto sent one hundred warriors against the Lolovenue clan. The battle was horrendous and Tagaro's men massacred every last one of Mweragbuto's warriors.

The day after this crushing defeat, Mweraguto sent one hundred fresh men and Tagaro's veritable killing machines finished them all off. Seeing this, he sent his last one hundred warriors. And again, the men from Lolovenue quickly took them down. The day after this last defeat, Mweragbuto, seized with panic, realised that all of his men were dead. However, he was quickly calmed. He put on Tagaro's clothing so that he would become invincible and able to defeat Tagaro and his warriors alone. He hung a conch shell from his nose, a *tamtam* from his right ear, and a woven coconut palm mat from his back. Then, he went to Lolovenue where he started to fight. Upon seeing

Mweragbuto coming, Tagaro's warriors were terrified and ran into the bush. Even the great Tagaro was worried when he saw his adversary armed to the teeth. It was, to be sure, the stolen magic powers of Mweragbuto the traitor that worried Tagaro the most. He advanced to meet his enemy. Mweragbuto shot poisoned arrows that Tagaro was able to dodge easily. Tagaro ducked, dodged, and jumped as if to catch something invisible in the air and he slunk close to the ground covered in his enemies' blood. It was these acrobatics that allowed Tagaro to get closer and closer to his enemy. Mweragbuto took out his one hundredth and last arrow. The arrow missed its target.

"Now, it's just you and me! The final hour of reckoning has come," cried Tagaro.

The clothing thief became frightened and ran towards the bush in order to escape his enemy. But before he could enter the safety of the forest, Tagaro jumped on him and pushed him to the ground. He called to his men and told them to tie the prisoner to a *namele* tree trunk. Tagaro then took back his clothing and killed his enemy with one blow to the head. He told his men to burn the corpse. Once this war had ended, peace returned to Lolovenue and Tagaro reigned for many years as supreme chief of Ambae.

This legend was given by Georges Ruru of Lolovenue, Ambae.
It was written in Bislama by Rita and Georges of Lolovenue.
It was translated into French by Patrick Rory
and into English by Kendra Gates.

Nabanga n°30 (05/06/76)

The legend of kava
(Maewo)

At one time on Maewo, there was a strange man who fed on human flesh. His name was Aso. He reigned in terror over the whole island. When his appetite pushed him to lurk near villages, men, women, and children would all run in fear screaming, "Be careful! the horrible man-eater, is coming!" The inhabitants of the island could never live in peace. They were always worried.

Aso had a wife who was very ugly. She was a witch who prepared his cannibalistic meals. Often, it was she who hunted their prey. While Aso liked fat bodies, well-fed on wild pigs, she preferred young children who were more tender and less fatty. This was no doubt because Tagaro had never allowed this terrible woman to have a child of her own.

In one of the villages where Aso often went to hunt his food, a man had just married a beautiful woman. They were both very happy. However, wars were frequent and one day, the young husband had to go off to fight. Alas, he never returned because he was killed by the first arrow that was shot. The woman cried a lot, soaking herself with the tears of love. Her only consolation was to see her stomach move. Indeed, she was pregnant by her handsome husband, her courageous warrior.

A little while later, she gave birth to magnificent twins on the island of Maewo. These children grew. They ate taro, yams, fish and pigs. As every man from Maewo needs to know how to fight, their mother taught them.

"I will teach you the work of a man," she said. "One day, you must know how to kill your enemies without them killing you first. That is the law of our island. Here is a bow. Take it and be careful when the string rebounds. Here is your father's *nalnal*. It is heavy so hold it well. In a little while, you will know how to use these weapons. Go and practise. But beware, my children. Aso is dangerous. His wife is a cunning ogress. They live in that direction, so you should never go there. They will eat you like they have eaten others. You don't have a father anymore, and I don't have a husband. I only have you."

The twins listened to their mother closely, but she had only peaked their curiosity. They told themselves that they had become men and that they had the necessary weapons to defend themselves. Thus, they dared approach Aso's house. It was the horrible woman that welcomed them.

"I am so sorry. Aso is not here, but he won't be long. Go and wait for him in the *nakamal* and I will call you when he comes," she told them.

The two children went into the *nakamal* to wait.

The evil woman then called her husband by singing,

> *Aso Aso Ruru netunku Aso*
> *Ruru netunku Aso*
> *Gandaru tamate mo toga lo gamali*
> *Gamu letuagi ganku letuagi*
> *Aso, Aso, Aso*

Aso, in his garden, heard the song. "There must be something happening," he said to himself. "Maybe my wife has found some fresh meat!" and he greedily rubbed his hands together.

As his wife continued to sing, he yelled, "I'm coming, I'm coming, evil creature that I love!"

Aso arrive in the *nasara* and said, "So, my ugly one, what have you prepared for me? At least a meal fit for Tagaro, I hope!"

The woman laughed, "My friend, there are two boys who have come to see you. They are waiting in the *nakamal.*"

She laughed louder and louder. Aso went to see the children. They were amusing themselves by making sand drawings. Aso tried to be very likeable.

"I am charmed by your visit and very pleased that you want to get to know me. But first," he suggested, "let's go eat in my house."

The children responded, "Thank you, Aso, we are so very hungry."

Aso sat them down in his house and went to get some *laplap.* However, the twins had understood his plan.

One of them said to the other, "He wants to kill us while we're busy eating. We should eat one after another, so that one of us is always on guard and ready to fight."

They organised themselves so well so that Aso was unable to attack them during the meal. So he came up with another trick.

"Now," he said to them, "you will kill the lice that is making my head itch."

"Good idea," said the children. "We will kill them and eat them. Lay down over there."

Aso laid down on the ground, and the children caressed him so gently that he was soon asleep. The twins smiled when they heard him snore. They then attached his braids,

one by one, to a beam in his house. When Aso finally woke up, he couldn't move. The more he moved, the more it hurt him.

One of the children told him, "We know that you eat men."

Aso groaned, "No, that's not true. Have pity and let me go."

The twins did not take pity on him, and killed him with a sharp blow of the *nalnal* and then set fire to his house. They then went to Aso's wife and said, "Horrible woman, spread your legs. We want to see what you have there."

The woman laughed and refused to obey. The children insisted. They had heated a black stone used to cook *laplap* and were holding it between wooden pincers called *"gaibala"* in the language of Maewo. The old woman finally spread her legs. Then, one of the twins shoved the burning stone inside of her and the ogress screamed in pain.

"Here is your payment," said one of the children. "We have killed Aso and now it's your turn to die."

They killed the woman with a blow of the *nalnal* and they set her house on fire. They left behind the stone with which they had burnt the witch's sex. The twins announced the death of Aso and his wife, and everyone from all the neighbouring villages came to see.

"Oh," one of the twins cried, "look at the plant that is growing from the place where we left the stone."

Another man asked, "Do you think that it is good?"

They saw a rat eating a branch from the young bush. Its behaviour became bizarre; it started to dance and sway its head from side to side. When the drunken rat left, it had problems getting back into its hole. Thus, the men grated the root of the plant and drank its juice. It tasted like earth but each man said, "I feel very good."

The men of Ambae came to buy some pigs on Maewo. They tried this new drink and took it back to their island. Kava made men happy: they love it like they love their women because kava was born of a woman.

This legend was given in Bislama to Peter Crowe by Albert Tovotu of Fingalato,
a little village in the heights of Ambae.
Adapted by Paul Gardissat.

Nabanga n°89 (07/10/78)

MALAMPA Province

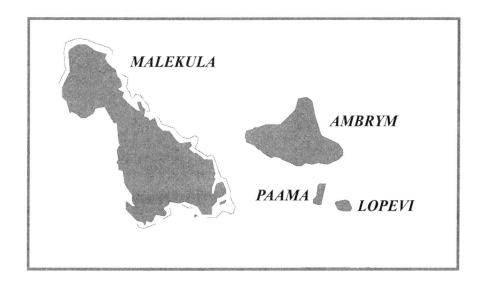

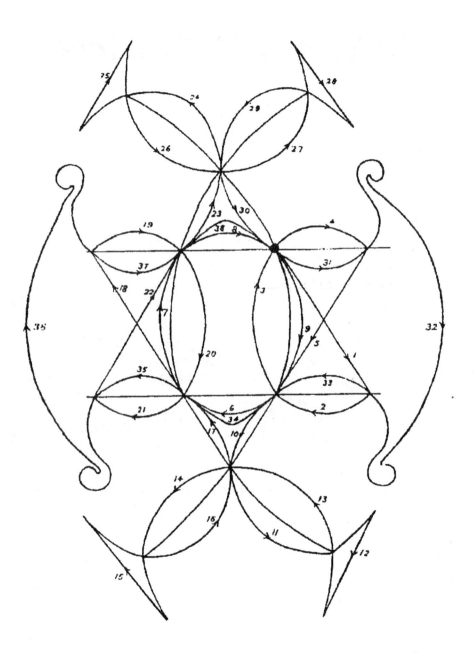

A sand drawing from South West Malekula representing the stone of the Nevinbumbaau (Deacon - 1934)

Ambat and Nevinbumbaau
(Malekula)

It is raining on the big island of Malekula. The clouds are full. However, the wind is soft today. In the early hours of the morning, smoke comes out of the huts in this village where a small people live their daily lives. We are on the side of those southwestern hills on that mysterious island where the people either don't know, choose to ignore, or make war with each other. There are devils everywhere. These devils can take on human form. There are also spirits. These spirits roam the mountains and the valleys chasing those unfortunate enough to be caught in their path. The bush is haunted by a strange world that is always looking for a man to eat. The smoke is coming from the huts covered in ivory palm leaves and the rain falls softly as Malekula wakes up. It is early morning, a chilly morning. Near the big bay in the southwest, there is the island of Tomman. It is here that the world started. It is from here that the first men came. This is most certainly because they were much safer on their little island than on the big one. Tomman island is a sort of fortified citadel. The sea that surrounds it acts as a rampart against those who might attack. Despite the security of Tomman, people also live in the mountains facing this little island. And on one of these hills live Ambat, Ambat and his brothers.

Ambat is the biggest. Ambat is the oldest. Ambat is the leader. Ambat is also white. White, you ask? Why? Well, we don't know. Ambat has four brothers: Awinrara, Awingotgot, Awinsapetliu, and Awinqitwas. This is his entire family. The rain continues to fall from the sky as the sun rises.

Ambat, who always leads, says to his brothers, "My brothers! Today, the sun is very wet. Take these small bananas stumps and we will go to the garden to plant them."

Ambat's family takes the little banana stumps and goes to plant them in the garden just as Ambat said. The trees grow, give a bunch of bananas, and the first ripe ones belong to Awinrara.

"Awinrara, your bananas are ripe. The spirits have deemed it so. Now, we will go fishing in the sea and make a *laplap* with the fish that we catch. Take your bow and arrows; we are leaving now!"

And they left. Ambat is in front and his brothers follow him. When they arrive at the shore, the brothers spread out. Ambat goes to one side and the brothers to another, each trying to kill a fish with his bow from on top of a boulder. However, a *sangalegale,* a *lisepsep,* is there, hidden behind a large stone. She is looking at the big family while they fish. This *sangalegale* is a terrible woman, very little, with long hair that falls all the way to her feet, and hands that end in claw-like nails. Her name is Nevinbumbaau. While the *lisepsep* walks, she always throws her long, flaccid breasts over her shoulders. A *lisepsep* is never beautiful and is always very small. And so, the tiny old woman is there watching these men.

"You, my pretties, I will have you and I will eat you! Ha ha ha ha ha ha ha ha ha!"

The men, who do not suspect a thing, continue to fish and to jump from rock to rock. As for the woman, she is planning her hunting strategies.

"This is what I need. I need a nice flat stone to sit on, taking care to lift my little old breasts. As soon as I get up, they will see me or at least hear me... one of them will come to investigate."

The woman prepares her stone and sits down. She sits and finally lies down, tired from waiting. Suddenly, she stands up quickly. At the same time, the rock explodes. The men continue to fish and catch a lot. Each of them is holding a long rope strung with many fish. Awinrara approaches the rock where the woman had been sitting and without realising it, he finds himself next to her. He goes even closer to the rock and ...BOOM! The rock explodes and the woman appears.

"Aha! Was it you that was on this exploding stone?"

"Yes, it was me. But what are you doing here? Are you fishing?"

"Yes, I'm fishing. My brothers are behind those rocks."

"Where are you going? Stay here... don't leave!"

"No, I told you that I'm fishing. Leave me alone. My bananas were the first to ripen and with them we shall make a *laplap*. So, I need to fish."

"No, come with me. You shall see that you will be more comfortable at the house."

"Bubu, I told you that I am fishing. My bananas are ripe, and I must find fish. The others are waiting for me."

"No, come with me. We'll eat the *laplap* there together."

"Stop insisting. The others are waiting for me."

"Come, I tell you. We'll eat the *laplap* and these fish by ourselves."

Awinrara finally lets himself be persuaded by the *sangalegale*. Both of them head for the hills. On the way, Awinrara becomes a little worried.

"Where is your house?"

"There, over there. It is so close by, that when you are there you will be able to hear Ambat and your brothers talking. It's not far off at all… it's right here."

The woman, the *sangalegale,* is lying and thinking of only one thing: eating the man! When they arrive at the woman's house, they both start to prepare the *laplap.* Awinrara prepares the hot stones while the woman grates the bananas, makes the pudding, spreads it on leaves, and closes it up. The two of them put this package on the hot stones and cover it up.

"Now, the *laplap* is done. We will take it off of the fire with the fish. You will enjoy yourself. You're happy here with me, right?"

"Yes, but as soon as we have eaten, I will return to my brothers. They might get worried."

"Worried? Why?"

The *sangalegale* harps on the idea of a feast. A *sangalegale* has reactions that can be very bizarre. A *sangalegale* can do many things, many things that no one knows about.

"Alright, I'm leaving now."

"Oh no, you're not leaving. Look outside! You know, I think that it is going to rain."

Awinrara put his head outside the low door of the hut and looked at the sky. There was not a single cloud.

"The sky is clear. I'm leaving."

At the same instant, the old woman farts. A lightning bolt rips across the sky and it starts to rain.

"You see! It's raining. You can't leave. You must stay."

In the old woman's hut, there is a very big hole hidden by a flat stone.

The *sangalegale,* who wants to keep Awinrara by any means, says, "Wait a second. I'm going to change my mat at the back of the hut. I'll be right back."

This is a trick that Awinarara, of course, is not aware of. The old women goes to the back of the hut to the big hole and lifts off the stone covering.

She comes back and says, "I look better like this, don't I?

"Oh, I don't know… I think I'll go now."

"No, I told you that it was raining. Here, will you at least go and put the rest of this *laplap* in a basket that you will find hanging at the back of the hut?"

Awinrara takes the *laplap,* wraps it in some leaves, and goes to the back of the dark hut. He does not see the big hole and falls in it.

"Aha! The first one! Ha ha ha ha!"

As for Ambat's other brothers, they aren't too worried. They think that Awinrara spent the night at a friend's house. So the next day, they start to fish again. Awingotgot gets further away from his brothers without realising that he is getting closer to the *sangale-gale's* flat rock. He approaches a little more and the old woman who has been sitting on the rock takes a step closer to him, making the rock explode again. The woman appears.

"Are you looking for fish?"

"Yes, I'm fishing. But did you see that? That rock just exploded!"

"Where are you going?"

"I told you that I'm fishing. Have you seen Awinrara around here? He disappeared yesterday."

"No, I haven't seen him."

"It's very strange. Something must have happened to him."

"No, I assure you. I haven't seen anyone. But you should come to my house and we'll make a *laplap.*"

Awingotgot doesn't want to go, but the old woman persuades him and Ambat's second brother follows her to her house. In the same way, the woman prepares the *laplap.* Awingotgot heats the rocks and as soon as they had eaten, he wants to leave. The *sangalegale* farts and the rain starts to fall.

"You can't leave. It's raining. Gather up the *laplap,* wrap it in some leaves, and go hang it on that bamboo. You see it...at the other end of the hut."

As planned, the woman had lifted the stone that covered the hole. Awingotgot goes to hang the *laplap,* doesn't see the hole, and falls in.

"Two now! Ha ha ha ha ha ha ha!"

The *sangalegale* is satisfied. Everything is happening according to plan. Two of her prey are in the hole. She doesn't need to wonder anymore; the system works. The *san-galegale* lays down on the stone on the beach and waits for Ambat's third brother, Awinqitwas. He arrives, still fishing. The stone explodes.

"Come to my house! We are going to make a *laplap!*"

In the same way, Awinqitwas goes to her house and the two of them prepare a *laplap.*

"Can you please put the rest of the *laplap* into the basket hanging at the end of the hut?"

"Aha! The third one! Ha ha ha ha ha ha!"

After the third one, the fourth one, Awinsapetliu, disappeared in the same way into the bottom of the hole. There is only one brother left: Ambat.

"It wouldn't be strange for Awinrara to disappear... I know him! He's always chit-chatting! However, to have all my brothers disappear one after the other, well, that's not normal. I will go and look for them. Yes, tomorrow, I will try to find them."

The next day, Ambat goes to the garden. The bananas are rotten.

"I have let my bananas rot. That is a bad sign."

Ambat, the oldest of them all, is more cautious. He gets some dry coconuts, husks them, breaks them, takes out the flesh, and attaches it to his hair along with some bananas and bamboo knives. All of this securely on his head, Ambat goes down to the sea and approaches the exploding rock. The old woman appears.

"Ah-ha! That is what has hurt my brothers. I think I understand. We'll see what happens..."

"Is that you, Ambat, in flesh and bone before me?"

"Yes, it is me! Ambat. Where are my brothers?"

"I haven't seen them."

"You haven't seen them?"

"No, I told you that I haven't seen them."

"Yes, you have."

"No, I tell you. But what are you doing here?"

"I'm fishing. My bananas are ripe. I want to eat some *laplap* with fish. My brothers' bananas have rotted. It's very strange."

"Oh! Come with me to my house!"

"Where is your house?"

"There, very close by."

"But I don't want to go to your house. I have my own and do not need yours."

"Come, Ambat, we shall cook the *laplap* at my house."

Ambat follows the woman. As soon as the *laplap* is done, the two eat it.

"I'm leaving. I've had enough."

"No, I'm sure that it is raining outside. I'll go look."

The woman farts and a lightning bolt rips through the sky.

"You see, I told you. It's raining, so you can't leave. You will stay with me and we shall sleep together!"

The rain is falling outside and poor Ambat is obliged to stay in the old woman's house.

"Put this *laplap* in the basket hanging in that dark corner at the back of the hut... then, come and get into bed with me."

The woman had again put the basket above the dark hole. In his confusion, Ambat doesn't see the hole and falls in.

"Ha ha ha! The fifth one! Ha ha ha! They are all in the hole! Ha ha ha!"

"Oh, my brothers."

"Ambat? You, too?"

"We are all at the bottom of this hole."

"The *lisepsep* wants to eat us. It's all clear to me now."

"How are we going to get out of this hole? We're all going to die! And we're starving!"

"Here, I brought some *laplap* and some coconuts. Eat, and tomorrow we'll try to get out of here."

Ambat and his brothers fall asleep. The next morning, Ambat gives them all a banana and satisfies their hunger.

"Now that you have eaten, take this. Here are some bamboo knives. We will try to dig. First, we must find some banyan roots."

Ambat and his brothers dig with their bamboo knives. They find some banyan roots and follow them. Ambat is sure that they will lead them to the banyan that is next to their village's *nasara*. The woman, however, still believes that everything is fine and that her prey is still at the bottom of their hole. So, she counts the days that separate her from the *namangki* that she has dream of for so long.

"In two days, it will be my *namangki*. I will be able to kill some pigs and rise in rank. I will be a *mwaluen!* In two days, it is my *namangki*. I will tell everyone. Sound the *tamtam!*"

And these wooden bells resound throughout the bush of Malekula to make known to those who were not aware that soon there would be a *namangki*.

"My *namangki*, my *namangki*, my *namangki*... My *namangki*, my *namangki*, my *namangki*...!"

Amabat and his brothers, at the bottom of their hole, continue to dig. When they are tired, Ambat sings. The five brothers dig and dig, throwing the ground behind them. They have found the banyan roots and are following them.

"Ambat, we're tired and we're hungry!"

"Have a little more gumption! Here is some coconut. Take it and shut up."

Ambat starts to sing again. They keep digging and eventually arrive at the foot of the banyan tree.

"The banyan is above us. We will soon be free!"

The people of Malekula had heard the news and are now arriving from all around. They are singing and dancing. Ambat and his brothers have arrived at the end of their imprisonment. Only a little bit of earth separates them from their freedom. So, Ambat, in order to encourage his brothers, sings for the last time.

"Let's go!"

Ambat pokes his head out of the hole. He finds a bare field and realises that he's in a corner of the *nasara*.

"My brothers! Listen! They are dancing and dancing. Soon, night will fall. They will all go into their huts. Then, and only then, can we come out. For now, we must stay hidden."

The people who had come to the *namangki* are singing and dancing. However, some people are worried at not seeing Ambat and his brothers. They are well-known in the area.

Some people were saying, "Where is Ambat? This *namangki* can't take place without him and his brothers."

Night falls. Ambat and his brothers sneak between the huts. They want to change their *nambas*. They wash their bodies and their faces, attach bells to their feet, stick flowers and feathers into their hair, and put croton leaves into their belts. When they are ready, they jump in with the other dancers. They dance this way until morning.

"Come, my brothers. Dance! Dance! Dance, and you shall see…"

When the sun starts to rise between the huts and the palm trees, Ambat, whom nobody had recognised thanks to his heavy makeup, goes to see the *lisepsep*.

"This is your *namangki*. Where is the pig that you must kill to feed the people who have been dancing and singing all night? Everyone is happy! Go and kill a pig to make them even happier."

The woman then runs towards the hole and peers in.

"But…but, where are they? There is nothing in this hole! What am I going to do? The pig isn't there… it has run away!"

"The pig has run away? When you organise a *namangki* of this size, people are generally extra careful that the pig doesn't escape! What is the only thing that can make the people who have sung and danced all night happy? A pig to eat! The people will eat the *laplap* with pork that we give to them. Then they watch the *namangki*. Then, they dance. Then, two more pigs are killed so that each person will have something to take back with them. Where is the pig? Where are the pigs?"

"There aren't any!"

"This woman doesn't have any pigs because she was going to use us as her pigs. She wanted to kill us! Yes, she was going to use us for pigs! She wanted to rise in the *namangki* ranks by killing us! Today, it is she that will die. You will die for your own *namangki* because you are a *sangalegale*. Your *namangki* ends here."

Amabat jumps on the woman and starts to hit her.

"You wanted to eat us, huh? Where is your strength? Speak! You have no more power. Hey, where are your pigs? Huh? Take this. And this. And that."

Ambat brings his club down on the old woman's head with all of his strength. She falls to the earth, dead.

"And now, you may kill all the pigs that you find. Kill them! Kill them all!"

And so, the men did as Ambat told them to. They went everywhere around the *nakamal* and killed all of the pigs that they saw. Some took them back to Tomman island and others to their own villages far away in the mountains near Southwest Bay. As for the woman, she is still there spread out on her own *nasara,* and there she will rot.

This legend was given in Bislama by Georges Eiler from the village
of Lembinwin in Southwest Bay, Malekula.
The radio adaptation was done by Paul Gardissat.

Radio New Hebrides

The two Lindenda

(A legend from Tomman Island)

Among the numerous villages on the big island of Malekula, there was, during ancient times, the village of Ymvanhna. In this village, there lived two women who were both named Lindenda, a name that came up quite often in custom. Indeed, it was through them that the first coconut palm was born. They constantly urinated in a spot, named *Ambweibwa,* reserved for just such an action. One day, a sapling sprung up in this place. They watered it with their urine. It is often the way in the legends from this archipelago that the mysteries of creation were explained.

Time passed, and the plant grew. It became a tree that unfurled itself against the sky, a new tree that the women decided to call *"namatou,"* or coconut. Then, as a challenge, they said, "No one will ever discover what we have called this tree, but if they do, we will marry them."

They returned to the village to announce the news. "A new tree has been born, and it gives round fruit. What is its name? The first to say it will be our husband," the Lindendas said.

From *nakamal* to *nakamal,* the news travelled across the plains and over the mountains. Everyone became aware of the mystery and then the game. The two Lindenda would be very kind to he who could solve the riddle. Oh, the two beautiful Lindenda, the two powerful Lindenda! The news even travelled to the inhabitants of Tomman island at the southwest tip of the big island. Of course, all of the men ran to see the tree and guess its name. However, none of them had the imagination or knowledge needed to find the answer. Each had an idea, but no one could reveal the answer. "It's a *nakatambol* - no! a *navele* - or maybe a *nakavika* - perhaps a *nandouledarle* - a *natapoa?"* people said.

No, this was a tree much more original that those, and much more difficult than a simple guess. Despite arrivals from the mountains and all directions on Malekula, much more talent than any man on the island possessed was needed to win the two Lindenda.

The news had also reached the ears of a famous family from Imaral of which one of the five brothers was named Ambat. Unfortunately, at this time, Ambat was ill. Sores covered his entire body. He was wracked with fever and pain. Ambat couldn't even walk. However, he told his four brothers to go without him to the village of the two Lindenda. While he remained in bed, the others left, travelling over rivers, climbing mountains, and arriving finally in Ymvahna only to find it chock full of men making their guesses. What could this strange tree be? Like the others, Ambat's brothers circled the trunk, looked at the strange, round fruits high in the tree, and discussed their ideas. Truly, the puzzle was too difficult and so they returned to their home without having solved it.

Avunrara told his bed-ridden brother about their trip and the ambiance at Ymvahna, describing the strange, new tree. Ambat pushed him to return to the two Lindendas village with his three brothers and continue to search for the name given by the women.

The next morning, the four brothers returned to Ymvahna. Once they had gone, Ambat rose painfully, so eaten was his body by the sickness and his sores by the mosquitoes. He worked his way into the bush, chose a tree named *"narbout,"* cut its trunk in two, entered inside of it, and all of his sores were pulled from his body onto the tree. Ambat came out of the *"narbout"* with a new skin, rid of his illness. He was once again handsome: he covered his sex with a new *nambas,* changed his belt, and attached a fresh branch of croton leaves behind it. Very proud and in good health, Ambat started off for Ymvahna.

Once he arrived, he went right to the famous tree. The crowd turned towards him to admire his good looks. Among the numerous people at this place were Ambat's brothers. However, they did not at first recognise him for they found it impossible to believe that his sores could have been healed so quickly and that his fatigue did not stop him from climbing the mountains. Yet, when he spoke, they knew that it was indeed Ambat.

Ambat said to the assembled crowd, "This tree is named *"namatou."* It's a coconut palm."

Then, the Lindendas exclaimed before the stupefied crowd, "Yes! This is the man that we will marry!"

This incident provoked both astonishment and jealousy from the spectators. But Ambat, exultant with joy, ordered his strongest brother to climb the tree. Avunrara did it. Arriving at the top, he marvelled at the beauty of the fruit and touched it. Ambat then told him to remove his hand and he shot an arrow into the coconut. Then, an extraordinary thing occurred; the pierced fruit turned itself upside-down. This is why the eyes of the coconut on the tree that once looked at the ground now look at the sky.

Ambat again ordered his brother to pick the fruit and all the coconuts fell to the ground, one after another. Avunrara came down. On the advice of his brother, he started to husk the coconut with a sharp stick and then cracked it on a rock. He put the white flesh into his mouth and cried, "By the family of Ambat and by all the ancestors whose skulls rest in our *nakamal,* this fruit is good!"

The whole village threw themselves at the coconuts and tasted them. Everyone proclaimed its excellence. In the general gaiety of the moment and at the request of the Lindendas, Ambat received the honour of killing the pig for the feast. The beast was skinned and gutted. Once this was finished, Ambat offered the head of the pig to his brothers and each went his own way. Ambat lead the two Lindendas to a hut by a round about way in order to defray curiosity. This hut, called *"Lohintange,"* was deep in the bush. Then, he returned to the split tree that held his sores and covered his body with them again. Finally, he wrapped in some leaves the pig's heart which he had kept hidden from the others.

At this moment, Avunrara came upon his brother and inquired as to what he was doing. Ambat replied, "These are outgrowths that eat illnesses. They grow everywhere on rotten trees." Avunrara insisted that he was hungry and that he wanted to eat something. Ambat gave in at such strong insistence and the two men started to eat. At length, the two brothers separated but not before Avunrara formed the desire for revenge in his clever heart.

On the way back, Avunrara discovered the hiding place of the two Lindendas. Soon, he was holding counsel with his brothers: he would like to take the second Lindenda as his wife. But what if they killed Ambat first? They would only have to ask him to go diving for the giant clams, called *Namanpig,* that were found on the reef next to Tomman island.

No sooner said than done. The brothers went to gather some *navele* and then to find Ambat. Once they had found him, Ambat, aware of his brothers' sinister intents, did not want to follow them. They insisted and finally Ambat conceded to their demands. However, before leaving, he warned his two wives of the danger, told them to stay locked in the house, and to shoot any bird that came near their hut. After he left, though, the two women went outside, cut some vines, and took them into their hut.

The five brothers continued on together to their planned destination. The first brother dived, went down and came up, his face full of pleasure and his mouth full of white meat. This white meat was, in reality, the meat of the *naveles* that the brothers had gathered. However, it looked like the flesh of the *"natalae,"* or giant clam, and it was on this that their plan was laid. Another brother dived, and then another, each acting the same scene.

"Oh, this *natalae* is great!" they all said together.

Ambat's turn came and he let himself be fooled by their well-played trick. Innocently, he dived, stretched out his hand towards the shell, and CLAP! It slammed shut on him. In this way, Ambat died.

The four brothers left in their canoe. Then came the inevitable quarrel: who would get the two Lindenda? A compromise was established: each of the two sisters would be shared between two brothers. They came ashore and climbed quickly up the mountain to their hut. There, they came upon a terrible scene. The two Lindenda had hung themselves from one vine. The four brothers buried them sorrowfully in the hut. Forever after, that place has remained taboo. And that is the story of the first coconut palm in the south of Malekula.

***This legend was recorded by Nase Robinson in Bislama from the village of Malvakal
in the south of Malekula (Nabanga n°98-99 (Feb. 1979)***

The legend of Tolambe Islet
(Vao)

A long time ago, in the archipelago located next to Vao and Malekula, there was an islet. This little piece of land was quite tiny, but there was still enough room for several villages. It was in one of these villages that there lived a particularly happy man and woman. Their happiness was soon completed by the birth of two adorable children, first a boy and then a girl. Their life was simple and peaceful. In this home, love united them. The parents showed all the love and affection possible to their children who were calm and obedient. Their existence followed the rhythm of the days and the seasons. The only events that perturbed this rhythm were the *namangki,* those custom ceremonies held on the islet. These were memorable occasions of singing and dancing. In the villages, the talk was mostly of pig killing. During the *namangki,* the chiefs sacrificed dozens of pigs. From a young age, the boy and his sister were allowed to participate in these much anticipated events. You can see that life was simple and calm for the children and their parents on this islet called Tolambe.

They often left for Malekula to get some food. While their children were still small, the young couple brought them along. For the brother and sister, it was a great voyage. Years passed. The children learned to walk and were no longer totally dependent on their parents. Finally, the trips to Malekula lost their charm; they were used to them. So, their parents went alone, leaving their children alone on the islet. However, they never left the islet without the father giving a very curious warning to the children.

"Never, ever, ever touch those two stones over there on the beach!"

There were, indeed, two big stones on the beach just across from their house, and they greatly intrigued the children. They had often got close to them, but they had never dared to touch them. The brother and the sister knew that it was strictly forbidden. They contented themselves with looking at them and pondering the mystery that they concealed. Curiosity and impatience burned strong, though, especially for the little boy. He had already asked many questions of his father. But the child could not eke out even the tiniest bit of information. He was told, however, that one day he would learn the truth.

One sunny day, while his mother and father were getting ready to leave for Malekula, the boy got it into his head to disobey his parents. As usual, he and his sister were treated to the habitual warning.

"Never, ever, ever touch those two stones over there on the beach!"

114

Alas, as soon as the parents had got into their canoe, the young boy grabbed his sister's hand and whispered to her, "Come on! Let's go see what those two stones are hiding."

The sister was surprised.

"You're crazy! Didn't you hear what mother and father said?"

The sister's attitude annoyed the boy.

"Don't be such a scaredy cat! They'll never know that we touched them. After having seen what's under them, we'll put the two stones back like nothing ever happened."

The sister was still a little unsure, but her brother's words persuaded her.

"Alright…ok. Let's go. But we have to do it quickly before anyone gets back!"

Once they were on the beach, the two children faced a problem. How were they to lift the two stones? They didn't take long to find a solution, because causing trouble is a child's forte. Two pieces of wood did the trick. The brother and sister used them as levers. However, they had barely placed the wood under the stones when a catastrophe occurred.

A huge stream of water several hundred metres tall shot into the air. What a horrible spectacle! Water submerged the whole islet. In the village, panic reigned. Some of the inhabitants were able to take flight and swim all the way to Malekula. Alas, many of the villagers were carried away by the waters and drowned. Among the victims were the two children whose curiosity had caused all the trouble.

Today, you can still go to Vao. Once there, you may ask villagers to show you where the islet once was and you will see that the water is very shallow there. While diving, you might even see statues and big stones stacked one on top of another. These are the vestiges of the *"namangki"*, those big ceremonies that once upon a time gathered together the inhabitants of Tolambe.

"Alors… raconte." Broadcast n° 7 Radio Port-Vila.

The pig from the Islet of Vao
(Vao)

A long, long time ago, on the islet of Vao, one of those coral islets in the northeast of the big island of Malekula, lived very happy people. Life was blissful, calm, and uncomplicated. Pigs had not come to the islet yet; they were still unknown.

The islet of Vao, while being small, was well populated by a people who had fallen from the heavens, surprised to find themselves on earth. Vao had fallen directly from the sky! In this way, one beautiful morning, everyone living on high found themselves falling; a piece of the sky had fallen into the water. This was Vao.

And so, the people organised themselves to start another kind of life. Naturally, they had to build houses, make gardens, and construct *nakamals*. However, they were missing something. Life seemed monotonous. People became bored on the little island. Songs didn't exist yet, and neither did dances. They didn't know what these were, and so their significance was ignored. Why should they dance? Why should they sing? When Vao was still an integral part of the sky their way of life was different. Here, the people of Vao were bored.

A man and his wife had two daughters, two very young and very beautiful daughters. On the nights when everything was calm and the wind had died down, the sea was like a lake and not one leaf would move on the trees. At the hour when the moon rose and the crickets started to sing, they would sit on the sand and dream. They dreamed of a time long ago when they lived up high.

One day, the two girls were sitting on the sand and watching the sun sink behind the mountain on the mainland of Malekula. That morning the sun had risen between Ambae and Raga; it had been very hot, very hot right away. Everyone had sweated all day. Now that the moon was rising, the air had become cooler. It was with a voice full of melancholy that the youngest of the two sisters said, "Big sister, this moment is so beautiful. Look at how the moon shines on the water around our little island. But I am bored. Do you think that one day we will marry?"

"No, I will never marry. If you would like to, you should find a man. As for me, I was made to live with the stars and perhaps it will be with one of them that I will marry. My sister, do you want a husband?"

"Yes, I want a husband. I am too bored alone. I want a man and some children. I want to get married."

In the silence of the evening, only the sound of the waves breaking on the beach seemed to be listening to the dreams of the two sisters; one of her husband, the other of her star. However, the star was watching his wife who spent her time on the islet of Vao missing the heavens.

The years passed, all of them the same. The two girls were still naked, showing that neither of them had found the husband of their dreams. One day, the youngest was married. Finally, the moment that she had been waiting for had arrived. Thus, she began to wear a mat around her waist. The older sister, still unmarried, would look at the stars each time she was on the beach and ask, "When will one of you think of me?"

In Vao, there were many villages. In one of these villages, Venu, there was a man and a boy, a tall, strong, handsome boy who was also bored. This boy had never left his village, no one knew him, and he lived naked because he was not married. One day, in one way or another, he heard that the people of Tokvanu had decided to take a trip to Ambae. It was a custom that the people of Vao would go to Devil's Point on Ambae to exchange mats and even women. The young boy said to his father, "Papa, I would like to go to Ambae with you to exchange mats and to see the island that looks like an over-turned canoe."

"Well, you are young, but you must learn. We will leave tomorrow in our canoe with the people of Tokvanu."

The next morning, many canoes were lined up on the beach. They all had their sails up. The woven *pandanus* crackled a bit in the wet breeze. Packets of mats were fastened into dry places. The young boy was very excited. Finally, they all left for Ambae. Once in Devil's Bay at Ambae, the wooden slit drums could be heard announcing the arrival of visitors from another island. Everyone was ready to exchange adventures, sing, dance, and barter.

After having been received in the appropriate custom manner, according to the rituals of that age of drinking green coconuts and eating hot *laplap,* the guests were called by dances. The young boy took his first dance steps and was given a mat, the *"singwotamarino,"* some highly coloured branches of leaves that he stuck into his thick bark belt, and finally some basil to perfume himself. The young boy from Vao was very happy because he had never seen any of this before.

However, just before leaving Vao, a young girl had seen him. He had seen no one, but she had seen him! This woman, this young girl, had always dreamed of marrying a star. That morning, at dawn, when everyone was packing for Ambae, among all of the men she had seen one that looked like a star.

Finally, after dancing and looking intently at the girls from Ambae, the men from Vao got back into their canoes and, one fine day, arrived in Vao. The whole island was there to receive them and among them was a girl who was looking for one man in particular amongst the *pandanus* sails of the canoes.

"My, how handsome he is! His arms are encircled by bracelets, he has a mat around his waist, and colourful leaves in his belt! He is so handsome!"

On seeing him, the star-girl felt right away that she wanted to marry him and made her wish known to her family.

"I want to meet that boy on the main island at the place that we call *Natovonaloa*. I would like to meet him under the big *Natapoa.*"

The next day, the young boy took his canoe and went towards the main island. The young girl did likewise and they both met under the *Natapoa*. They looked at each other and understood the other's wishes.

"You will give me your mat, the one that you bought on Ambae. Then, I would like your *Nasasa* leaves. I will put them on my arm."

The young girl undressed the boy and covered her waist with his mat. She attached the *Nasasa* leaves to her arm, and went back to islet of Vao. When she arrived there, she went directly to her father's house. Her parents saw her running with a mat around her waist. They said, "Something has happened, the girl is wearing a mat from Ambae!"

The young girl breathlessly asked her father to take her to the main island. The father looked at his daughter and his response surprised her. "My daughter, I have not yet been to the garden. There are no yams in the house. I cannot let you go like that!"

The girl, anxious, insisted and so her father went to fetch some yams from the garden and then they set off towards the mainland. Arriving on Malekula, they both followed the coast. They passed one village, and then another. The old father had trouble following his daughter because she was walking so quickly. When they had reached the village of Venu, the father finally understood that his daughter wanted to marry. He could smell the odor of many *laplaps* baking on hot stones! The *nasara* was well-swept and mats were there, ready to buy a wife for the young boy. At this time, women were bought with mats because pigs had not yet come to the island.

And so, the young girl was bought by her husband with the mats called *Magha*. These were narrow mats with long *pandanus* fibres that hung from the sides. These mats were never unrolled; they stayed in the hut smoking until the fibres disintegrated.

Days passed, and months too. The young wife gave birth to her first son; his name was Muronturala. She then gave birth to a second, Rory. Time passed slowly and the woman began to forget her stars. She got older and her sons grew.

One day, Muronturala married a girl from Lebu, next to Atchin. They both came to live with Muronturala's parents. However, the young wife did not like Vao. She was bored on the small islet; she often ran away and returned to her parents' house at Lebu. Tired of her antics, Muronturala decided one day to go and get her. He arrived in Lebu and asked to see her. The wife cried. Her parents tried to console her, but her husband was furious and cut short their sympathetic cooing.

"I am taking my wife back. She is mine. I have paid for her."

Both of them left for Vao, he in front, she behind. On the way, a snake spotted them. He climbed a tree and hid himself, all the while watching the couple's progression. When the woman walked under him, the snake jumped on her and bit her. The wife screamed and called to her husband.

"Oh! Look! The snake has bitten my sex!"

The husband was surprised to hear her voice. It was the first time that she had spoken in his presence. However, the wife was even more surprised to see blood running down her thigh. She had been a virgin, but she was no longer. The serpent had deflowered her. Muronturala advised her to go wash in the sea. Both of them continued on to Vao and the woman finally gave herself to her husband for the first time. Both of them were quite happy after that.

A little while later, the woman, still happy with her husband, went with him to Lebu to see her parents. They stayed for four days but then started to get bored. They decided to make their way back to Vao. On the way back, at the same spot where the snake had bitten her not so long ago, she cried out.

"Look! I have just given birth to a pig!"

Thus, the pig made its first appearance on Malekula. Muronturala, her husband, advised her to leash it, so the woman took a vine and attached it to the young swine. The three of them continued on their way, the husband first, his wife behind, and the young pig following both of them.

Arriving in Vao, the wife fed her young pig. It grew and became fat. It was a sow, and this sow gave birth to ten piglets. These ten piglets grew. One of the ten became enormous and his tusks began to turn and turn. Muronturala and his wife would go to the garden and the pigs would follow them. They went everywhere! They would even follow them to the beach and when the couple would swim, the pigs would swim with them! The sows gave birth to five piglets, ten piglets, and then ten again. Muronturala finally had one hundred pigs.

The pig with curved tusks was born in Vao. He is the *Namangki* chief. Muronturala killed the one hundred pigs and organised the first *Namangki* in Vao. This was the first grade taking ceremony. Every village from Vao was there in the *nasara* to feast and dance. Muronturala and his brother Rory were the genesis of ranks on the island and that is the reason why, in memory of the apparition of the pig, the Rory family does not eat sow.

This legend was given in French to Paul Gardissat by Albano Rory from the island of Vao.

Nabanga n°85-88 (August 1978)

The birth of the sea
(Malekula)

A long time ago on Malekula, there lived men who were said to have been the first inhabitants of the New Hebrides. Of course, their lives were rather rudimentary but they knew how to organise themselves and their days were not too different from life as it is now in the islands of this archipelago. They even knew how to make *laplap*. But to tell the truth, their *laplap* was not very tasty because they didn't salt it; they didn't even know what salt was! However, this did not stop the first men on Malekula from being very, very content.

One day, a villager left to go hunting in the deep forest. Imagine his surprise to see a giant bread fruit tree lying on the ground in the middle of the bush. Why had it been chopped down like this and who had done it? What a mystery! What particularly struck the hunter was the length and thickness of the trunk. There was also a strange liquid oozing from it. The man tasted it. It resembled water but had a bit of an aftertaste. Wanting to gather a little of this precious liquid, the villager went in search of a bamboo. He then filled it up, thinking that he would like to add a little to his *laplap*.

The man that made this amazing discovery was married. He was also the father of an adorable son. He loved his family very much and was proud to offer them a *laplap* that was unlike any other. Nonetheless, he wanted his new creation to be a surprise.

"It is I who will make the *laplap* this evening. I don't need you for the moment. I will call you when it's time to come," he told them.

The woman and the child obeyed without asking any questions. The son starting to run through the village in order to join his friends in a game. Without hurrying, the wife of the hunter went to chat with a couple of her friends. The child was enjoying himself, playing with the other boys his age, but running and laughing between the huts had made him hungry. Indeed, he felt so hungry that he decided to go and find his father. The man had just taken the *laplap* out of the oven where it had been baked.

"Papa, papa, I'm hungry!" exclaimed the small boy on seeing the dish his father had prepared.

"You came at just the right time because it's ready! But listen! This *laplap* is unlike any other. Don't tell this to anyone and don't give any of it to anyone. If you do, you will betray the whole world. Do you hear me? You will betray the whole world. So, don't say anything!"

The child was intrigued by the words of his father but he promised to obey. Immediately, he took a bite of the piece of *laplap* that he had been given. He had never tasted one as good!

"This is so delicious!" he said, proud that his father had prepared such a succulent dish.

When he went back to see his friends, the child held his tongue. Soon, though, he could no longer keep his secret.

"I'm sure that you have never eaten a *laplap* as good as my father's. It's delicious!"

His friends wanted to taste the dish in question.

"Alright, but only a little," said the small boy, "because my father will not be very happy with me. He told me not to tell anyone about it."

The other children were impressed by the new flavour of the *laplap.*

"What did your father do?" they asked impatiently.

"What is it? What is it?" they demanded with curiosity.

"I don't know."

The other children were disappointed. They wanted to know the secret.

"Don't worry! I have a plan!" said the son of the hunter suddenly, proud of himself.

The next day, he followed his father into the forest. The man arrived at the fallen breadfruit trunk. Calmly, he filled his bamboo with the salty water. Hidden a little further off, the child discovered the secret. He was so excited that he forget to be careful and went a little closer. His father saw him. He was furious!

"Go back to the house! You shouldn't be here! You had better leave now before I get really angry! Go! Now!"

However, the man knew that it was too late. He son now knew the place where the precious liquid sprung from. Resigned, he waited for the worst… and quickly the water started to gurgle… several huge bubbles burst all along the trunk… little by little the churning quickened… and the water overflowed! It ran and ran, covering the entire village: everyone was drowned. It invaded the entire world, leaving pieces of land only here and there.

That is why, now, if you look at a map of the world, you will see the continents and the islands separated from each other. This is because a long, long time ago, those large stretches of saltwater (now called "the ocean") didn't exist. A long, long time ago, the world was one. But now it has been broken up because a small boy disobeyed his father a long, long time ago on Malekula. And now, men live separated from each other, separated by the SEA!

Nabanga N°15 (08/11/75)

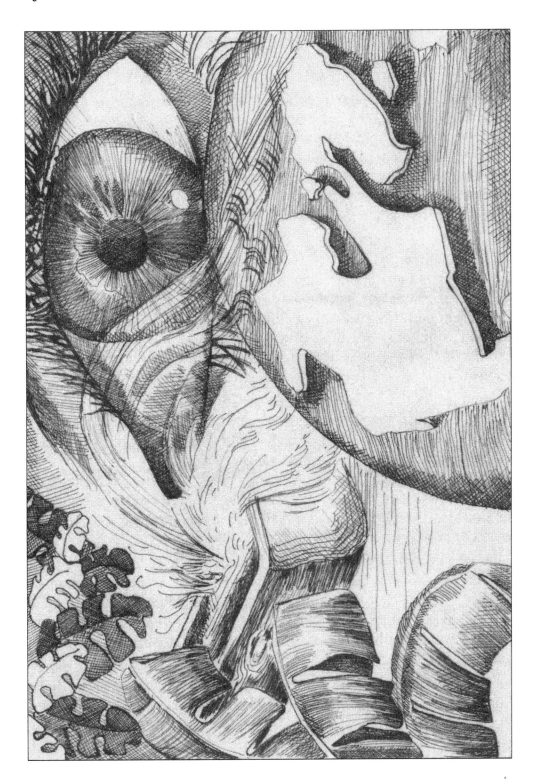

The dwarves of Malekula
(Tenmaru, Malekula)

A long time ago on Malekula, there used to live mysterious and kind beings: dwarves, humans that do not grow and thus never exceed the size of children three or four years in age. At this time, there were many on the island; they lived in high grasses in which they could disappear. The humans living in villages nearby were ignorant of their existence. That's why they were always surprised by certain phenomenon for which the dwarves were responsible. More than anything, the dwarves preferred working in the garden, and it was there that the villagers received their biggest surprises.

In fact, when a man went to his garden and started to weed in one corner, the next day, to his big surprise, he saw that the whole garden had been weeded. Again, when the weeds were good and dry, a villager returned to burn them. Often, he didn't have enough time to finish; he left, and the next day, to his big surprise he saw that the whole garden had been burnt! Sometimes, a villager from Malekula wanted to plant some bananas. If he could only finish planting some of them, the next day he saw that the whole garden had been planted. The whole island was surprised without knowing who was responsible.

Life continued in the same way. When a man planted a yam, the next day he saw that his whole garden had been planted with yams. Everything that the villagers started, the dwarves finished.When someone put a stake up to support growing yams, the next day he saw that every yam had a stake to support it. All this was very good. However, the dwarves' activities had a downside. When a villager came to dig up one yam to see if it was ready, the next day he saw that all the yams had been dug up. The result of finishing everything that the men started was that the dwarves ravaged the gardens and destroyed their bounty.

Enough was enough, and one day, the villagers from Tenmaru were fed up. They wanted to know what was happening and decided to watch their gardens overnight. They didn't have to wait long. The villagers quickly discovered the dwarves' occupation. A plan was rapidly hatched. In the evening, while the dwarves worked in the gardens, it would not be difficult to find them and catch them.

"Even better! We will get rid of them once and for all. Listen, I will carry my flute with me. When I play my flute for the first time, you will approach the dwarves. The second time I play my flute, you will burn the dry weeds..."

The chief had spoken and everyone agreed with his decision. They knew that with him as their leader, the battle would be won.

The plan was put into action the next day. Every man in the village carried a torch to guide him through the moonless night. Silently, they crept to their gardens. Suddenly, the chief's flute pierced the night. Quickly, the men made a circle around the dwarves, forming an impenetrable wall. The flute was heard once again and the men understood. With their torches, they set the weeds on fire. The crackling made the dwarves jump; they could see the smoke but they did not move. To them, the fire was far away. They could hardly believe their eyes when they saw the fire coming closer and closer. The dwarves started to run hither and thither, but it was too late. The flames encircled them. They couldn't do anything: they were caught in a fatal trap.

The next day, the villagers savoured their victory. Certainly, their gardens had been turned to charcoal, but the fire had also freed them from the dwarves. This story is a little cruel, but the result is obvious: the dwarves have disappeared, the gardeners have a lot more work to do, but at least they can take advantage of their produce and eat what they have cultivated!

Nabanga n°20 (17/01/76)

The legend of the carnivorous stone
(Ambrym)

A long time ago, on Ambrym, one of the islands in the New Hebrides, there lived an enormous marine beast. It was a beast that didn't look like any other beast in the world, except perhaps a wild boar with a large horn in the middle of its head. Where did it come from? No one could say. It was only known that it lived in the bay of Olal and that it was, in some way, its guardian. Indeed, the inhabitants of this area were not mistaken: they had named it the "Pouviaserole", or the guardian of the sacred bay.

The beast was truly a monster. It fed on human flesh, particularly appreciating the tender flesh of small children. When it was hungry, the Pouviaserole would crouch down on the beach and turn itself into a log. It waited and waited. Sometimes, it waited for hours until one or many children would come to play on the shore. The children would amuse themselves joyously along the beach. Unfortunately, several of the children would come to sit on the log, or perhaps three of them would swing the log back and forth between them before throwing it as far possible into the ocean with a great splash. It was such fun! However, their joy did not last. The log would transform once again into the "Pouviaserole". The children would be paralysed with fear and surprise. Thus, the beast would be able to catch some of them, letting the others run away, sobbing. Without hurrying, the beast would slink back into his underwater lair to devour his victims. He would fill his belly with children from the villages in this way. His trips to the beach were so well spaced that his existence was often forgotten. That was how he could always catch some local children unawares.

One day, however, the chief from a neighbouring village, shocked by the disappearance of the children, decided that the beach should be taboo. Nobody would have the right to walk, swim, or play on the beach where the monster regularly transformed himself into a log. Ignorant of the decision that had been made, the Pouviaserole left his lair one day, hunger driving him on. Approaching the beach, he was already licking his lips at the thought of the feast that would be his. As usual, as soon as he arrived on shore, the monster changed his appearance and became a log on the beach, deserted except for a couple coconuts. The beast waited… and waited… and waited. This time, the wait was by far the longest. Finally, the monster understood that no one would come.

Thinking that the inhabitants had finally become wise to his game and had put a taboo on the beach, the monster decided to go into the village nearest the bay. Hiding in the bush, he glided silently towards the nearest huts. The villagers were busy with their daily work and of course, were unaware of the danger at hand. The animal

watched the children playing, laughing uproariously. He chose the strongest and most handsome from among them. The Pouviaserole waited until the child had separated himself from his friends, and SNATCH! The monster grabbed the child and made off with him into the bush. Little did he know that he had taken the son of the chief!

The chief, he who had declared the beach to be taboo, knew that it would be useless to go after the monster. He cried, knowing what was awaiting his son. He swore revenge on the monster. In a grave voice, he announced to the hunters that he had assembled, "The Pouviaserole must die! You must kill him!"

The men left for the hunt, ready to strike as soon as the monster would show himself.

The beast had gone back into the water to savour his victim. However, the chief's son was quickly digested. Used to being able to catch and eat at least three or four children, the monster's hunger was not satiated. He decided to return to the village, and imprudently set out along the coast. The beast left the water and had taken only a couple of steps on the sand when the hunters were upon him. They had been hiding behind a rock and waiting for a very long time. When they saw him, their hearts leapt! My, how enormous he was! Without more than a second's thought, they set to work. The hunters tightened their bows: an arrow cleanly pierced the beast's left eye. Another hit him in the stomach.

The beast was proud. Even though he was grievously wounded, he did not want to die on the beach before his adversaries. The Pouviaserole backed slowly towards the sea. He wanted to breath his last breath in his own lair. Fearing the escape of the beast, a hunter threw his lance violently. The weapon planted itself in the neck of the animal. Blood stained the water. The monster remained immobile. To protect itself from the arrows and lances that had begun to rain upon him, the Pouviaserole transformed itself into a rock.

This is how the legend of the carnivorous rock came to be. The stone is still visible today in the bay of Olal on Ambrym; it reminds us that there was once a monster that lived there named "the guardian of the sacred bay."

Nabanga N°13 (11/09/75)

The snake of North Ambrym
(Ambrym)

A long time ago on the island of Ambrym, next to the two big volcanoes Benbow and Marum, was an immense ash plain. Around the edges of this plain of black sand were villages, lots of villages. In these villages, there lived many men and women. Each had their own gardens, pigs, *nakamals,* and places to dance. Life there was very normal. Of course, there were wars, but people were used to them and often made peace through marriages between villages. And then it was time to celebrate!

One day, a man from one of these villages decided to walk down to the ocean alone. His intention was to collect shells and crabs. So, without saying a word to anyone, he took his bow and arrow and left, hiding himself the whole way so that nobody would notice him. When he arrive on the beach, the reef was exposed and the tide was low. Standing before the multitude of wet rocks, he felt very tiny, just a small man from the mountains. However, it was with a certain satisfaction that he took in these sights so unfamiliar to his eyes. He inhaled deeply to fill his nostrils with the fresh scent of the sea.

Suddenly, he saw two people walking along the edge of the reef. This worried him because he thought that he had been alone. He looked a little closer and realised that they were two women. Two women on the reef?

"Where did these two women come from? I didn't see them. Could they have followed me?" he asked himself.

The two women finally noticed the man, but his presence didn't bother them at all. They continued to collect shells. The man watched them do this, and realising that they didn't mind him being there, he approached them. When he got closer to them, he realised that these two women were actually young girls, very beautiful young girls, who were much prettier than the girls in his village.

He came a little closer to them and said, "I'm not familiar with you. Where are you from?"

"We are sisters…"

"But where do you come from?"

"We come from the mountain" the sisters said.

Realising that they were shy, he started improvising a conversation with them.

"Have you collected many shells?"

"Yes, we already have a basket full. We're also collecting white coral to burn. Once it has been reduced to a powder, we'll burn it over there under a big tree. After, we'll use the lime to colour our hair. Does this surprise you?"

"No! You are both so beautiful!"

The two girls, rather embarrassed, didn't answer. They took up their baskets and went towards the shore. The man, bothered, quickly gathered some shells. From time to time, he glanced towards the beach. On the sand, near a big tree, the two girls had made a fire. The smoke drifted upwards slowly. The man continued to gather his shells; he filled his basket little by little, all the while approaching that big tree and the drifting smoke that so strangely attracted him.

"Those two girls are so beautiful!" he thought.

Both of the girls were smoking their shells and looking at the man out of the corner of their eyes. As for him, he was busy thinking.

"I would be very happy to marry one of those girls. I could marry that one because she is so very beautiful. However, the other one isn't bad either!"

The two girls started to pick up their baskets and leave.

"Don't leave! I would like one of the two of you to marry me."

"No, if you want only one of us, it's not possible. We are two sisters, so you have to take both of us."

"Both of you?"

"We are two, however we are only one. We can't be separated. We will always be together."

The man didn't understand a thing that they had said, but the two girls were terribly attractive. What should he do?

"Stay here. You will wait for us here. We are going to visit our mother and then we will come back. Then, you can follow us" the sisters said.

The man followed their instructions and when the two girls arrived at their mother's house, they told her what had happened.

"We met a man on the reef and he wants to marry one of us. We told him that it wasn't possible and that he must marry both of us."

"And how did he respond?"

"Oh! Mother, he agreed right away!"

"Good, very good, that's excellent. However, be careful…"

The two girls left and went back to the beach where the man was waiting for them, questioning himself. He was worried that the girls were tricking him. He hadn't understood anything that they had said to him. He would have been even more worried had he known that the girls' mother was an enormous serpent that lived on top of the mountain Tuyo, in the north of Ambrym.

"Where is your mother, then?" the man asked.

"Up there, on top of the big mountain that you see."

"When you told her that you were coming with me, what did she say?"

"She said that it was very good. We didn't hide anything from her. We spoke to her about you. She has given us permission to follow you. She only told us to be careful."

While they were on their way, he wanted to know more about them and started asking some questions.

"Are you happy to follow me?"

"Oh, yes!"

"Do you have brothers and sisters that live with your mother?"

"We have neither brothers nor sisters."

"I would like to meet your mother."

At the same time, in chorus, the girls firmly responded, "No, our mother is horrible."

However, the two girls didn't say that their mother was a snake.

Before arriving in the village, the man hid the two girls in a corner of the bush near his house. When night fell, he sought them out and brought them into his house where they would be safe. He then blew into the big *pupu*, that giant shell that summons every man in the village. That night, the *nakamal* was very crowded. The chief quieted everyone down.

"My friends, Wurwur Naim wants to speak to us. Let's listen to him."

"I plan to be married. Tomorrow you will all prepare what's necessary for the feast and the day after tomorrow will be the big day!"

The crowd was surprised.

"Who is Wurwur Naim going to marry? We haven't seen anyone yet!"

Wurwur Naim didn't say anything. Nobody knew that the two girls were there, only a couple of steps away, in his house.

The next day, the whole village went to work. The women went to find dry wood. The men informed the other villages. On the way, they gathered yams and taro, each one pulling a pig behind him on a leash as custom demands. Others tried to get more information.

"Who are you marrying? Which village is she from?"

Wurwur Naim, imperturbable, responded, "I am the only one who knows, and tomorrow you will see. Be ready for tomorrow, and I will show you."

The chief put the taro and yams into big piles. The pigs were attached to poles, one beside the other. Then the chief blew into the *pupu* and the old men started to play the tamtams. This was when Wurwur Naim, holding one girl with his right hand and the other with his left, made his appearance. They then went towards the pile of taro and yams, making the round of honour and greeting the crowd. Next, they went to the chief whom the Wurwur Naim greeted. The chief was surprised, but could do nothing because Wurwur Naim seemed to have made up his mind.

"Those two girls are extremely beautiful!" said some.

"But there are two of them!" said others.

The chief separated the taro and yams as well as the pigs brought for the ceremony by the villagers and friends of the family. Finally, in the smoky evening, the dancing started.

"Where did you find these two beautiful girls? What village do they come from?"

Wurwur Naim responded, "I met them on the beach..."

The dances continued until the next day. Pigs with rounded tusks were killed and cooked in hot-stone ovens. Pigs with tusks curved twice around were set apart to give to the mother of the two wives. Wurwur Naim knew very well that their mother would not come because his wives had already told him so.

"Our mother is too horrible. We will take her the presents ourselves."

Once the pigs were cooked, the two girls took the pieces reserved for their mother and left to take them to her. Wurwur Naim wanted to follow them. The girls once again demured.

"We have already told you that our mother is awful. It is better that you stay here. We'll come back quickly."

"I want to meet my mother-in-law."

"You are not big enough to meet her, and certainly not strong enough."

"I would still like to meet her."

"You can't."

"I have known worse people, uglier even…"

Finally, the two girls gave in.

"Alright, let's go see our mother."

Wurwur Naim followed them up the big mountain called "Tuyo." The man became impatient.

"Where is your mother's house?"

"We're here. There's the entrance."

Wurwur Naim looked but could only see reeds. He looked a little closer, squinted his eyes and realised that he had just entered a strange place.

"Wait for us here," said one of the girls. "We're going to take her meal to her."

Big reeds hid the entrance to a cave, an enormous black hole hidden behind grasses. The two girls parted the reeds, went closer and closer to the biggest reed and then disappeared.

The girls were at the bottom of the hole. It was very dark. One of the two presented a parcel to her mother.

"Here is the *laplap* and the pork that our husband's family has prepared especially for you."

"Put it down over there."

"Our husband wants to meet you, so when you have finished eating, come and see him. He is waiting behind the reeds."

The two girls left.

"Our mother will eat first and then she will come and see you."

A little while later, the ground started to shake and a terrible noise like an angry volcano came from the hole. Wurwur Naim started to tremble with fear.

"You wanted to meet your mother-in-law. Here she is."

Next, the wind started to blow cyclonically and the snake brought its head up above the rocks. Its slithery body moved between old lava flows. Each time that it opened its mouth, a huge wind crushed the surrounding vegetation.

Wurwur Naim found it impossible to remain standing; he shivered, he sweated, he was very afraid.

"You wanted to meet your mother-in-law. You asked for it, so here she is…"

The snake's head was now leaning on a stone. The earth shook and Wurwur Naim started running, tripped, got up and took off again. On the way, he lost his *nambas* but, naked, ran on. His wives followed him and picked up his penis sheath.

Wurwur Naim arrived at his village, bathed and ran towards the *nasara*. He hit the *tamtam* and called all of his friends. They all came running, surprised to see his frightened face.

"Come into the *nakamal* quickly. I need to talk to you!"

In secret, they prepared a plan of attack. That night, Wurwur Naim said to his wives, "Tomorrow, I will go to the garden and build a house for your mother. You two will go and get her."

The next morning, the two women went to get their mother and Wurwur Naim went to build a house in his garden. The roof was made of dried banana leaves. Once the house was finished, he went home. The two women and their mother arrived at sunset. They settled their mother into the house and then started to heat the stones to bake a *laplap*. While they were doing this, their mother spoke to them.

"My daughters, I know that something is going to happen. I know that they want to harm me; I feel that they might even kill me. When they do kill me, you will know by a sign that you will surely recognise. I don't need to tell you what it is. When I am dead and you are planning a meal in my honour, don't forget to put into the middle of your *laplaps* this thing that you will see. Everyone must eat on this day, the old, the young, the women, the men, the children and even then *"meleun,"* the least powerful in the village. Don't forget anyone; they all must eat. While they are eating, you should blow into the conch. Then you will see what happens!"

The mother kissed her two daughters and went to bed. The two wives went back to the village to be near their husband. That night, Wurwur Naim said to his wives, "Tomorrow, you will go with the other women to burn the dry grass and the old stumps in the chief's garden. As for us, the men, some will hunt pigeons and others wild pigs."

The next morning, the women left to go burn the chief's garden and the men pretended to leave for the hunt. A little while later, they had all surrounded the mother-in-law's house. They covered the hut with dried palm fronds and old wood. Then, they set it alight. Hidden behind some trees, they watched the house burn. The serpent writhed in the blaze. Again, she twisted herself and the earth began to tremble. One last agonising twist and she was dead. Only a pile of ashes remained.

During this time, the women in the garden didn't suspect anything. One of the two girls felt something fall on her shoulder. She picked it up, called her sister and showed her the snake skin that had fallen from a tree. It was the skin of their own mother.

"The sign that you will recognise...," their mother had said.

The two girls fell into each other's arms and sobbed. Their mother was dead.

Once they had returned home, they asked Wurwur Naim, "Did you kill our mother?"

"No, we were hunting."

"You killed our mother! Don't lie, we know it, you killed her!"

"Yes, we killed her!"

The two women started crying again and went to cover themselves in the ashes of their mother. Calm again, they returned.

"You must organise a feast in memory of our mother as custom demands."

The chief called everyone together again. The women gathered wood and the men collected taro and yams as well as pigs held on leashes. The stones were heated once more and *laplap* were baked. This was another feast, a different sort of feast.

The two sisters looked at each other. Each broke a piece of the snake skin between her fingers. They crushed it into powder and discreetly slipped a little of it into each *laplap*. When everything was ready, the women opened the ovens and did exactly as their mother had asked them. Very kindly, they asked the women to make themselves comfortable in one hut. They did the same for the men. When everyone was ready to eat and the chief had taken the first bite, the two girls looked at each other and blew into the *pupu* together. Nobody had the time to realise anything. Instantaneously, the elderly and the men were transformed into pigs and were left to finish the feast that they had started as men.

Today, on the immense ash plains of Ambrym, live thousands of pigs. The inhabitants of this island hunt them continuously but can never fully deplete them.

The two women also live in this region. You can meet them sometimes when they bathe in the river. They call to you, but you can't see them. To speak to you, they sometimes change themselves into women from a neighbouring village. These are the two women of whom I spoke in my legend. They are still alive. If you ever go to Ambrym, you might just meet them!

This legend was given to us by Damelip Taso from Sinai, in the south-east of Ambrym.

Nabanga n°47-49 (February 1977)

The legend of the Vermelap stones
(Ambrym)

A long time ago, on the island of Ambrym in the village of Craig Cove, there lived a man and a woman. Very close to one another, they had been able to lead simple, happy lives. One day, their happiness was completed by the birth of two beautiful twins that the mother loved with all of her heart. In the village, everyone had a soft spot for what they called 'the happiest family in Craig Cove." The two boys grew quickly. They grew so fast because their lives were very calm. They became strong and vigorous. Full of life, they asked their father to make them some bows and arrows. They had become strong enough to pull a bow cord taut. Armed with these tools, the children quickly became excellent fishermen. Life passed without fuss. Everyday, the man and the woman went to the garden which they wanted to be clean and without weeds. They took very good care of it. They gathered ripe fruit, picked sizeable vegetables, or repaired the fence that kept the pigs from destroying their hard work. While their parents were doing this, the boys followed the tide and fished. They swiftly put arrows to their bows and never missed their targets. The fish could never be careful enough around these able fishermen. When evening came, the family gathered together happily. With the excellent vegetables from the garden and the fresh fish caught in crystal waters, the mother prepared succulent meals. The four of them, seated on a mat woven from coconut palms, told each other about the little adventures of the day. Every evening was pleasant and quickly became the whole family's favourite time of day. Suddenly, however, the twin's mother died.

Death struck quickly and no one could say what the woman had died from. The twins could have died from their grief. They couldn't be calmed. Perhaps, subconsciously, they knew that this day marked the end of their happiness. Misery and despair set in. After having mourned his wife for a certain time, the father realised that he could not maintain his garden, feed, and take care of his children alone. So, he decided to remarry. Knowing that he could never find a wife as wonderful as his first, he married the first woman to show interest. Alas, she was mean and egotistical. From the very first day, she started to hate the boys who made extra work for her. Family life became very sombre. The twins continued to fish the days away, but only because the sight of a fish had become a sort of consolation for them. Their father and step-mother cleaned the garden during this time, but it was done with a lot less love. The produce that they brought back was not as good. Especially during the evenings, one could feel that times had changed. Laughing was a thing of the past and the meals were nowhere near as tasty. The new mistress of the house put the taro and yam peelings in a separate pot and, without telling her husband, served them to the boys. The twins didn't dare say a word because they feared the violent reactions of their step-mother. Also, fishing made them hungry, and so they contented themselves with the peelings.

One morning, when the twins had just turned ten, they went to the shore. Sitting on a rock, they looked pensively at the horizon. Their hearts were heavy. Without saying a word, they considered their plight. Suddenly, one of the brothers spoke.

"Brother, I've had enough of eating like a pig. Our real mother was good and kind, preparing only the best meals for us. Our new mother isn't the same; she terribly cruel! She doesn't love us. Brother, I think that we should follow our real mother..."

Absorbed by these macabre thoughts, they returned to their home a little before noon. There was nothing to eat. So, the two children went back towards the sea with even heavier hearts. Evening came and they were still on the beach. Out of habit, they returned to their home when night fell. In the saucepan, they found a half cooked *laplap.* They ate it because they were starving, meanwhile swearing that they would join their mother in death.

The next day, as always, the father and his new wife went to the garden. The twins went to the beach. They were in a dark mood. They were even sadder than the day before. Depressed, they climbed high up into an ironwood tree. Then, they started to cry. They thought of their mother and their former happiness. In his garden, the father heard the children's moaning.

"Woman, let's go back to the house! I think that the boys are in danger. I can hear them crying from here!"

"No, you're wrong. We can't hear them from this far away! It must be those big flies around the banana trees."

"I should go. Then I won't worry anymore."

The man hurried home. When he got to the house, he put his things down and ran to the shore. He found the twins at the top of the ironwood tree.

"My children, what are you doing up there? Come down! We must go back to the house now."

One of the twins replied tearily, "No! We don't want to go back with you! Our real mother was good and kind, she fed us well! Your new wife is mean and she hates us!"

"No, you'll see! Everything will change. It will be better now. You'll be happy!"

But the twins were too sad. They asked their father to go away.

"We want to die like our mother."

The man insisted and called to them a third time. Hopelessly, he started to climb the tree. The two boys climbed even higher. They climbed so high that they reached the top of the tree. The father got closer to them. Seeing that he was about to reach them, the twins threw themselves into the water below. They swam for a moment and then one of the twins went under. The other did the same only two metres from his brother.

Today, the inhabitants of Craig Cove can still see two stones in the water in the exact places where the twins drowned. These two stones are called the Vermelap, meaning twins. On the beach near the water, the ironwood tree that the boys jumped from, in order to join their mother, still grows.

Nabanga n°9 (11/08/75)

The lisepsep's son from Ambrym
(Ambrym)

On Ambrym Island in the archipelago, there lived a very happy young couple. The man and the woman got along marvellously. Their days spent on the flourishing green island were made of pure happiness. Of course, they had a garden that they enjoyed cultivating. One beautiful day, their happiness was completed by the birth of two children, two handsome young men who were as charming as their parents. At first, the father left his wife at home in the village to take care of the children while he went alone to the garden. But he felt that he could not be away from his wife for long. Soon, he asked her to once again accompany him. As for the children, there was no need to fear because they had only to weave two small hammocks and let the twins relax in the shade of the trees. It was not really all that difficult. One beautiful day the man and the woman went to the bush with their two children, ready to lay them under a cool, green tree. It is here that the story really begins.

While the parents were weeding their garden, the two boys slept peacefully in their hammocks. Suddenly, one of the twins started to cry. His tears didn't bother his parents very much because they had got used to hearing him cry at all hours of the day and night. However, the cries attracted a woman that was passing close to them. This was a woman not exactly like other women because she was, in fact, a devil. In her arms, she held her son. The cries of the other child made her turn from her path and she approached the hammock. At a glance, she made sure that no one was watching her and swiftly she snatched the crying child and put her son in his place. Then, very quickly, she ran away.

The couple continued to work but the sun had sunk to the horizon.

"I think that it is time to go home."

The man and woman gathered together their things and went in the direction of the two hammocks, never guessing the dirty trick that the devil woman had played on them. The village was not very far, the young family quickly reached their destination. Without paying attention, the young mother put her children to bed. Suddenly, the devil child started to cry because he did not smell the scent of his mother. It was then that the new mother examined him closely. You cannot image her surprise when she realised that this child was not her son! Anxiously, she called out to her husband.

"Come quickly and look at this child! It is not our son! Look at him closely!"

The man didn't know what to say, but he became frightened once he saw that this child didn't want to eat anything. Indeed, in an effort to console the child, the man had tried to give him something to eat. The baby refused everything; truthfully, he was behaving strangely. The man thought for a moment and then said to his wife in a grave voice,

"Listen. I think that we should throw him into the sea."

The woman ran towards the sea, the child in her arms. It was dark and, feeling bewildered by this rather supernatural occurance, she was afraid to turn around. Reaching the beach, she calmed down. She took several slow steps, ready to execute her destructive action. But at the precise moment that she was going to abandon the child to the waves, a voice spoke up behind her.

"Do not throw this child into the sea. He is my son! Keep him, take good care of him and you will see that when he grows up he will help you and your husband. He will help you and save you from danger."

The young women stayed still, not knowing what to do. She didn't dare turn around for fear of facing an evil spirit. Panicked, she didn't know what to say or to do, but she was especially overwhelmed by a wave of shame at throwing this baby into the sea. Feeling desperate, she responded, "But he doesn't want to eat anything!"

It did not take long for the voice to answer,

"Give him coconut milk."

The voice disappeared and a heavy silence reigned on the beach. The woman didn't even hear the noise of the waves, such was her fear. She finally turned around and ran towards the village.

On arriving at her house, the young woman told her husband about her adventure. The man also felt rather ashamed at having wanted to abandon the baby.

"Well, there is nothing to do but to keep the baby. So what if he isn't ours, he's still a human being… and we have to feed him like the voice said. He will only eat coconut milk because that's what he needs."

As soon as it was said, it was as good as done. The woman held out a coconut to her husband which he cut cleanly in two before gathering the precious milk in one of the halves. The man would repeat this gesture for a long time, indeed every day to feed the child.

The parents rather forgot the predictions that the woman devil had made on the beach until one day they realised that the child that they had raised was capable of marvels. He was no longer a child but now a man, and a sort of a warlock by nature. He was famous on Ambrym but it is said that he came to Port Vila one day and even there people came to consult him because his reputation had preceded him across the ocean.

This legend was given by a listener of the broadcast « Alors…Raconte ! » of Radio Port-Vila

The Titamol
(Paama)

Once upon a time, there was the Titamol, a spirit that lived inside a great banyan. Not far from this tree, in a village by the sea, there lived two men who survived by fishing and gardering. Everyday, they woke up at dawn and went to work in their gardens until the crickets started to chirp. They loved this calm life which nothing disturbed except the crashing of waves on the shore. One beautiful day, while they were in the garden, they heard a wonderful song. It was the Titamol who was singing to announce that low tide had come. His fascinating song went like this:

Ouwii amat mémésé, séivaké kéil akékéla'o
Ouwii amat mémésé, séivaké kéil akékéla'o

This meant, "Hey! It's low tide, the shellfish have come out of their hiding places. It is time to come and collect them!"

However, the first time that the men heard this song, they didn't pay any attention at all. Another day, while they were hunting, they killed a big boar. Once they had got it back to their village, they skinned it and roasted it over the fire. While the boar was cooking, a delicious smell wafted from their hut directly into the nose of the Titamol. The Titamol then climbed all the way to the top of his banyan tree and learned that the smell was coming from the village. The sun started to sink into the west. There was an amazing low tide that day, lower than ever before. The idea to trick the two men suddenly occurred to him. So, from the top of his perch, he started to sing.

Ouwii amat mémésé, séivaké kéil akékéla'o
Ouwii amat mémésé, séivaké kéil akékéla'o

The song did the trick. Without suspecting a thing, the two men took up their baskets and went to the reef to gather shellfish. During this time, the Titamol went into the village and ate everything it saw. Then, overwhelmed by the call of nature, it relieved itself in the oven and buried everything where the boar used to be. When they returned to the village, the two men were starving and ran to the oven to dig up their food. Surprisingly, they only found the Titamol's waste. In their extreme anger, the men decided to take revenge.

A lunar year had just come to an end when the two men, during a particularly profitable hunt, brought back two fat boars. When they got back to the village, they decided to cook the beasts in two different ovens. No sooner was it said, than it was done. Then, from the top of his banyan, the Titamol began to sing.

Ouwii amat mémésé, séivaké kéil akékéla'o
Ouwii amat mémésé, séivaké kéil akékéla'o

The two men immediately knew that the Titamol was planning to play another trick on them in order to eat their feast. Swinging their baskets beside them, the men went to the reef. However, while they were walking to the beach, one of the men took a side path back to the village. He then hid himself in a hole that had been dug especially to surprise the Titamol. Believing that both men were on the reef, the spirit entered the village and went directly to the first oven. Bowing once again to the call of nature, it relieved itself in the hole that it found there. The Titamol had extremely long hairs hanging from its rear-end. These hairs hung right above the hole where the man was hiding. Without losing any time, the man tied the hairs to some roots. Then, he called to his friend to alert him that their prey had been caught in the trap. Having no recourse to escape, the Titamol was at the mercy of the two men who immediately clubbed it to death.

Since this day, the Titamol, represented by a sand drawing, has haunted the younger generations.

This is a legend from Paama written in French by Jacques Gédéon.
Previously unpublished.

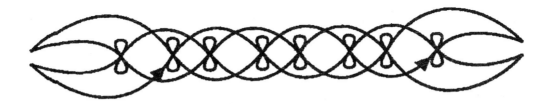

A sand drawing from the island of Paama representing the spirit of Titamol (Cabane, 1995)

The namele's child
(Paama)

Vatimato lived on a heavily wooded island. He lived alone and raised pigs. He took good care of his pigs and they were very handsome. He kept them in a big enclosure close to his home. Once a day, he fed them, sometimes in the morning and sometimes in the evening. He gave them coconuts, papayas, and ripe bananas. One morning, as usual, Vatimato went to feed his pigs.

"I don't understand," he said. "I feed my pigs everyday, but they don't seem to be getting fatter."

This was, indeed, true. His pigs seemed to be getting thinner and thinner as the days passed. Vatimato went back to his house with an empty basket. He was very worried about his pigs. Suddenly, he heard a strange voice coming from the enclosure. He didn't know what it was. He had never heard it before.

The voice said, "Wh-a wh-a wh-a," like a child's cry.

At the same time, Vatimato heard his pigs running round and round in their enclosure.

"Maybe something's chasing them," he thought.

However, he knew that this could not be true because he was alone on his island.

"What could it be?" he asked himself.

The next morning, Vatimato got up before the sun had risen.

He said to himself, "Today, I must find out what is happening to my pigs. They are getting so thin!"

Vatimato thought that his pigs might even die.

"Before anything, though, I need to find out what is making them run round and round in their enclosure."

As usual, he prepared his pigs' food and put it into his basket. He went to the enclosure and fed the pigs. Then, he went back to his house and hid behind a big tree trunk to see what would happen. From there, he watched and saw something extraordinary: a tree, a *namele* that grew and grew, blowing up as if it had air in its trunk. It wouldn't stop growing. Vatimato watched it very closely. He wondered what would happen. He was terrified.

All of a sudden, the *namele* opened up and a child came out. He looked like all other boys of his age except that he was very thin and had long, straight, black hair. His hair was so long that it hung way down his back.

"What is going on?" Vatimato asked, trembling in terror.

He stayed hidden behind his tree without ever taking his eyes off the little boy with the long hair. The boy looked around him a little. Of course, he was not aware that Vatimato was looking at him from behind the tree. Then, the boy quickly went over to the pigs' enclosure.

When he reached the fence, he cried, "Wh-a, wh-a, wh-a!" and then jumped over.

The pigs were very frightened. They left their food and ran to the other side of the pen. The little boy then started to eat. He was very hungry and he quickly finished everything. Vatimato was boiling with anger.

"Now, I know why my pigs are getting so thin. I must do something about this."

When the boy had finished his meal, he jumped the fence once again. He was going to leave when Vatimato jumped out from his hiding place.

"Hey! Wait!" he yelled. "Who are you? Where do you come from? And why are you eating my pigs' food?"

The child stopped short. He hadn't realised that Vatimato had been watching. He bowed his head and then, raising it very slowly, spoke to Vatimato.

"My name is Vatmah. My mother is *Namele* and I do not have a father."

Vatimato knew that Vatmah's mother could not work in order to give her child food. He looked so thin and so sad that Vatimato had pity on him.

He looked at the boy and said, "I will be your father. I will take you to my house and take care of you."

Vatmah replied, "I will come with you on one condition. You must promise never to cut the *namele's* leaves. If you do, you will hurt me and I will leave."

Vatimato promised. He took the boy back to his house and took care of him as if he were his real son. He taught him everything that a boy must know. They went hunting and fishing. They built a canoe. They spent some very good times together. Vatmah often helped Vatimato to feed his pigs.

One day, there was a big feast on a neighbouring island. Everyone was invited. Vatmah and his father went in their canoe. They pulled it up onto the beach and walked all the way to the village. There were many men, women, and children there. Vatmah was very pleased to make so many new friends. Everyone was making merry. Vatimato and Vatmah ate much *laplap*. Then, Vatimato went to join the men's dance. He asked Vatmah to wait for him in the village. However, Vatmah had never seen anything like this and so he stood a little to one side and watched the dancers. There were *namele* trees all around the dancing grounds. Vatimato wanted a leaf to dance with. Without thinking, he went and picked one. When Vatmah saw what his new father had done, he felt awful. He was sad that Vatimato had so quickly forgotten his promise. He started to cry and then ran away and hid himself in a *namele* in the middle of the bush.

When the dance was finished, Vatimato went to look for Vatmah. However, the boy was not where he said he would be. Vatimato couldn't find him anywhere. Then, he thought to look under the *namele* trees. He wasn't there either. Vatimato looked every-where. He sat down near the dancing grounds and thought. Suddenly, he remembered Vatmah's words on the day that they met. He understood that the boy must have run away. He looked all around and called and called, but there was no answer. Night was falling, and Vatimato had to return home. He went back to his canoe, and went back to his island all alone and very sad. He never saw or heard of Vatmah again.

This legend from the island of Paama was written in French by Jacques Gédéon.

Previously unpublished.

SHEFA Province

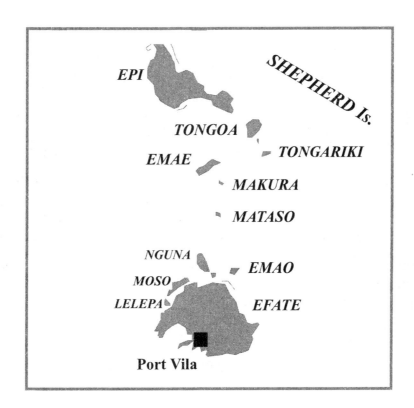

EPI

SHEPHERD Is.

TONGOA

TONGARIKI

EMAE

MAKURA

MATASO

NGUNA

EMAO

MOSO

LELEPA

EFATE

Port Vila

The old woman and the bananas
(Epi)

A long time ago, on the Island of Epi, there lived an old woman that loved bananas. She loved them so much that she had planted banana trees all around her house. One day, when everyone in the village had gone through the bush to visit a neighbouring village, the old woman stayed at home with her granddaughter. Suddenly, they heard a strange noise next to the house. It was coming from the banana trees that the old woman had planted!

Lovoe lovoe talmbe rere a bomae rambe ninive
Tera tera terel terelbue terelbue tere terealbue terelbue

"Who is singing in my garden?" asked the grandmother.
"Bubu, there is no one outside!" responded the granddaughter.
A few minutes later, the same song pierced the silence.

Lovoe lovoe talmbe rere a bomae rambe ninive
Tera tera terel terelbue terelbue tere terealbue terelbue

The little girl peered outside. To her great surprise, she saw the banana leaves moving even though there was no wind. She told her grandmother what she had seen and the old woman became very angry. She grabbed her cane and went straight to the banana trees. The old woman hit the trees again and again until they were all broken.

This is the reason why, today, all of the banana trees are so small. The old woman's anger had stunted their growth. If not, they would have grown as tall as coconut palms and we would still be able to hear them sing.

Lovoe lovoe talmbe rere a bomae rambe ninive
Tera tera terel terelbue terelbue tere terealbue terelbue

This story was told by Joseph Yona from Mabfilau on Epi. It was translated by Nancy Yona.

Previously unpublished.

The prisoner of the stone
(Epi)

Once upon a time, an old man fell in love with a much younger woman. To tell the truth, she was little more than a child. The old man went to the child's father and asked his permission to marry her. The father was happy enough to marry his daughter to the old man and it was decided that a last feast should be held before the daughter left to live in her new home. The day after saying her goodbyes, the girl, escorted by her father, went to her husband's house. As soon as she saw the old man, she became very sad because she knew that she could never love him. He was too old. However, the young girl didn't dare say a word and so her father left her there alone and returned to his house.

That night, the young bride waited until her husband was sleeping deeply. Then, she crept out and returned to her village. The next day, her father brought her back to her husband. She continued to run away like this but, each time, her father brought her back. One day, the girl had an idea. She wouldn't return to her village! She would hide herself in the bush so that no one could find her. A few days later, the girl ran away again but this time, into the bush.

She had been walking for days and days without food. She was on the edge of total exhaustion when she found a *navara,* a germinated coconut. She picked it up and continued on her way until she came to a big stone. She wanted to break the coconut on the stone so that she might eat its contents and gain some strength. So, intent on her purpose, she climbed up on the stone. But, at the very moment when she hit the coconut on the stone, something very strange happened. The stone started to grow and grow, taking the young girl prisoner and pushing her high into the air. Scared to death, she tried to jump but saw that she was already too high up. There was no way off the stone. All alone on top of the rock with no food except the *navara*, the girl started to cry. She cried and she cried. When she finally looked down from her rock, she realised that she was now in the middle of a big lake. She also saw that a giant eel was swimming round and round the rock. Now, there was definitely no way to escape.

The young girl's family, after some time, found out what had happened and where she was. They made their way to the stone and saw their child on the peak of the stone. They tried their best to get her down, but all their efforts were in vain. It broke their hearts, but they were obliged to leave their daughter all alone. They finally returned to their village, abandoning the girl to her fate.

The young girl lived up there, a prisoner of the rock, until her death. This stone is just behind the hill that we now call Maemoral.

This story was told by Joseph Yona from Mabfilau on Epi. It was translated by Nancy Yona and Peter Murgatroyd.

Previously unpublished.

The legend of Sakora and Tiara
(Makura)

There were two
Two men from Makura
Sakora and Tiara.
And each day the sun sank into the sea
And each day they saw it sink.
And a desire filled them to see where the sun slept.
Thus, Sakora took his canoe and went, went towards the sinking,
Always towards the sinking
And the sun told him as he neared
Stay, stay away, far away, my heat is too strong;
You would die…
Thus, Tiara took his canoe and went in search of the moon.
And the moon sunk into the sea
And the sea became cold
And the moon said: Man, do not approach, absolutely do not approach
But the man did not listen
And the moon touched the water
And the water covered the man
And Tiara drowned.

But him, but Sakora, he touched an island
He touched Merigh
The island of women
And he hid himself in the bush
But a woman saw him, hidden in the bush
A woman who had come to fetch salty water.
Woman, who are you?
What are you doing?
Come
Come with me to the house.
And him? And your husband?
What will your husband say?
Your husband will kill me.
The woman said again
Never during the day does my husband come
Never during the day, always at night
And the man followed the woman and the woman hid him in her house.

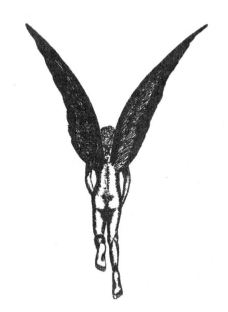

And your husband
Who is he?
Is he like me?
No.
But when night falls, he will come.
Then…
Then, they went to bed.
During the night in each house, in each house, on top of the roof,
Come the flying foxes to unite with the women.
There is my husband, said the woman, pointing to a flying fox
Who had come into the house.
And Sakora exclaimed
In my country, far, very far, they are eaten, the flying foxes,
They are never men

Men look like me
And Sakora killed the flying fox so that he could sleep with the woman.

And hour after hour
And day after day, the months went by
And their secret life continued.

Then, the woman became pregnant. She grew, became heavy
Her friends saw her, believed her sick, questioned her,
I am not sick, said the woman,
A man, a true man
A man came to my house, came with me.
The flying foxes, all those flying foxes are not men.
And the women wanted to see the man
And the man united with each woman, in each house
Each day, each in their turn.

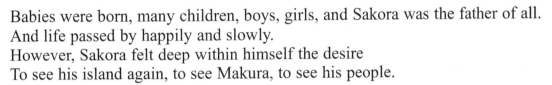

Babies were born, many children, boys, girls, and Sakora was the father of all.
And life passed by happily and slowly.
However, Sakora felt deep within himself the desire
To see his island again, to see Makura, to see his people.

At the edge of the reef, one day
A woman, an old woman was sitting at the edge of the reef
And Sakora saw her, Sakora greeted her
And asked her what she was doing.
And the woman said:
"I am with my people who fish on the reef
I am a Siviritot
With my people we fish, we fish everwhere
On the islands, on every island".
Then Sakora said: Will you go to Makura?
Yes Makura
Efate.
Then Siviritot, I want to return to Makura, to see my people again
All of my people
I have been here for a long time, a very long time, too long a time
But how to do it? I don't know how to return to Makura.

The voice of the old woman, she was a goddess, raised slightly.
Go Sakora
Go and find six reeds
Do not, absolutely not, peel away the leaves
Instead attach them one to the other with their leaves.
Go Sakora and find some coconuts
And the old woman split the coconuts
And the old woman removed the white meat
And the old woman gave her rags to Sakora to cover himself
And the old woman hid so that he could go in her stead.
When the Siviritot fishermen returned to bring fish to the old woman
Sakora received them
But Sakora did not eat them, he fooled the Siviritot fishermen
He fooled them as the old woman had told him to
He ate instead the white meat of the coconut.
Thus fooled, the Siviritots led Sakora from island to island, as if he were the old woman
In the night, they fished from island to island.

After the Torres
After the Torres the Banks is Merigh, the island Merigh.

Sakora and the Siviritots touched Ambae
And Sakora asked
Where will we go next?
Ambrym.
And the night continued
And always Sakora asked
Where will we go next?
Epi.
Emao.
And the night continued.

Now, he knew
He, Sakora, knew
That they were approaching Makura.
At the beginning, since the beginning, he held tight the reeds
The bundle of reeds
Reeds enchanted by the old woman.

"That the day should be delayed from breaking
That the sun should be delayed from showing on men
That the night be long
That the course of the moon be protracted
So that all the islands might be reached
So that Makura might be reached before dawn."

And in the night appeared Makura, his island, his people, all of his people.
Makura his life his blood.

Thus, to fishing, fishing in the night, fishing with the Siviritots
The Siviritots that left their garments, abandoned their garments and their
Wings, there, on the shore
In the care of the old woman
In the care of Sakora.
But Sakora saw
He saw among them
Among the Siviritots
A beautiful girl
A young girl
She pleased him.

Then…
Then, he hid her wings
The wings of the girl.
Reeds. Their turn now. Your work
Your work to bring the light
Your work to snuff out the night.
And Sakora undid the reeds
And took up the first reed
And hit the ground with force with the first reed
So that the night would stop
So that the moon would dive
  into the waters
So that the sea would swallow it up
So that the day would appear, new and yet dim
And he hit the ground with the second reed.

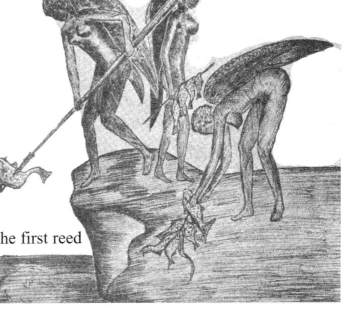

The sea became blue, a blue tinged with black
The horizon lightened
And he hit the ground hard with the third reed
And the ocean became rosy, and the sky reddened
And the wind started blowing
And the great star climbed climbed
And he hit the ground hard with the fourth
With the fifth, with the sixth reed
And it was explosive, enriching, completely bewitching
It was the day that in all its glory
As on that first day
The Light that was the gods to diffuse.

The woman was alone.
Silence…
But she, the girl, the Siviritot, she was looking for her wings.
She wondered, and did not understand.
On the beach she ran
She returned towards the rocks, left.
She felt trapped.
"My wings,
Where are my wings?
Who took my wings?"
Only the sound of the waves,
The sound of the waves on the rocks responded to her cries.

Sakora was anxious
Very anxious. He wanted to see Malakoto, his village, his family.
In the early morning, when he finally arrived at the dancing place,
The *nasara* was empty, around a big wooden drum.
The grass had covered the ground trampled by so many feet in times past.
Since he had disappeared, Malakoto had been in mourning.
No more dancing; the drum sounded no more.
Mourning, deep mourning.
Sakora saw the drum. Sakora beat it.
The sound that issued from the long wooden slit was as yet weak.
Sakora had lost his ability.
He beat it, beat it again.
"Who beats that drum?

Who beats that drum when we are in mourning for Sakora?
Who dares to do the forbidden?"
And Sakora continued to beat the drum.
Confusion, amazement everywhere.
"Who beats our drum thus?"
And to the people to run.
And to recognize and to cry.
The first to arrive called to those still far off, too far to recognise.
And the noise of the *tamtam* and the cries of joy melted into each other.
And the dances were taken up where they had been left off,
And the grasses were bent by a thousand trampling feet,
And every drum was beaten.
And thus the cries
And thus the chants
And thus the trampling of the grass,
The deafening sounds of the drum,
The drums.

Joy.
Sakora was alive
He was there
There among them.
The chief spoke.
"One of us has come back.
Have a great feast in his honour!"
The women prepared the ovens,
Reddened on the blackening wood.
The men went to harvest the best yams and the best taro
That they then gave to the women.
The village was busy: Malakoto reborn.
Night fell. The women opened the ovens.
The stones, still hot, were put into piles.
The old women placed onto big leaves hunks of steaming yam
And the pig still smoking.
In the *nakamal* the men sat
Sat around Sakora.
And Sakora told of his adventures: Merigh, Ambae, Ambrym, Epi.

The girl.
Where was the girl?
He had forgotten the beautiful
Siviritot without her wings, waiting on the beach.
He got up.
He ran.
He arrived on the beach.
"Siviritot, where are you?"
But it was too late: the beach was empty.

Malehakera, a god that lived under a stone had seen the girl
The girl hopelessly alone, the girl running along the beach.
"What are you doing here alone?"
"I am looking for my wings. Have you seen my wings?"
"We shall find them. Come with me. Come to my house."
And the girl followed him and asked,
"Where is your home?"
"There, under that big rock."
"What? You do not have a house?"
"Then, man, go and find some wood. I will teach you
Teach you to build a house."
Melehakara came and went, came and went with everything that the woman asked for.

And day by day, month by month, the time passed.
The woman became pregnant and gave birth to her first son. His name was Karisipua.
And then another, Tafakisema.
And finally a girl, Leipuapua.
The two boys grew.
One day they said to their father:
"We want you to make us a bow and arrow."
And the father found some wood and made a bow for each of his sons.
And the brothers went hunting, hunting for lizards.
Under a rock, a lizard warmed itself in the sun.
Kairipua pursued it.
Tafakisema jumped from one rock to another. The lizard hid under a big rock.
Thus, the two boys lifted the rock,
Cried with fright, and ran away.

Under the rock were nestled the wings, hidden by Sakora.
Home, trembling with fear, shivering with fear,
The brothers told their story,
Told it with difficulty to their mother.
"An enormous bird was hidden under the rock," said Karisipua.
"No, feathers. Only feathers," said Tafakisema.
"Let us see," said the mother.
Now near the rocks, the mother lifted the stone and found her wings
Then her face changed, then her voice became different:
"I am going to leave you alone with your father."
But the children did not understand, and the three returned to the house together.

At this time,
Exactly this time, Mekehakara was in his garden, not suspecting a thing.
He had readied some yams that he was preparing to bring to the house.
The sun was still high, high in the sky.
The mother said to her children:
"We shall kill a pig.
A pig that we will cook with the *laplap,* a *laplap* which has already been prepared."
They killed a pig and the mother said:
"The head will be for your father.
He will eat it on his return from the garden."
When the *laplap* and the pig were cooked the mother left.
The mother gave a part to each of her sons, and went to try her wings.
She stroked the feathers carefully, carefully with trembling hands.
And attached them to her back.
"That the wind might carry me lightly as in the old times,
That the wind would push me, that it would carry me high,
That light would I be, like a Siviritot."
And the woman rose in front of her sons,
Her two stupefied sons.
She rose and she descended, she rose,
Rose once again towards the sun as if she wanted to take a closer look.
Like a bird, she glided.
However, in one swoop, she descended.
Around her, the wind from her wings flattened everything,
And Melehakara in his garden was pushed to the ground,
And the branches of the trees broke and covered him.

Yams from the pile flew everywhere...
And the woman flew, and the woman dived, dived right towards her children.
She landed lightly, kissed her two sons, and flew away
Only a white speck in the sky.
The two children were alone
Alone and crying.
Malehakara who did not know anything, did not know a thing, about all this disaster returned,
Returned from his garden, breathless.
"Mother has left. She flew away.
The head of this pig is for you."
To Malehakara to eat the head of the pig left by his wife and to die.
To the two boys and their sister Leipuapua to be left alone with their sorrow.
And to them to attach to the door of their *fare* ten mats made from woven palms
And to them therefore to put themselves into mourning.

This legend was given in Bislama to Jean Guiart by Shem Mwasoeripu from Makura.
We have tried, in the translation, to conserve the rhythm of his poetry. Adapted by Paul Gardissat.

Nabanga n°32/37 (1976)

The magic shell
(Makura)

Once upon a time, on the island of Makura, there lived an old woman and her grand-daughter. The girl adored her grandmother who took good care of her and surrounded her with love. Her parents had died of a strange sickness whose cure had not yet been discovered. What surprised the little girl the most was how the grand-mother did her hair. The old woman often put her hair up with a magic shell. This shell made her hair smooth and shiny without any work. This peaked the little girl's curiosity to such a point that she decided to find out more.

One day, taking advantage of the grandmother's absence, the little girl took the magic shell. She hid it, promising herself that she would come back to inspect it later at her leisure. As always, in the afternoon, the grandmother took her nap. What a chance for the little girl! She took up the treasure, examined it, and was very disappointed. She inspected the shell, turning it this way and that in her hands. No, the shell was not unique, neither uglier nor prettier than most shells. Truly, it must be magical only for her grandmother. It was too sad! In her anger, the child threw the shell far, far away.

The grandmother did not notice that her shell had disappeared until she woke up the next day when the sun was still low and pale on the horizon. She looked for her magic comb everywhere in the house. Seeing that her granddaughter looked ashamed, she realised that perhaps she had had something to do with her shell's disappearance.

"Where did you put my shell?"

The child felt her heart beat faster.

"I threw it away," the child said quickly as if sighing.

"Go find it! And fast!" the grandmother cried angrily.

Her face reflected her dismay even more because her hair was not beautifully done that day. The little girl obeyed without further delay. She left in search of the shell. She looked everywhere around the village. Nothing. The child began to think that her search was hopeless. The tall grasses revealed nothing. The shell was lost for good. Slowly, she made her way back to the village and told her grandmother the horrible news.

"I couldn't find it... perhaps it fell in the river down the way."

Neither yelling to frighten the child nor saying soft words to console her, the grand-mother took off in the direction of the river.

161

"Come with me. We will look together."

Both of them went to the river. All along the river bed, where the water was clear and limpid, there was nothing to be seen. Of course, the two found some shells, but none of them were magic. The grandmother had lost her treasure. Full of despair, the little girl had only one thing on her mind: to disappear forever. She found it impossible to bear her grandmother's pain. So, she played a trick.

"Look! In the village! Our house is on fire!"she cried, pointing to the village high on the plateau.

The grandmother turned around to look. This is exactly what the little girl wanted. Splash! She jumped into the sea. When she came back up to the surface, she had been transformed into a rock. The grandmother, not understanding what all the fuss was about, turned back to the child. To her surprise, the little girl had gone! She called very loudly. Nothing. Without a doubt, she must be in the water. The old woman, in turn, jumped in. When she came to the surface, just like her granddaughter, she had been transformed into a stone.

Since that day, in the sea, near Makura, one can see two stones. Perhaps this is the effect of a lost shell...

Radio Port-Vila broadcast "Alors...Raconte!"

The legend of Kuwae
(Tongoa)

A long, long time ago, in the centre of Vanuatu, between the islands of Epi and Makura, there rose up a big island with, here and there, little volcanoes, extinct volcanoes, peaceful volcanoes. This island was called Kuwae. In the *nakamal,* during the evening, the old men told stories and the younger men listened. The old men said that a long time ago, the island had been shaken by a huge earthquake that had caused a large part of the east coast of Kuwae island to slide into the sea. At this time, the volcanoes spat fire. Above Ambrym and Lopevi, the sky was stained red.

Years and years ago, on Kuwae, there lived a great man, a tall and very strong man. He had long hair, a bushy beard, and a splendid necklace of shells around his neck. On his arms, pigs' tusks and brass bracelets accentuated his muscles. This man was named Pae. On the whole island of Kuwae, he was known as the best bow shooter. He was very talented and he never missed his target. Pae was a very proud man. While hunting, it was always he who killed the best pig. While fishing, the best fish were for him. No one could come close to Pae. This, of course, provoked jealousy. Pae was admired but not liked.

"He is always the one to kill the best pigs."

"The biggest fish are always on his line!"

The people of Kuwae became tired of Pae's prowess. One day, a group of young people got together.

"Friends, do you not find Pae too proud?"

"Yes, the girls only look at him!"

"Everything is for him!"

"I think that we should play a trick on him that will make him ashamed to show his face in public..."

"What a good idea! Let's go!"

After this discussion, the youth from Kurumembe village decided to act. That evening, the *nakamal* was dark. There was no moon, only a small, dying fire in one corner of the building. The boys went to get the girls and bring them to the *nakamal.* They were all there laughing and joking. On Kuwae, women were allowed to enter the common meeting place. They could even sleep there. Laughter echoed in the dark, and a woman slipped onto Pae's mat. Pae felt the female body next to him and he entered her. Suddenly, the mood was broken by a loud cry.

"Ah! My son! My son! I have just slept with my son! Ah!"

163

The woman had just touched a raised scar on Pae's chest. She then ran away, leaving Pae speechless.

"My mother! It was my mother! I slept with my mother... oh, horrible incest!"

Alas, it was too late because in Pae's head, the idea of revenge had already taken form.

"I will have revenge. They'll see... They'll see who they are dealing with!"

One day, the people from Ikatoma and Anabong decided to go to the south east of Ambrym where they had some family. To make this voyage, they had built an enormous canoe. Pae thought that the best solution was to leave for Ambrym, the country of fire. His uncle lived over there, and his uncle knew everything. He knew how to use poison and leaves, everything necessary for him, the perpetrator of incest, to take revenge on the others. So, he left with the people of Ikatoma. Once they arrived on the beach, his uncle, who had seen the canoe arriving, went to meet him.

"How good it is to see you! But what's wrong? You face is drawn. You must have a problem."

"My uncle, the people from Kurumembe tricked me and I slept with my mother! It was their fault! Their fault!"

"My son, I understand your anger at the trick they pulled on you. What do you want to do about it?"

"I want to take revenge... I want the fire of my fathers..."

"The fires! Pae, my son, think a little bit. Think of the innocent living on Kuwae."

"Uncle, I want my revenge."

"Alright, tomorrow morning at sunrise, we will go and get what you want."

And the next day, the men climbed high up into the rocks where nothing grew and a sinister smell of sulphur pervaded the air.

"Here?"

In front of them, there was a strange hole. It was very hot and there were many lizards around it. The uncle then called the spirit of the volcano and said to his nephew, showing him the big lizards swarming around the hole, "Which one do you want? This one? The big one?"

"No, it's too big. Much too big. I won't be able to carry it."

His uncle then showed him a small one, like those with blue tails that warm themselves on the beach.

"Yes, that one! That's the one that I want!"

"But Pae, this lizard is too powerful. It is capable of destroying everything..."

"That's the one that I want."

"Alright, Pae, if that's the one that you want. However, I'm warning you that it could destroy everything at once. Here, take this yam and dig a hole in the inside. Put the lizard in it and close it back up. Close it well."

Marakipule, the man who had rowed the canoe that had brought Pae to Ambrym, came back to get Pae. Pae attached the yam containing the lizard to the mast of the canoe still known as Warasole. The big sail made from woven pandanus filled with wind, and they were off. When they were half way to Kuwae, the lizard's power was so great that it split the canoe in two. Marakipule, the rower, did not understand what had happened. The canoe continued to stay afloat, however. Water could be seen in the crack in the canoe, but it did not come into the boat. Warasole continued its trip. When they had arrived at Kuwae, Pae went and buried the yam containing the lizard at the foot of an ironwood tree, next to the *nakamal*.

Then, he covered it with a big stone and said to Marakipule, "Leave! Leave quickly! Take your canoe and go with your family to Efate. Direct your canoe towards Emao Point. You know, the point that we can see on clear days that we call Aken. When you arrive at Aken, you will see another point on Efate. This is Maniura, right next to Forari. You should go to Maniura. Stay there for six years and only return to Kuwae once these six years are up."

Marakipule didn't ask any questions. He knew that he must listen to Pae and that something beyond his comprehension was going on. Marakipule's whole family took their places on Warasole and left in the direction of Aken. Pae then asked his brothers to organise a feast.

"Ha! He's organising a feast when he's slept with his mother!"

"Laugh all you want! You won't be laughing soon!" Pae thought to himself.

A pig was sacrificed, and Pae took its bladder, blew it up, and hung it from the top of an ironwood tree. The next day, a pig was again killed and the feast continued. Pae took the bladder from the second pig and hung it under the first. The third day, another pig was killed and Pae hung its bladder under the first two. He repeated these actions until six bladders were strung on the tree. Six pigs had been sacrificed, eaten, and had had their bladders hung from the tree at differing heights. As soon as the feast had ended, Pae said, "You will see now!"

He climbed up the tree and popped the first bladder. The ground started to shake.

"What's happening?"

"Hey! It's an earthquake!"

He climbed down a little and popped the second bladder. The ground shook again, but stronger this time.

"Oh! What's going to happen? The ground won't stop shaking!"

"This is strange," some of the elders said, "the ground hasn't shaken like this for some time."

Then, Pae burst the third bladder and the ground shook even harder.

"What is going on? The ground won't stop quaking!"

Others said, "What is Pae doing, bursting those bladders at the top of the tree?"

"Don't forget that you slept with your mother. Stop showing off!"

"He's bringing us bad luck by acting like this. The ground won't stop moving."

Pae, not listening to the others, popped the fourth bladder and the ground shook, the land started to tilt, and caused the people of Kuwae to be very afraid. Women and children from all around started to run into the bush. The men tried to stop them, but they were too afraid. The elders threw themselves to the ground.

"Pae! Stop! Take pity on us and stop!"

But at that moment, Pae burst the fifth bladder and the island started to explode.

"Fire! Lava!"

"Fire! Fire!"

"Lava! The volcano!"

Pae had just enough time to burst the sixth bladder.

"Your time has come! And my time as well!"

A volcano opened at the base of the tree. Lava covered everything and the volcano spat glowing blocks of stone. Pae's head was thrown all the way to Ambrym, and Kuwae broke loose. A good half of the island slid into the sea and Kuwae was destroyed.

At Maniura, that point on Efate between Eton and Forari, Marakipule had watched the explosion of Kuwae. The ground had shaken terribly on Efate and a tidal wave had followed. For six years, Marakipule waited. He did exactly as Pae had told him. Then, at the end of the six years, he went to the now displaced Kuwae. The island was nothing but a pile of ashes. There was neither plants nor a single tree. Only one little bush with yellow fruit could be found amidst the silence in that barren place. This was the *waratongoa*. This is the reason that the island that has taken the place of Kuwae is called Tongoa. Kuwae exists no more. What is left of Kuwae today is called Tongoa, Tongariki, Ewose, and Falea.

This legend was given in Bislama by a chief of Tongoa, Tom Tipoamata.

Radio New-Hebrides

Six brothers and the snake
(Tongoa)

Once upon a time, on Tongoa island in Vanuatu, in the village of Panita, there lived a poor woman with her six handsome sons. Her husband was no longer of this world, but she was able to raise her sons with all the love given to a woman who must play the roles of both mother and father. When the boys were grown, they learned to use a bow and arrows. Their biggest joy was to go hunting. The mother, though, did not like this activity. She was always afraid that something bad would happen to her boys. She was never at ease when she left her boys to go to the garden. So, she usually told the boys to stay in the village and play with other children of their age. They would be safe that way. The bush hid so many dangers...

One day, as usual, the mother headed off to the garden. Bothered by a premonition, she told her boys to stick close to the village. She was so sure that something bad would happen that she warned them several times. However, the six boys really wanted to go hunting. Some of the boys felt bad about disobeying their mother, but their desire to go hunting was too strong. Their mother had just gone out of sight when the boys left in the opposite direction, armed with their bows and arrows. The children had been walking for some time when, around a bend in the path, they came face to face with a snake. It was an enormous beast that looked them directly in the eyes. The boys were seized with terror. But their fear increased when the snake started to speak to them.

"Go away, children! You are bothering me! I'll let you live, though. Go. Now. I only ask that you don't tell anyone about me. If you do, they will come to hunt me. Know that if you speak of me in your village, I will kill you before they kill me! Go, now."

Overwhelmed with panic, the boys ran away. They ran all the way to their village where they barricaded themselves in their house. A little while later, when their mother had come home, she found her boys still overcome by fear. Of course, the boys could not hold their tongue. They told her what they had seen. And, of course, the mother couldn't keep quiet either and soon, the whole village of Panita knew about the giant snake in the bush not far from where they were. The next day, the poor woman left for her garden. Before she left, though, she warned the boys to stay close so that her worst fears would not be realised. Once their mother had left, the boys couldn't hold still. The beast had fascinated them and they wanted to show it that they, though small, were good hunters. After all, there were six of them and only one snake, no matter how big it was!

Encouraging each other with brave words, the six boys headed for the snake. The youngest are always the proudest. The oldest boy, bringing up the rear, made sure that no danger could approach them from behind. While inspecting the bush for perils, he fell further and further behind his brothers. He ran to catch up with them and was surprised to see the snake coiled around his brothers. He was dismayed by this sight but realised that he could do nothing against the giant animal. Without waiting, he ran to the village for reinforcements. In haste, he went to warn his mother. The villagers walked hopelessly towards the bush but found themselves forbidden to enter. The path was blocked by an enormous stone that was in the exact place where his brothers and the snake had been. There was nothing to do; the boys were dead and the snake had disappeared.

Today, this stone still bears witness to the drama. It still blocks the path and is called Neimaru. If you go to Panita, you will definitely see it.

Radio Port-Vila broadcast, "Alors...Raconte!"

Mauitikitiki, the fisher of islands
(Emae)

Mauitikitiki lived on Emae, just behind the village of Finongi, at the foot of Mangarufu, one of the three mountains on the island of Emae. It is even said that he built his house at Katapuae. One day, he wanted to go to Efate. He took his club and went down to the shore. Once he got to the reef, he saw a shark passing.

"Shark, I want to go to Efate. Can you take me there?"

The shark, looking at him apologetically, said, "I am so sorry, Oh Great One, but I must stay in this bay. I was made to live here."

A little disappointed, Mauitikitiki continued to fish and, from rock to reef, he eventually arrived at Monoliu village. A turtle then swam close to him.

"Turtle, can you take me to Efate?"

The turtle, very happy to be of service, looked at him happily.

"Yes, come with me! We shall go on a trip. Get on my back and hold on tight to my shell!"

And so, the two were off. When they were under way, the man started to get hungry.

"Turtle, I'm hungry!"

The turtle, not surprised, answered, "Put your hand under my tail. You'll find something to eat there."

After having eaten, Mauitikitiki was thirsty and, a little shamefacedly, asked, "Friend, my tongue is dry. It must be the salt water making me thirsty... what should I do about it?"

The turtle pushed up its head ever so slightly and answered, "You are a great man on the ground, but apparently I'm more at ease than you in the water! So, you're thirsty? Put your hand under my tail and you'll find something to drink."

The voyage continued and the turtle forgot that he had a passenger. He started to dive into the water, and Mauitikitiki, completely soaked, spoke up.

"Turtle! I am wet and you are making me swallow sea water!"

The turtle excused himself by saying, "I had completely forgotten you!"

After having passed to the south of the island of Emao, after having swum alongside the villages of Epau and Purari, after having visited Rentapao and Maniura, the turtle rounded Epangtui Point and entered into Fila Bay. The two of them, tired out, arrived at Raolua. At the point of this bay, Mauitikitiki went to pee on a rock. Now, he felt better and mounted the turtle's back once again and said, "We shall go to see the white men!"

"Oh Great Man, you will kill me with all of this travel!"

And so they were off. A little while later, Mauitikitiki and his friend the turtle came back to Raolua. There, on the stone that he had peed on, a woman was waiting for him. Her skin was black. She used to live inside the big stone. Now, she was pregnant, pregnant by his urine. Realising what had happened, Mauitikitiki turned to leave.

"Friend, let us leave quickly. I don't want that woman there. She is too black!"

The woman, seeing that he was about to leave, stood up on the rock and cried, "Man, I am pregnant by you. If you leave, who will feed this child and give it a name?"

Mauitikitiki took a red yam and a fish and, giving them to the woman by way of a present, got back onto the turtle and cried, "If it's a boy, you will call him Tamakaia."

Then, he left for Emae abandoning the black woman with her big belly. While they were travelling, the Great Man again was thirsty and asked, "Turtle, I am thirsty. Do you have anything to drink under your tail?"

"Look well, Oh Great One, and you should find a coconut."

"How will I open it?"

"Great One, you really are very awkward in the water. Silly man, you forget that I have claws. Give me the coconut. Here, my friend, now you may drink."

Mauitikitiki drank. When they had gotten to the reef in Emae, the Great Man, furious at having been called silly by the turtle, cracked the coconut over the turtle's head. Before dying, the turtle said, "Now that you are in the land of Supwe Na Vanuau, you forget your friend."

And it died.

Without a single tender thought for the turtle, Mauitikitiki gave the animal to a friend of his from Taripoa that was passing by. Then, he walked along the shore in order to return to his own village of Katapuae. During this time, at Raolua, that little bay that is just across from Fila island, the woman had given birth to a boy. He had grown and grown. From time to time, he would go to Fila to play with children of his own age. He liked to sharpen reeds and throw them. It was his favourite game. With the help of a cord made from coconut husks, a bundle of ten sharp reeds were launched the longest distance possible. The boys would stand in a line and see who could send their reeds the furthest. Tamakaia, because that was the little boy's name, won each time. The other boys eventually stopped playing with him. They didn't like him and were very jealous.

"Tamakaia is always winning our games. He is not from our island. He is from Ranboa and his father is from Emae. He is a stranger."

One day, the children were ready to eat and Tamakaia got into his canoe and paddled off to see his mother at Raolua. She gave the boy a piece of yam and a piece of fish from those that Mauitikitiki had given her before he left. Tamakaia returned to Fila with these provisions and everyone went to work. His friends grated their white yams and he did the same with his red one. After the stones were very hot, the young boys took them off the coals and put together big packages of banana leaves in which they had placed their grated yam. Tamakaia put his red yam in a corner of one of these leaf packets. Then he brought the hot stones and put them on top of the leaves. When the time came to pull the *laplap* out of the oven, everyone was stupefied. The red yam had risen; it had risen so much that it covered the white yam. The whole *laplap* was red.

Tamakaia then said triumphantly, "This *laplap* is mine because it's red," and he took it with him.

If the boys from Fila were angry, they were, however, not without hope. Time was on their side. Yet again, they decided to prepare another meal together. Because they were suspicious, though, they wanted to know what Tamakaia would do. When everyone had left for the gardens in search of banana leaves, dry wood, and yams, one of the boys pretended to have a fever and laid down. Once everyone had left, Tamakaia decided to go to his mother's house at Raolua. He saw the faking sick boy and asked him if he would like to go with him. Both of them got into the canoe. Just as the faking invalid was about to take up a paddle, Tamakaia told him, "Hold on to my bark belt and close your eyes."

When he was told to open his eyes, both of them were inside a rock in a big, echoing cavern. Tamakaia's mother, that woman of the black skin, was happy to see her son again. But the faking invalid was afraid of this humid cavern. He looked all around him and, pulling on Tamakaia's belt, said, "Let's get out of here. Now."

Tamakaia asked his mother for some yam. Like the last time, she gave him a red yam and some fish. Tamakaia realised that his friend was frightened to death and, giving him the same instructions, the two of them found themselves off the shore of Fila.

The other boys came back from the garden carrying the dry wood, banana leaves, and yams. Then, they all started to grate their yams into a paste that would eventually become *laplap*. While grating, they chatted and the brother who had pretended to be sick asked what had happened.

"I went to Tamakaia's home in the rock at Raolua. We saw his mother who was all black and his house that was a big, damp cave full of things."

The *laplap* was ready. The stones were pulled off the leaves and when the children had opened the packets, at the same instant that the wonderful odour of *laplap* hit their noses, they all leaned in to look. Tamakaia's red yam had risen and again covered his friends' white yam. No one was pleased. Some of the boys started to scratch the ground with their feet to show that they were upset.

Tamakaia once again smiled and said, "This laplap is like the last one. It is all red. My yam was red. This *laplap* is mine."

His friends exploded with rage. "You have beaten us twice: at the game and at the meal!"

Another said, "You are a stranger. You are not welcome here. We don't know your people on this island. Your father is from Emae."

At the same moment, a wild fowl walked by the nasara. One of Tamakaia's friends said, "Ha! That's your father!"

Tamakaia ran after the fowl with the big feet and, out of breath, caught it and asked, "Are you my father?"

The fowl, angry at having had his feathers ruffled, responded, "How could I be your father if your father is from Emae?"

Tamakaia let the bird go and went to see his mother in her rock. When he saw the black woman, he told her his story.

"The other boys told me that my father was a wild fowl. I caught the fowl. It was really vexed with me. But what could I do? The fowl told me that my father was from Emae."

The black woman took her son in her arms and said, "Yes, son, you father really is from Emae."

Tamakaia pondered her answer and, taking his mother by the hand, left the rock and said, "Mother, we are going to build a canoe. I want to go to see him."

The next day, Tamakaia set fire to a tree in order to fell it. The day after, when he came back to the tree, it had already started to be fashioned into a beautiful canoe. This was the work of his grandfather, Supwe Na Vanua, the god of the Earth. After three days, the canoe was finished. Tamakaia had not done a thing. His grandfather had done all the work at night. Tamakaia called to the children from Fila. They pulled the canoe into the sea.

Tamakaia said, "Who among you would like to come to find my father on Emae with me?"

The young boys talked amongst themselves and decided that the youngest boy of each family should go with Tamakaia. Tamakaia and each of the youngest children took their places in the canoe 'Samararua' and took off in the direction of Mataso. The wind filled the sail of woven pandanus. They passed Pango Point and arrived at Mataso. At Mataso, Tamakaia asked Kalorana to row the canoe. Kalorana accepted and Samararua, its sails swollen with the good wind 'Ruatu,' arrived during the night on Emae, at the point of Makafaneya. In the dark, they saw a red light. Tamakaia thought that it might be a fire on the shore and noticed that his friends were half frozen.

He said to one of his friends, "Go and get some of that fire. That way, we can warm ourselves while waiting for daybreak."

The boy got out of the boat and when he arrived near the fire, a beast hit him and he fell down dead. Tamakaia, seeing that his friend had not come back and thinking that he was selfishly warming himself alone, sent another boy to go get him. The second boy went towards the fire and in the same way, the beast hit and killed him. Tamakaia, now a little nervous, sent another boy and the same thing happened. The six members of his team including the rower Kalorana, one by one, got out of the canoe and were, one by one, struck down. So, Tamakaia decided to go himself.

He took his club and went towards the fire where he found all of his friends splayed out, dead. Seeing something shiny, he moved closer to it. The beast wanted to hit him, but Tamakaia had just enough time to duck out of the way. Only his hand had been slightly hurt. Realising what had happened to his friends, he took up his club and walked away. Tamakaia went to rinse his bloody hand in the sea at the place called Worakoto. He then continued on his way, his hand still bleeding. So, he dipped his fingers in the sea at Ifila next to Sangava. You can still see the places where he washed his hand. Always walking, he met a man on the beach. This was Mafoa, a very worried man.

"Where are you going?" he asked.

"I am going to continue my walk."

Mafoa left Tamakaia, making him believe that he was walking away. Taking another route, he went into the bush, walked on some twisted, steep paths, and came out in front of Tamakaia, lance in hand.

Tamakaia frowned and said, "Didn't I just meet you back there?"

"Yes, that was me."

And Mafoa tried to spear Tamakaia with his lance. However, he didn't even have enough time to raise it above his head when Tamakaia hit him over the head with his club and, very dignified, continued on his way, leaving Mafoa prone on the ground.

Tamakaia's hand was still bleeding. So, he washed himself at Ranboa, hid his club at Finongi, and climbed up into the hills to see Mauitikitiki. While Tamakaia was climbing, Mauitikitiki was coming down, and seeing him coming, Tamakaia turned himself into a silver bird, those beautiful silver birds called *nawimba* that live in the bush. Mauitikitiki, seeing this *nawimba* in his way, tried to catch it. The god hadn't tried very hard before the bird came to rest on his hand. Mauitikitiki hid the bird and took it back to his house. Once inside his house, he perched the bird on his sceptre. The *nawimba,* however, did not want to stay on the top of the sceptre and let himself fall to the ground. Mauitikitiki, not understanding what was happening, tried the same thing with other pieces of wood that he would stick into the ground, but the *nawimba* always fell down. The god, angry at the bird, took his club, planted it in his roof, and set the bird upon it. The latter felt comfortable on the club and did not move again. Mauitikitiki had another bird that would never leave him. It was a *hoknait,* an owl, that would only fly at night. During the night, the *nawimba* became Tamakaia once again. The boy took down his father's club and left to go and kill everyone on the island, particularly Mauitikitiki. The owl, who sees everything at night, started to hoot in an effort to encourage Tamakaia.

"Kill them! Kill them all!" it said.

Unfortunately, this noise had alerted the inhabitants of the island to Tamakaia's plan. He was obliged to transform himself once again into the *nawimba* and settle on the club planted in his father's roof. The next day, everyone went back to work and forgot the fears of the night. Mauitikitiki went to feed his chickens and pigs. Tamakaia watched him doing this, hidden behind a banana tree.

"If all of these animals belong to my father,"said Tamakaia, "they will stay calm. If not, they will run away when I scare them."

Tamakaia, still in the form of the bird, beat his wings and the chicken and pigs ran off into the bush. Another day, Mauitikitiki went to weed, straighten, and generally clean up his garden. When the garden was cleaned and the weeds ready to burn, Tamakaia flew up into a tree and looked at the finished product.

"If this is my father's garden, it will stay this way. If it is not, it will be covered in weeds once again."

Mauitikitiki heard a noise behind him and, turning around, saw all the branches and weeds that he had just cut start to grow again. The god was furious.

"There must be a reason for all this misfortune!"

Tamakaia finally decided to show himself in his human form. He climbed into a *navele* tree and picked a piece of fruit. He dug his nails into the fruit's pulp and in this way drew his symbol. He then threw the fruit down at his father. Mauitikitiki was hit on the shoulder by the fruit and jumped in surprise. The *navele* rolled at his feet and he noticed the imprint of nails in the fruit. Knowing the character of his son, he quickly understood that Tamakaia was in the area and that all this trouble was because of him. He turned around, looked up into the *navele,* and saw his son.

"I am sure that you are the one that made my animals run away. Come down here!"

Tamakaia came down and the two left together. Once they got to the house, Mauitikitiki told Tamakaia to be good and he went back to the garden. Tamakaia watched his father leave and smiled. Supwe Na Vanua, the god of the earth, the boy's grandfather, lived secretly in a small hut near his son's house. On days when there was a high wind, Tamakaia was worried because he had heard a strange noise coming from somewhere inside this hut. However, Tamakaia was not allowed to enter the hut. The fact that entry was forbidden, the strange noise, and the fire coming from this place made Tamakaia all the more curious. He decided to go see for himself. When he went inside, he saw the old man seated on the ground, his knee on fire. Yes! A strong wind was blowing from a fire in the old man's knee.

The god, surprised, said, "Tamakaia, what are you doing here? I thought you were on Efate."

"Old man, I didn't know that you were here either. My father has always forbidden me from coming inside this house. That wind worried me and I wanted to see what it was."

Tamakaia looked all around him. If Mauitikitiki had forbidden him to come inside, it must have been for a good reason. Supwe Na Vanua, too old to move very much, tried to stop Tamakaia from going through the belongings in the house.

"Child, behave yourself, those things belong to your father."

A vine was hanging in the middle of the hut and Tamakaia stared at it.

"Grandfather, what is this vine for?"

"Your father often likes to swing on it. He's quite a child!"

"I'm going to swing on it and you, Pappy, will push me!"

"Tamakaia, I'm too old to push you. I don't have any strength left. If the vine were to hit me, I would die."

"Grandfather, push me. I want to try."

Tamakaia held on to the vine and Supwe Na Vanua pulled him back and then let go. Tamakaia swung into the sky and saw, shining in the sea, all the islands in the archipelago. Then, he understood. He understood that this was how his father could see everything that went on around him.

"Your turn, Grandfather. You must see all of these islands."

"Tamakaia, you are crazy! I am too old!"

"Grandfather, I want you to see this. It's marvelous!"

Supwe Na Vanua got a tenuous grip on the vine. Tamakaia pulled him back and then let him go. He climbed into the sky and saw all the islands. Then, at the end of his strength, he asked Tamakaia to catch him. Supwe Na Vanua, however, was too heavy and knocked Tamakaia down when he tried to cushion his fall. The old man lay sprawled in a corner with a broken leg. Tamakaia, sorry to see his grandfather in such pain at his expense, went and made two bamboo splints with which he set the broken leg. When the splints had been attached with a vine, Supwe Na Vanua was healed. So, Tamakaia asked the old man to make him a vine just like his father's so that he too might see all the islands. Supwe Na Vanua made him a long rope out of woven coconut husks. Tamakaia hung the rope and his grandfather pulled him back and let go.

Tamakaia felt happy. He saw all the islands coming into focus on the sea. At this time, all the present day islands had not yet come out of the water. Out of all the islands in Vanuatu, only their summits could be seen. Tamakaia swung back down and Supwe Na Vanua gave him another push. He went up and up until he saw an island. He threw a rope and caught the peak of this island and pulled it towards him, running towards Tapuae where his footprints still exist today. Then, with all of his might, he pulled the rope into the air and the island followed. Then, he did this again for another island and another until all the surrounding islands had come out of the water. Satisfied with what he had done, Tamakaia swung one more time, throwing himself even higher into the air. In the distance, there was a very big island.

This was the island of the White Men. Tamakaia threw his hook and started to pull. He pulled and pulled with all of his strength. The island was too heavy and his rope broke. Tamakaia fell backwards, surprising his grandfather. Disappointed, he took a handful of ashes and threw them on the island that would not move.

"In this way, that island can never approach us. If that island does not want to join us, it can stay where it is."

Mauitikitiki also had a stock of fish. Between two great stones, he had piled pebble upon pebble to form a wall so that the fish could not escape. When the tide was high, the fish went to hide in this pool and could not get back out. Tamakaia did not know about this stock. One day, though, he heard the noise of jumping fish and went to see his grandfather to ask him where this noise was coming from. Supwe Na Vanua told the boy that he didn't know what it was, thinking it better to protect the fish.

Tamakaia, hearing the noise once again, said, "It sounds like fish jumping in the water!"

One day, he went towards the bay and saw the pool. Thousands of fish were there jumping in the water.

Tamakaia said, "If all these fish are my father's, they will stay in the pool. If they are not his, they will all swim away!"

At that moment, the pebble wall crumbled and a hole opened up. All of the fish swam away.

Mauitikitiki, from up high on the rocks, looked at his son hopelessly and said, "You have destroyed everything that we had... what will we eat now?"

And that is how this story ends.

This myth was given in Bislama by Kalotapa.
It was collected by Paul Gardissat and is based on the research of Jean Guiart.
Nabanga n°55-62 (1977)

The myth of Sina
(Emae)

In the mythological family tree, Tisamori was born of the goddess Sina and her husband Kusuwe. These two heros are actually rocks. Sina and Kusuwe live next to their rock called Luku. The local version of this myth says that the first man to live off this island was Supwe Na Vanua, the god of the Earth. Supwe Na Vanua lived at Epau, at the summit of the mountain that went by the same name. Epau is a little village in the north of the island of Efate. Supwe Na Vanua's son is Mauitikitiki, the fisher of islands. He had a son, Tamakaia, and a daughter, Sina. Sina lived at Bulaiua, the Cook Reef.

Sina lived on the island of Bulaiua, the current Cook Reef, next to the big island of Kuwae which was destroyed in a giant cataclysm and split into the islands of Tongoa, Tongariki, and Ewose. Sina's brother, Tamakaia, lived with his mother in the village of Raolua, her namesake. Raolua is the little bay next to Fila islet. Supwe Na Vanua, the god of the earth, was Sina and Tamakaia's grandfather. He lived in Epau, a village in the mountains of Efate. One day, Tamakaia called his men, got in his canoe, and left. He was heading towards Emae, his canoe filled with men. He steered his canoe near the point of Emae called Nanguisululuwi. Here, the canoe broke into two pieces and all the men drowned. Tamakaia was the only survivor. With his club in hand, he started on his way. While walking, he met Kusuwe. Kusuwe had just come from Faitini. Both of them, surprised to see one another, greeted each other.

Kusuwe said, "Hello, friend! What are you doing here?"

"I have come from Efate. My canoe splintered on Nanguisululuwi Point. All of my men have drowned. What are you doing here?"

"I have come from Luk."

So, the two of them sat down in the shade of a great banyan tree and began to talk.

"Kusuwe! I would like you to marry my sister. Do you know her? Her name is Sina and she lives at Bulaiua. On your way home, you'll see some burao trees along the shore. A lot of dead leaves will be on the sand. There, you will see a *burao* that is smaller than all the rest. We call it *"Nabulelonumatasso,"* the *burao* from Mataso. The leaves of this tree are used to wipe the sweat from chiefs' brows. You should find some of these leaves and crush them in your fingers. When you find some that smell like human sweat, turn around and you will see the island of Bulaiua."

Kusuwe did exactly as Tamakaia had instructed him. He went to the shore, looked for the burao, saw one that was smaller than the rest, and smelled its leaves. He recognised the characteristic odour of human sweat. It was a black night, and not a leaf was moving. Kusuwe turned around and there, on the sea, he saw something glowing.

He said, "It's her! It's Sina! That must be the marvellous goddess, Sina, that Tamakaia told me about... the one who will become my wife."

Kusuwe, happy and certainly proud that he was going to marry a goddess, went back to his village and called on his ten brothers.

"Come and look! At Bulaiua, there is a very pretty girl. We can see her from here... come and see!"

"How can you make her out from here?"

"Come, and I will show you!"

When the brothers got to the shore, they were stupified. Just as they had been told, in the distance, in the same direction as Bulaiua, there was a sparkling light.

"Let's go, Kusuwe! We want to see her too!"

"Brothers, before going to see her, we need to have a big feast and kill some pigs. Then, each one of us will bring her a piece."

The ten brothers organised a feast. First, they danced, and then, as at every feast, pigs were killed.

"Who will go first?"

"I will go first because I am the oldest among us and I will take the pig's head."

The oldest got in his canoe and headed for the island of Bulaiua. When he got near the beach, he started to sing.

"Boulato no Boulata?"

"Boulato. I saw you coming. What do you want? What do you want from me with that piece of meat in your hands?"

"I have come to see you, Sina, and have brought you this piece of pork to eat. When you have eaten it, we shall leave together."

"I don't love you. Eat your own meat and go back to where you came from."

"You don't want me?"

"No, I don't love you. Go home."

So, the oldest brother, severely disappointed, got back into his canoe and paddled for Emae, singing his sadness the whole way. When he had got near to the beach, the brothers, who had been waiting impatiently, saw him coming.

"Here is our brother returning with Sina!"

"No! He is alone!"

"I am going to try! It's my turn!"

The second brother took a thigh from the pig and left in his canoe, paddling towards Bulaiua. When he got near the beach, just as his older brother had done, he started to sing.

"Sina, Boulata no Boulato?"

"Boulata, I don't want you! Go back to you island. I don't want your presents and I don't want you. Leave quick. Boulata!"

The second brother got back into his canoe and left. And like the first one, he sang the whole way home as if to say goodbye to Sina. When he arrived on Emae and saw his brothers, he hung his head.

"She doesn't want me."

Each brother, in his turn, took a piece of the sacrificed pig, and went to see Sina who, in the same way, rejected each one of them. There was only one brother left: Kusuwe. Kusuwe was a man that looked like a rat. He was ugly, he was dirty, and when it rained flies came and buzzed loudly over his hair.

"My brothers, I will try to see Sina."

"Kusuwe, you are as ugly as a rat! You smell bad and the flies form a circle around you whenever it rains. Why would that woman want you?"

"My brothers, let me try. I will take the pig's tail and offer it to her."

"What does she want with a pig's tail? We took the best parts of the pig to her and she didn't want them. We are handsome and you are ugly and look like a rat. The flies love you when it rains. Do you really think that she will want you?"

Kusuwe didn't listen to them but instead took up a piece of sugar cane and hit the central roof pole of their house. Suddenly, a curtain of rain separated him from his brothers. Then, he took the pig's tail and left in the direction of Bulaiua. The rain followed behind him, but in front of him it was sunny and the sea was calm. Everything was crystal clear before him and behind him an ominous black cloud and a torrential downpour separated Kusuwe from his brothers. He arrived on Bulaiua and, like the others, started to sing. Sina, who saw him coming, was worried.

She was so worried that she said, "Foulavano. I have been waiting for you for so long. Why did all of those terribly ugly men come to see me before you? Why did you wait so long? All my things are ready. I will follow you, my friend."

The two of them then took off in the direction of Emae. When they got near the beach, the canoe broke and today, you can still see the prow of the canoe, transformed into a rock, in the water. Then, Kusuwe took Sina to a secret place. There, she undressed and hung her mat from a stone which can still be seen today, next to the village of Marae.

"I have prepared this house for you, inside this stone."

Kusuwe kneeled down on a flat rock and by rubbing two sticks of wood together, started a fire. One can even now see the place where Kusuwe prepared Sina's fire. Then, he went back to his brothers and started to prepared a *laplap*. Naturally, he had hidden Sina well so that no one could see her. When the *laplap* was done, he took the best piece from the centre of the *laplap*.

He said to his brothers, "I am taking this piece of *laplap* to give to the pigs."

His brothers, feeling a ruse coming on, said, "Kusuwe said that he would give the best piece of *laplap* to the pigs. That is too strange to be a coincidence. He must be hiding Sina somewhere. That piece of *laplap* is for her! Let's follow him!"

Sina, who understood the danger following her husband, said, "Those men want to kill you. I can see it. I can feel it. You will take this piece of wood with you. If the men ask you to go look for some crabs, and if while you are looking under some stones for them you hear a sort of groaning, look out! You can stop the rock that was meant to crush you with this piece of wood."

Kusuwe then went off to look for crabs with his brothers. They went to the beach and climbed up on the rocks.

"Kusuwe! Kusuwe! Come and see! There are plenty of crabs under these stones! Kusuwe, go and get the big one at the bottom."

One of the brothers gave him a basket, and Kusuwe slid under the stone. He felt that something bad was going to happen and so he was very careful. The moment his brothers loosened a giant stone meant to crush him, Kusuwe did exactly as Sina had told him and stopped the rock with the piece of wood. His brothers were extremely angry. They had to think of a new plan.

"What should we do? He has beaten us once again. Let's try again and push this stone."

And once again, Kusuwe stopped the stone with a simple flick of the wood.
He then said, "Here are the crabs that you wanted, my brothers."

The basket was swarming with crabs which he gave to his brothers before going off to see Sina.

"Sina, those men do want to kill me. That piece of wood that you gave me saved my life, but I still feel as if my end is near. Take this comb."

Kusuwe stuck a comb into the *natangora* roof of their house.

"When you see blood coming from this comb, you will know that I am dead."

Kusuwe went to find his brothers.

"We are going to fish on the reef. Come with us, Kusuwe. We are going to catch some clams, some *natalae.*"

Kusuwe's brothers looked at each other and nodded. Each of them went off to find some germinated coconuts, some *navara,* which they then broke on some stones. They took out the sweet insides and put them into their baskets with their *laplap.* They then left for the reef. The first brother dived into the sea and when he came back up his mouth was full of chewed *navara.*

"This clam is excellent! All I had to do was reach my hand inside to get some. Your turn, Kusuwe!"

In turn, Kusuwe dived into the sea. The clam was there on the ocean floor with its mouth wide open. Kusuwe dived further down and reached into the clam which promptly closed on his hand. Kusuwe was trapped! It did not take long for him to drown. At the same moment, Sina saw blood dripping from the comb planted in the roof.

"Kusuwe is dead!"

Sina took all of her mats and her things and went towards the reef. The men were happy because their enemy was dead. They were now free to marry Sina.

They saw Sina and said, "Sina, Kusuwe, who's over there on the beach, told us to come and get you."

"Go away! I know that you are lying! I know that you killed Kusuwe... I despise you! I hate you all, do you hear? Leave! I am going to find Kusuwe..."

Sina ran down to the beach, crying. She ran to find the man that she loved. But, on the rocks, a man was fishing. He had just caught a fish that was flopping on the stones, and Sina watched him. The fish was still alive, but instead of eyes it had two black holes. Sina then understood that it was Kusuwe, at the bottom of the sea, who had eaten the eyes. She looked all around her and then, far away, at the furthest point possible, she saw the man that she loved: Kusuwe. She ran and ran. When she reached him, she was out of breath.

"Kusuwe!" she gasped.

But Kusuwe did not respond.

"Kusuwe," she gasped a second time.

He did not answer. Sina then understood.

"I am speaking to you and you do not answer. Now, I know that you are dead, but I will give you back your life."

Because Sina was a goddess, she was able to bring him back to life. Both of them then went off to the last point on Makatea, a place called Monoliu. When night fell, both of them slept in different places. In the night, Kusuwe, who was a man, thought of Sina, who was a woman, and wanted to be with her. Consequently, he sent his sex to her like a snake. When Sina saw this, she took a pandanus leaf and cut off a piece of the sex. She then threw the piece delicately into the sea. But the sex continued to come closer and so she was forced to cut off another piece. In the same manner, she threw the second piece into the sea. But the sex continued to come closer and so she was forced to cut off yet another piece. In the same manner, she threw the third piece into the sea. All of these pieces that were thrown in the sea are called *neliku,* and these are the holothurians, or sea cucumbers. The sea cucumbers are, in fact, quite numerous around Monolui Point. The sex came even closer and Sina, who understood that Kusuwe was close to her now, cut off the last piece and threw it into the sea. Then, and only then, did Kusuwe become a real man.

"Now, you are my husband. You will stay here."

From their union made possible by these events, were born two children: Karisipua, the eldest, and Tafak, the youngest. These two men, children of Kusuwe and Sina, are still venerated today by a large portion of the population in the Shepherd Islands.

This legend was given in Bislama by Chief Charley Tisamori of Marae village on Emae.
Adapted by Paul Gardissat.

Radio New-Hebrides

Seganiale, the Forari devil
(Mataso)

On the island of Efate in the New Hebrides (Vanuatu) there used to be a devil. His name? Seganiale. He lived at Forari in a very dark cavern. This cavern was very special because it was equipped with three doors, each one behind the other, that only the devil could open thanks to a magic wand. It was in this cavern that the devil, after he had hunted them, held men, women, and especially children prisoner to enjoy them as a tasty meal. However, Seganiale didn't only savour human flesh; he appreciated pigs, cows, and fruit as well. He was ferocious and voracious.

One day, having just got up, Seganiale left his cavern. The wind was blowing violently. The devil breathed deeply to fill his body with this fresh air when what did he smell? A powerful odour of bananas, bananas with such a perfume that it tickled his nostrils.

"Mmmm, that smells good! It makes me hungry for bananas!"

The devil inhaled again and realised that the odour came from the island of Mataso.

"I must go!" he said immediately. Seganiale ran towards the coast, put his canoe in the water and was off in the direction of Mataso.

Arriving within a hundred metres or so off the island, the devil could see two children who were walking innocently along the coast. Seganiale paddled his canoe in an effort to draw along side of them. Without a sound, he went ashore near the two children and started talking to them as gently as possible.

"Hello, my friends! What are you doing on this beach?"

"We're looking for fish, sir," the children responded confidently.

"Oh, my poor children, you will not find any here. I know a place where there are many fish! Come, I will take you there, but first I would like you to give me some of your wonderfully ripe and delicious bananas."

Happy to discover a reef teeming with fish, the two children gladly agreed to go in search of some bananas. They didn't drag their feet, and it wasn't long before the canoe was full.

The two children were impatient.

"Where are you taking us?" they asked, trailing behind the devil who was getting into his canoe.

"Come with me and you will see! On my island there are many fish!"

185

"But who are you?"

"My name is Seganiale and I live at Forari."

The devil's mouth was already watering from inhaling the odour of the bananas and contemplating the two children who would also make a savoury meal. The children were sitting in the canoe naively unaware of Seganiale's thoughts. Meanwhile, they were moving steadily towards Efate. The canoe had but just touched ground when the children jumped ashore and started helping the devil to unload his bananas. Seganiale directed his unfortunate prey towards his cavern. The children followed trustingly and soon they arrived in front of the devil's cavern.

"Now, you must close your eyes."

"Why?" asked the two inquisitive children.

"Because you must not see what I'm going to do. Come on now, obey!"

The two children followed his orders. They closed their eyes, but one of the two, overwhelmed by curiosity, kept his head lowered and opened his eyes just a crack. He was able to distinguish the devil's strange ploy. Seganiale, in fact, lifted a big stone and removed his magic wand. With the wand, he hit the first door which opened immediately with a "shsht."

"Walk straight ahead, my friends, but keep your eyes shut!"

The two boys moved forward but the clever child continued to peek. Nothing escaped his notice as Seganiale opened the second door with a tap of his wand... "shsht"... and then the third one... "shsht."

The devil and his two victims found themselves in the dark cavern. Only now did the children understand their danger.

"I'm going to devour you now!"

"Not yet! Don't eat us yet!" cried the clever child. "You can see that we are too skinny! Why not first eat the delicious bananas that we brought for you?"

"Hmm, good idea!" The devil sat down and started to eat the savoury bananas. "They really are quite delicious!" And Seganiale kept on eating.

He ate and he ate. He greedily swallowed all of the bananas. Finally, he couldn't eat any more. He took up the last banana, but no, he was obliged to lay down and satisfied, he slept.

"How are we going to escape?" asked one of the boys.

"Don't worry," answered his clever friend. "You know, I didn't close my eyes before. I know what he did to open the doors, so we can leave. I was sure that he would eat too many bananas and that he wouldn't be able to watch us anymore. Look here!"

The child took the magic wand and, silently so as not to wake Seganiale, he was able to open the three doors... "shsht".... "shsht"... "shsht."

The two children were free. They ran towards the beach, threw themselves into the canoe, and made towards their island, Mataso, that they deeply regretted having left.

The next day, the devil had a hard time coming out of his deep sleep. He looked all around.

"Where are the children?" Seeing the doors open, Seganiale quickly understood. He ran hastily out of his cavern, and following the odour of the children, he arrived on the beach. "My canoe, they took my canoe! Oh well, I'll make another one fast!"

Thanks to his enormous strength, the devil was able to make a magnificent boat in no time at all. He didn't even have time to admire it though, before he was already in the middle of the ocean following the odour of the boys that was leading him to Mataso. It was there that they had found refuge!

"Hahahahahahaha!! They won't get away from me for long!"

But the devil did not have time to enjoy his victory. Right when he was coming ashore, a giant wave rose up. He couldn't do anything; his canoe flipped over and was thrown against the reef. The devil was crushed against a rock. "Ouch!!"

His blood ran freely, attracting several sharks. Weakened, Seganiale couldn't fight against the animals and he died, eaten by sharks.

And this was how Seganiale, the Forari devil, disappeared forever on the coast of Mataso.

Radio Port-Vila, broadcast « Alors...Raconte ! »

Wotanimanu, the Rock Monument
(Moso)

"Wotanimanu" is the rock monument; that stone that rises alone above the water next to Mataso, right next to it. But, before it was there, it lived on Erromango. It was born on Erromango. During the great cataclysms, it came out of the sea. On Erromango, it spent its time fishing along the shore and didn't worry about gardening. It is said, certainly by the people of Erromango, that it was lazy. One day, it was on the reef fishing. There, it saw a clam, a *natalae*. It tried to pry it from the stones, but instead received a big pinch. This made him angry. This made him angry because, close by, the people of Erromango only thought of dancing. The music made him angry, the dancing made him angry, he who had been wounded. He took a *burao* leaf, a red *burao* leaf, a *nadibibou,* and he bandaged himself with it. While he was suffering and listening to the dancers, the *tamtams* began to call all those in the surrounding areas. These *tamtams* also made him angry. So, he took his canoe and left in the direction of Efate.

In his canoe, were his subjects and his two wives, Wanov and Ono. Everyone followed him. When he arrived at Efate, he entered Purari Bay, a little village that was next to the great Maniura. This was Purari. And there, once again, people were dancing to the music of the *tamtam.* They were dancing in Purari and Wotanimanu, angry, went a little further and found himself at Epau. Here, he felt good. There was no more noise. So, he left his enormous canoe on the beach. Then, one day, while fishing, he arrived at Emae. Emae's chief's daughter was named Sina. She was beautiful. She was standing on the shore collecting sea water for cooking. Wotanimanu saw her and he wanted to talk to her.

"That woman is so beautiful...do I dare...?"

But he didn't dare and so returned to Epau with an abundant catch of fish in his canoe. The next day, he returned to the same place to fish. He found the same girl. This time, he spoke to her.

"I see that you are even more beautiful today than yesterday. Yesterday, I did not dare speak to you."

"I want you," she responded.

"But I come from far away..."

"Come to the house and talk with my father if you want me."

"Alright, let's go and see your father."

And so, he came to live on Emae and continued to fish. The chief of Emae had decided to abandon his title and leave it to someone else. So, he told his subjects to prepare several large plantations and big pig pens where those animals that were already on the island and those that came from afar could live. Then, he noticed that Wotanimanu wouldn't plant or take care of the pigs and he reproached his daughter for marrying a man that didn't follow his instructions. The woman repeated her father's speech to her husband and accused him of being lazy.

"Alright," he said, "let's go and weed the garden."

The two of them went off and weeded a small part of the garden. But, on the way, Wotanimanu saw that it was low tide and he soon went to fish. The father then asked his daughter what she and her husband had done.

"We weeded a small part of the garden and then we went fishing."

The father started to reproach his son-in-law again and the daughter transmitted the message.

"Why did she bring such a lazy person to live with chiefs if he won't help with the preparations for *naluan?* Why?"

Wotanimanu took his wife to burn the clippings from their work the day before. She didn't know that some of her husband's subjects had come from Epau during the night and continued their work in the garden. When she saw that the garden was completely clean, she was surprised.

"Who did this?"

"It was me!"

He then burnt a small portion of the weeds and left to go fishing. The father again asked his daughter what they had done and, as a result, repeated his criticism. She relayed the message to her husband.

"Let's take some yams and go plant them in our garden," was his only reply.

They went to the garden and found it completely cleaned by a fire that had burnt all the weeds. They then planted a yam, a sugar cane plant, and a banana tree, and left to go fishing again. The woman eventually spoke with her father about what had happened.

"Who cleared this land?"

"He said that it was him."

"He said it was him! What did you plant there?"

"One yam, one sugar cane, and one banana."

The next day, Wotanimanu took his wife to see the garden. It had been planted in neat rows.

His wife, surprised, said, "Who planted all of this?"

"It was me again!"

"When?"

"During the night!"

She still did not know about her husband's workers. So, she went to speak with her father again, but she had no other explanation for what had been happening except what her husband had told her.

When the plants had started to grow, the father grumbled about the pigs that they did not have.

The wife said to Wotanimanu, "Everyone is raising pigs and we don't have any!"

One day, he took his wife to attach the growing plants to some stakes. They did this for only a couple of plants. Then, they went back the next day. The plants had all been staked and the garden completely weeded. The daughter again talked with her father and told him what had happened. Both were completely flabbergasted. Wotanimanu told his men to build a large pig pen.

Then, the father said to his daughter, "What are you going to do with this pen? You don't have any pigs!"

The husband, alerted by his wife, made his men go back to work. During the night, pigs could be heard squealing. In the morning, the wife went to the pig pen. There she found many pigs with rounded tusks.

"Whose pigs are these?"

"They're ours! I brought them here last night!"

She went to get her father to show him the pigs.

On the date that had been set, the villagers went from garden to garden, harvesting all that they had prepared: they uprooted sugar cane and unearthed yams still on their vines. Wotanimanu pulled the plants up with one hand without digging around them like the others did. He had asked that his garden be the last one to be harvested. When the people arrived to do their work, he told them to take everything. It took them three days to take away all the produce in the garden whereas it had taken only one for all of the others. Then, it was time to herd all the pigs together and take them to the *naka-mal*. Wotanimanu again asked to be last. He was able to pick the pigs up by one hoof while the other men were obliged to truss them to a pole with a man bearing either end.

One day was enough to herd all the pigs on Emae together. The next day, it was time to deal with Wotanimanu's pigs. Wotanimanu did not help and it took the men three days to round up all of the pigs. The day after, all the pigs were slaughtered and put into a great pile in order to better divide them between the people of Emae. While they were doing this, the people started to talk amongst themselves.

"Who is this man that is stronger than all of us?"

"We don't know anything about him."

"He is not from here..."

The *naluan* lasted for one week until everyone went home with their share of the riches.

Wotanimanu then said to his wife, "It was me and me alone that made this feast so wonderful for the chief that called me lazy. Those men were asking about me and they called me a stranger. They asked me where I came from. I must leave. Tell your father that I can no longer stay with you. I must find another place to live."

So, he took his workers, his two wives, and he left. He left in spite of the chief's supplications and offers of his title. Then, Wotanimanu killed one of his wives and left her on the reef in the form of the rock "Bongaroa." He turned to leave with his remaining wife and his subjects. As he was leaving, the rock "Bongaroa," spoke to him.

"I can still see you. You need to go further away."

He arrived at Mataso near the village Alikaou. At this time, the inhabitants did not dance to the rhythm of *tamtams* but in their place used sticks which they beat against bamboo called *natale*. He heard this noise and it made him happy. He expressed his desire to live there. Because his reputation had preceded him, the chiefs of the village knew all about him.

"You may stay here, but you should set up your household outside of the village. The people are afraid of you."

"Yes, a little further... a little further..."

Wotanimanu got further and further away, asking, "Is this alright? Or should I go a little further?"

"No, that's good. You may stay there."

And he is still there with his subjects, the birds, who will always be with him.

This legend was given in Bislama by Chief Kalfao of Moso.
Wotanimanu, also called "Monument Rock", is still next to Mataso.

Radio New-Hebrides.

Nising and Turig
(Mataso)

Wotanimanu: he was the rock monument. He was born a very long time ago, just off the island of Erromango, in the southern islands. He came out of the sea, just like that, one beautiful morning during the time of the *tamtams* constantly beaten by the people from Erromango, he ran away to Efate and then, from Maniura, he left for Emae. He became angry with the people from Emae, though, and soon left for Mataso. Once at Mataso, he decided to leave them alone and settle next to them with his birds. He was there with his birds and, one day, he was petrified. He became the rock monument. One of his subjects was a woman. Her name was Nising. She was there, washing her face on the shore. It was morning. She took up *burao* leaves to wash her hair and then threw them into the sea which carried them away towards the Mataso shore. The chiefs of the island went to the shore. They picked up the leaves, crushed them in between their fingers, and smelled a sweet odour. Timataso, who was also from Erromango, spoke.

"Wotanimanu came from Erromango and must have brought that woman with the light skin, like the women on our island, with him."

The next day, the same thing happened. The chiefs saw the leaves again and again they smelled sweet.

"Timataso must be right," they said and decided to take the woman if they ever had the opportunity.

So, they built four canoes, cutting the hulls in one day, the seats the next, and then finally attaching them. They laid mats on the bottoms of the boats and raised the sails made of woven pandanus. Alikaou decided to be the first to go. So, he went to the rock and started to sing.

His song went like this, "Are you staying here? Or shall we go off together ?"

The woman was offended and answered, "Go away, go away! It makes me sick to look at you. You are too black. When I look at you, excrement fills my mouth."

Alikaou returned to Mataso and told the other chiefs, "Oh, she's there alright. She's very young and very white. Her hair falls over her shoulders. But she doesn't want me because I'm too black."

Timataso left in his turn, sang the same song, and received the same harsh rebuff.

"Go away, go away! It makes me sick to look at you. You are too black. When I look at you, excrement fills my mouth."

There was only one last chief to go, Malakoleo. Malakoleo left and went to sing in front of the rock. He was rebuffed in the same way.

"Go away, go away! It makes me sick to look at you. You are too black. When I look at you, excrement fills my mouth."

Turig, a man who did not belong to any *farea,* who did not have any house because he had no title, a man whose body was covered in rashes and who lived by working for first one person and then another, a man who everyone hated, Turig said, "I will try!"

"Invisible man, you want to go see her? Ha! She will choke on her own vomit when she sees you."

"I will try all the same."

He arrived behind Matasumsum at the rock we call Witimasom. He laid his club in the canoe and dived into the water. When he came back up, he had been transformed into a handsome man with light skin. He then left for Wotanimanu and sang.

Before he had even finished, the woman said, "Do you want to kill me? Paddle quickly so that we can leave together!"

She gathered her chickens, bound all of her mats, and went towards the rock to get her other things. She filled the canoe and left with Turig who paddled around Matasumsum so as not to be seen by the chiefs. He went into the deep water and moored at Valetuia on the reef where his canoe cracked, spilling the mats, baskets, and all the chickens. The prow of the canoe is still there today; it is called Savalararo.

Turig took the woman to a hole in a rock and said,"Stay here. I am going to the house."

He then went down to the shore, dived into the water, and assumed his rashy appearance once again. The chiefs questioned him and he lied to them by saying that nothing had happened.

"But where is your canoe?"

"Only my water scoop is left. Nising threw up when she saw me and almost died."

The next day, the chiefs decided to go to the gardens and get some red yams to make *laplap* with. Turig took a small white yam. Others noticed that he was acting differently.

"We shall see what happens to the *laplap.* If there is a red piece, it will be for you. If there is a white piece, it will be for me."

When they took the *laplap* from the oven, just a little part of it was red and the rest of it was white. Turig started to tease the others.

"I am going to eat all of that!"

"We shall eat together and not fight about it."

The next day, they decided to make a *laplap* of white yams and Turig again distinguished himself by digging up a red yam. The *laplap* was, for the most part, red and the same discussion ensued. When they had finished eating, he took his pieces of *laplap* and hid them in some leaves. He took the leaves, telling the others that he was going to throw them in the sea. Then, he went to wash himself. He once again took on the aspect of a light skinned man, ate, and made love to Nising. Later, he went back and took on his rashy appearance. The chiefs realised that something was up and the next day, they went to cut some wood. They chopped a tree until it was ready to fall and then told Turig to go and see in what direction it would fall. He stood under the tree. One final chop and the tree fell onto Turig's shoulder.

The man was able to carry it without a problem and asked, "Should I take it to the *nakamal?*"

The chiefs wondered how they could kill Turig. They went to hunt coconut crabs, dug a big hole, placed a rock, set to fall, above the hole, and sent Turig to see if there was any prey in the hole. He went and the chiefs pushed over the big rock. Turig stood up quickly, clutching a coconut crab.

"Here is our food!"

The rock had rolled off his back and fallen harmlessly to the ground. While the chiefs were thinking hard about another way to kill Turig, they started to prepare some food. Turig again pretended to throw the rubbish away and went to see Nising.

He said, "They want to kill me so that they can have you."

So, he gave her a comb called *nakiwas.*

"Work on your mats and look at this comb. When you see blood dripping from it, you will know that I am dead."

Turig went back to see the chiefs. He left in their canoe with them, but did not know that they had secreted pieces of coconut and *navel* under their belts. They went to the reef. When they saw a clam, a *natalae,* each chief dived in turn and came back up with pieces of coconut in his mouth.

Turig asked, "What are you eating?"

"We are eating *natalae!*"

"When you see another one, I will dive and taste it like you."

They found a big clam and told him, "Come quickly! This one's for you!"

"What should I do?"

He dived and put his hand inside the shell. The clam instantly clamped down. The chiefs then took up their lances and speared Turig until he was dead. Then, they returned to the shore in order to discuss who would get the woman.

"She is mine!"

"No, she is mine!"

"I told you, she is mine!"

They sent some children to tell Nising that Turing was at their house and that she should come to prepare them some food.

"Nising! Come see! Nising, come and see Turig! He's on Mataso and he's waiting for you."

However, Nising had seen blood on the comb. She was preparing to go and find her husband when the children arrived.

"That must be another Turig," she said. "Mine is dead."

The children went back and repeated this response.

"She said that Turig was dead."

"Go back and see her."

Nising had buried herself in the ground up to her knees when the children came back to talk to her.

"Turig is at the chief's house. They have asked you to come and prepare something to eat."

The children ran back with her answer and told the chiefs that Nising was buried up to her knees.

"She's buried all the way to her knees!"

The chiefs didn't believe the children.

"Only crabs dig themselves in the ground."

So, they went back and saw Nising buried up to her shoulders.

"She's buried herself in the ground all the way up to her shoulders!"

They quickly returned to the chiefs who decided that they had to see this to believe it. They only found her hair above ground.

"What are you doing, crab?"

"Turig is dead and I have to find him."

They tried to pull her out by the hair but couldn't do it. The men brought their fingers to their noses and Nising's odour hit them. This odour pushed them to dig in the ground, but they only found stone. Nising crossed the island and came out into the sea.

She then asked a sand crab, "Have you seen Turig?"

"No, I haven't seen him."

She swam a little further. She then spoke to a small fish.

"Have you seen Turig?"

"No, I haven't seen him."

Still swimming, she met a shark.

"You haven't seen Turig, have you?"

Yes, look over there!"

She then saw his corpse. She took her fan, the *narivirivi,* and she beat the spears until they all fell out of his lifeless body. Turig once again came to life and both of them dived down to the bottom of the sea. They then met a turtle and asked if it could take them to Wotanimanu.

"Sit on my back and hold on tight to my shoulders."

In this way, on the back of the turtle, they returned to the rock where they have lived ever since. Now, there are two black rocks, one named Turig and the other, right next to the first, named Nising.

This legend from the island of Mataso was given in Bislama to Paul Gardissat by Kalo Manamuri.

Radio New-Hebrides.

The legend of Sosolobeng
(Mataso)

A little behind the big island of Kuwae, the island that exploded more than four hundred years ago leaving nothing but the islands of Tongoa, Falea, and Buninga, just at the door of the island group called the Shepherds, there is Mataso. Mataso, what is it? It's a little spike, a spike in the middle of the ocean. Moreover, these two rocky islands, unequal in size, are linked by a band of sand where men and women, who are not very rich but who certainly wear their heart on their sleeves, live. On clear days, one can see Mataso, that little spike, from Efate. It rises out of the sea, majestic and worrying. A little further, one can see the rock monument Wotanimanu which is also, for the people of Mataso, a living being that turned into rock in the middle of the waves. Wotanimanu means 'the chief with a million subjects.' As you know, Wotanimanu came from Erromagno and stopped, like everyone at that time, at Maniwora. Then, he married on Emao and, tired of the remonstrances by the people of Emao and the men of Efate, he left in the direction of Mataso. Once there, the chiefs asked him to move away a little further. So, he backed off and was transformed into a rock. He is still there today.

Mataso, then, is a little spike coming up out of the water, a spike five hundred metres in altitude, a dry spike, always swept by high winds. A long time ago, there were four villages there: Worakoto, Mataaso, Saouia, Sinmauri. They were spread out along the southwest coast of the big island. Next door, there was Matasusung which had always been a cultural bastion. Further away, Wotanimanu, surrounded by birds that pelt him constantly with guano, looks over the two great stones. Today, there is only one village left on Mataso, Naasang, named after the sand dunes cut by the wind. Mataso is quite isolated from other islands and this is the reason for the sad look of the inhabitants of this lone village left to the mercy of the tides, the cycles of the moon, and the ferocity of cyclones. The last of these big winds completely destroyed Mataso. The great Mataso suddenly found itself separated from its neighbour, Matasusung. The sea could now pass between them. The whole village had been razed to the ground. The only walls left were those of the church. The ancestors' great canoes were smashed on the rocks. Matasusung, the garden island, was flattened and Wotanimanu, in the distance, was unable to help. Of this island, only rock was left. The men and the women of Mataso cried bitter tears as happens after every cyclone. Then, gathering up their courage, they rebuilt everything, like they rebuilt everything after each cyclone. So, this is Mataso, a dry rock.

A long time ago, on the poor island of Mataso, there was no water, not a single river, well, or spring. Nothing. At the summit of this peak, there lived a man known by the name of Sosolobeng. He was an old man. He lived in Leela. In the language of Mataso, Leela means 'I see everywhere.' Sosolobeng lived alone on top of this peak and had a spring, a source of clear, fresh water that came directly from the rocks and burbled to brighten the days of the old man. This spring belonged to him and he was proud of it.

One day, the sun came out. The sun came and with it, it brought a drought. From the months of July to December, it had not rained. Not one drop of water had fallen from the sky. The whole island was dry. The trees had lost their leaves and the water problem had become serious for those who lived along the shore. The people of Worakoto, Saouia, Mataaso, and Sinmauri tried in vain to find a source of fresh water by scratching the sand during low tides. Nothing trickled out. So, one day, the four chiefs of the four villages got together.

"My friends, for more than five months, we have had a drought. Our island is so dried out that the stones will not give off any more water. If this drought continues, we will have nothing left to drink. What should we do?"

"There is only one solution left... only one solution."

"What is that, friend?"

"At the summit of the mountain lives Sosolobeng. Sosolobeng has a fresh-water spring. If we go and ask him for a little of that water, perhaps he will give us some."

"Yes, just a little, just enough to make *kava* with. The water that we are using now is too dirty; our *kava* has no taste left. We shall send our children to ask for some water."

The next morning, the children took some bamboo without knots in it, and went in search of water. They climbed the big peak, singing and making a lot of noise.

> *Sosolobeng!*
> *Sosolobeng!*
> *We are coming to get some water!*

Sosolobeng, who had been sleeping, woke up and heard the children's noise.

"I think that I hear some children singing. They are getting closer. The men who live on the shore must be having some water problems. I know what they are like. They don't dare ask me for water, but send their children instead."

So, Sosolobeng grabbed the cane that he often used to help him on his walks, and went towards the spring. The water was clear and all around, birds were singing. This was the only place on the island that they could get something to drink.

Sosolobeng looked at the spring and said, "Oh, my water, that gives me so much strength. I want you to become dirty, very dirty!"

With his cane, he stirred up the bottom of the spring and the water became black. Then, he went back to his house. When he got there, he saw the children.

They said, "Sosolobeng, the men from below want to drink their *kava,* but there is not a drop of water left. The wells are dry. Can we take a little water from your spring?"

"Yes, my children go and take some water."

"Thank you, Sosolobeng, you are a good man."

The children, still singing, went towards the spring.

> *Sosolobeng!*
> *Sosolobeng!*
> *We are coming to get some water!*

When they got to the water, they were surprised.

"The water is dirty!"

"Look, there is nothing but mud here!"

"Let's go back to see Sosolobeng."

The old man was waiting for them on the doorstep.

"Old man, we went to the spring and found the water all dirty! What happened?"

"The water is dirty? It must have been the birds that dirtied it while bathing there this morning."

The children, severely disappointed, dipped their bamboo into the dirty water and went back down to the shore. The villagers, seeing the children arrive, went to meet them.

"Did you bring us back some cold, clear mountain water?"

"The water was dirty!"

"The water was completely black! Sosolobeng told us that the birds had dirtied it while bathing this morning."

Disappointed, the men went back to their homes and that evening, they discussed the problem over their *kava.*

"What should we do? We can't go on like this! The children shall go back to Leela tomorrow."

The next day, the children left again, singing.

> *Sosolobeng!*
> *Sosolobeng!*
> *We are coming to get some water!*

When they arrived at the top of the peak, they were out of breath.

"Old man, the men on the shore want to drink their *kava*. They still don't have any water. Can you give them some?"

"Go ahead, take some!"

When the children got to the spring, they were once again disappointed.

"Oh no! The water is dirty again!"

Sosoloneng, hearing them coming, had again gone and stirred up the bottom of the spring. And, like the first time, the children came to complain to the old man.

"The water is dirty again! What should we do?"

"The birds often bathe there. Indeed, they are there every morning."

When they got back to their parents' houses, the children again told what had happened.

"The water was dirty!"

"The water was very muddy! We went to see Sosolobeng and he told us that the birds had come back."

"Sosolobeng must be lying. The birds are not muddying the water, he is!"

"What can we do?"

"Let us find a way..."

Chief Alikaou stood up and paced around the *nakamal*.

Angrily, he spoke up and said, "One of my assistants, my *atavi* from Tongariki, is Chief Sosomake who can make it rain in all of our islands. What if we go and see him? He can make the winds pick up. Let's ask him to help us. I will take my canoe and go see him on Tongariki."

Alikaou got in his canoe and left to see Sosomaki, his *atavi,* on Tongariki. Once he got there, Alikaou spoke.

"Sosomaki, I have not seen you for a long time. We are having serious problems on Mataso. We cannot drink *kava* anymore because there is no water. We asked Sosolobeng for some water from his spring, but each time the children go to see him, he dirties the water with his cane. You know that he lives at the top of the island. The children cannot get to the spring without being seen by him. Sosomaki, can you help us?"

"I can help you. Rain comes from the clouds and I can direct the clouds with the winds that I command. What wind do you want? Do you want the Ruatu, the wind from the southeast? Or perhaps the Tokelao, the wind from the northeast? The wind of the south? The east?"

"I don't know. What do you suggest?"

"If I send you the southern wind, Sosolobeng will see the cloud arriving and take precautions against the rain. It will be the same with the east wind and the north wind. Sosolobeng will see both of them coming. However, with the north wind, he will see nothing. It will take him by surprise."

"Sosomaki, send us the north wind."

Alikaou returned with his *atavi*, Sosmaki, to Mataso. The next day, Sosomaki called the north wind and it started to blow.

> *Come, come, come!*
> *Blow, blow, blow!*
> *Blow harder, stronger, faster!*

The north wind arrived, blowing stronger and stronger. Sosolobeng's house, on the peak of Mataso, could not stand up against the gale. Sosolobeng hopelessly tried to anchor the *namamao* pillars of his home. The wind, however, was too strong and the house blew away and was dashed against the stones on the shore. Sosolobeng started to sing.

On the shore, the chiefs watched the wind and heard Sosolobeng singing sadly.

"That's it! The wind has destroyed his house! Listen to him. He will come down to see us now."

Sosolobeng, lost in the wind, came down the hill, singing all the while. When he got to the shore, he went to see Chief Alikaou.

"Alikaou, I don't have a house anymore. Can you help me to carry dry wood?"

"We have a lot of work to do here. We need fresh water. You had some but did not want to give us any. We cannot help you. Go away."

Sosolobeng dejectedly went to see Chief Timataso.

"Timataso, my house was destroyed by the wind. Can you help me to carry dry wood and some salt water for my kitchen?"

"We have a lot of dry wood here and we have enough sea water in our kitchens. You were the one that always stirred up the water that we needed to drink. You did not want to help us then, so we cannot help you now."

Sosolobeng went next to see Chief Taravaki.

"Chief Taravaki, can you lend me some men to help me carry some dry wood and sea water for my food?"

"There are many men here that could help you do that. But did you think of us before this? You have always refused us fresh water. Leave now."

Sosolobeng carried his cane, his *abuitok,* and went to see Chief Malakoleo in his village. When the chief saw the old man arriving, he spoke to his men.

"Here is Sosolobeng, the man that always denied us the water we needed to make our *kava.* Get your clubs ready!"

Sosolobeng did not even have the chance to speak before Malakoleo told his men to beat the old man.

"That's him! Hit him with your clubs!"

Sosolobeng tied to run away but an arrow pierced him flesh and then a club was brought down on him. Sosolobeng ran a little way and on the shore, right next to the water, he fell. There, his body turned into stone.

A long time ago, on Mataso, there was no water. Coming down from his perch, Sosolobeng also brought the water along with him. You can still see the path that he made coming down from the mountain, the water trailing behind him. And there, if you dig down far enough, you will find Sosolobeng's spring.

This legend from the island of Mataso was given in Bislama to Paul Gardissat
by Pastor Siviu Muerik.

Radio New Hebrides.

The Mutuama of Ifira
(Ifira)

In Vanuatu, when the sun shines, Nature smiles. The seashore is a marvellous sight and the huge *nabangura,* which hang over the white sandy beaches, look at their reflections from morning to evening in the ever clear water. From the seashore up to the highest of the tall mountains, Nature breathes, the *notous* warble and the trade winds blow airily through the large forest. Here and there, lost in the thick bush of our islands, live happy people. Here and there, people from the small villages that are perched on rocks or hidden along the banks of streams or rivers, live a daily life unburdened by big difficulties and problems. A village in Vanuatu is often a place for dancing: in the *nasara,* the *nakamal* or meeting place. Little houses with woven bamboo walls and roofs of *natangora* thatch surround the *nasara.* And there are the gardens, where the inhabitants of Vanuatu spend a good part of their lives, and with great respect, even with love itself, planting yams for their ceremonies, taro, sweet potatoes and bananas. There are the pig enclosures. Pigs are used in grading ceremonies, in circumcision feasts, in peace-making ceremonies, on occasions of war and even for burial rituals.

When the sun shines, travelling from the Torres Islands, passing through the Banks Islands down to Espiritu Santo and on to Malakula, not forgetting Pentecost, Ambrym or Efate; and letting itself slip towards Tanna, to alight on Aniwa and finish on Aneityum, everything shines; all is light and security. One feels good in this country, as long as the sun is shining. But as the sun sets and disappears below the horizon to light up other places, things change. When night falls on all the islands, it falls suddenly. Darkness invades everything and transforms the sea, the sand, the trees, the bush and the mountains, the villages and even the people. Then, out of the darkness, emerge all the night beings. The owls wake up and the devils appear.

Devils can take all kinds of forms. If they don't have claw-like feet, they can have long hair and ears that sometimes reach right down to the ground. You can find these devil-beings on the branches of trees, hanging upside down on the branches of the banyan trees, just like flying foxes do when they perch. Night time in Vanuatu is sad, even when the moon is shining. Behind each tree there is a life, a spirit, a devil, a half-devil, a shape or a ghost. Don't forget that, in this country, you can die, only to return and annoy the living! These supernatural beings that come and tickle the feet of sleeping people are called *tui* in Tagaro's country. On Tongoa they have long hair and in the Shepherd Islands and even on Emau and Nguna they are called *sangalegale.* On Ifira Island, situated just across from the large town of Port Vila, the devil-spirits are called *Mutuama.*

And, to conclude, I will tell you again that, even as you are reading this legend, these devils are roaming around a little, everywhere. We call them *lisepsep* in Bislama. And beware! As you read this story, one of these devils may be right behind you! But, whatever you do, don't turn round. Read this first.

In front of Port Vila, there is Iririki island. Behind Iririki, there is the island of Ifira. Next to Ifira, on the main land to the left when one is looking at the sea, one can see Waraolua bay. The village of Waraolua is also located here. Behind this village, there is a hill called Tumo. A long time ago, on the top of this hill, there lived a small, long-haired, flabby-breasted devil. It was known as the Mutuama.

When the village was cooking its meals, when they had taken smoking *laplaps* from the ovens, the odour of burnt leaves and cooked yams rose to the top of Tumo hill and tickled the Mutuama's nostrils. From his perch, he surveyed the village and licked his lips in anticipation. The Mutuama often drooled when thinking about all the wonderful things that were being prepared for him in the village: small pigs, seafood cooked in coconut milk... The Mutuama sniffed, unhappy that he didn't have anything to eat, unhappy not to have a single thing.

One day, the Mutuama, tired of smelling all these good things, sat down with his head between his legs and started to think hard.

"When the sun is high in the sky, I will go down into the village. I will be very careful and I'll go very slowly. I'll break into their kitchens and steal every last thing!"

The sun was high in the sky. The men had left for their gardens and the women and children were gathering shells on the reef. The Mutuama threw his hair behind him, tumbled down the hill and arrived in the village. He looked to the left and then to the right. The village was empty. The Mutuama went into a kitchen, looked all around, and found the basket called *"savaka."* This basket is very special. The old women and mothers fill them with good things and hang them on a pig's tusk in the middle of the kitchen. After having inspected it, the Mutuama started to gorge himself. He had waited for this moment for a long time. It had been a long time since he had had an opportunity like this one. He went into another kitchen, looked for the *savaka,* and then devoured its contents. He did this until he had emptied every kitchen in the village. Satisfied, the Mutuama climbed back up his hill with a full belly and a silly grin on his face.

The people of Waraolua came back from the garden and the sea. They were shocked by what they saw. They had been robbed! But by whom? Who would dare do this? Who could the thief be? The villagers, still furious, resigned themselves to bed. On another occasion, the people of Waraolua had prepared a wonderful feast with yams, taro, cabbages, small fern leaves mixed with shells, coconut milk, and small pigs. The smell, carried by the wind, rose up to the summit of the hill Tumo. The Mutuama had been watching the people prepare their feast and the mounting smells excited him.

Soon, he found himself thinking gourmet thoughts.

"Those imbeciles are preparing the best meal of my life: yams cooked with young pig, yams cooked with small fern leaves that give them such a wonderful smell, *nasese,* fish, *nawita.* I even think that I smell some roasted pigeon and flying fox! Thank you so much! When you go to the garden, I will think of you while I'm stuffing my face. With my little fingers, I'll rip apart the chicken and I'll eat every last pig. Thank you my little friends for having thought of me! Thank you!"

The sun rose and the entire population of Waraolua came to life: some went to the garden, others to fish, and yet others to hunt. The Mutuama on top of the hill watched everyone leaving.

"Yes, go, go my children and be happy. Bring me back good things!"

The Mutuama tumbled down his hill and arriving in the village, looked left, looked right, and slipped into a house to ransack the kitchen. He found a *savaka* and started to devour it. He went into another kitchen and ate everything that was there including the baskets of *savaka* that were hung right in the middle of the room. Happy with his full belly, the Mutuama ran away, delighted with his findings. However, night had fallen and the villagers had returned. The Mutuama was forced to hide behind some trees until he could escape into the darkness. In the middle of the village, there was a beautiful papaya tree with many leaves. The Mutuama was surprised by the villagers and so he climbed into the tree and hid himself amongst the leaves. He thought that he would thus be protected from any strange looks. Nevertheless, he soon found it difficult to hold himself in this position on such a full stomach.

The children were the first ones to arrive in the village. They wanted to play a little before their parents arrived. One child approached the papaya tree, looked up, and exclaimed, "Look! The Mutuama is hidden in the tree! Come and see! There's the Mutuama! He was the one that ate everything that our parents prepared! Come and look! Quickly!"

So the other children came, shouting with surprise and joy. They surrounded the papaya tree and danced around it. In the village, there was an old man who had not gone to the garden. When he heard the children say the name of the Mutuama, he came out of his house and went towards the ruckus. He spotted the Mutuama hidden in the tree. Then, he quieted the children and said, "Don't make all that noise. It won't bring you anything. I know a song, a special song that the Mutuama doesn't like. You will see. I will sing and the Mutuama will fall from the papaya tree. When he does, you can shoot him with as many arrows as you like. The Mutuama will die and we will be rid of him. Don't make all that noise. Get your bows and arrows ready and follow me."

The children did exactly as the old man had told them. They went to their houses, got their bows and arrows, and went back to the papaya tree. They looked at the old man and waited. The old man came a little closer to the Mutuama, looked at it with a little smile on the corners of his mouth, and said, "My children, I am going to sing. I am going to sing so that first his right arm with shrivel inside his body. Next, I will sing so that his left arm will shrivel. When his arms disappear, I will sing so that his legs shrivel up. However, be very careful. While I am singing so that his legs will shrivel up, you should pull your bows taut and be ready. When the Mutuama falls, it will be up to you to pierce him with your arrows. Are you ready?"And he began singing:

> *"Mutuama mama wito wito lapa*
> *Nasawama ke mosusu*
> *Ke mosusu e"*

The right arm of the Mutuama became smaller and smaller until it couldn't be seen anymore. He was left holding on to the papaya tree by his left arm and his two legs. The old man began to sing once more.

> *"Mutuama mama wito wito lapa*
> *Nasawama ke mosusu*
> *Ke mosusu e"*

The Mutuama's left arm got smaller and smaller until it couldn't be seen anymore. Now, he was left holding on to the tree with his two legs. The old man started to sing once more.

> *"Mutuama mama wito wito lapa*
> *Nasawama ke mosusu*
> *Ke mosusu e"*

The Mutuama's right leg got smaller and smaller. He was left with only his left leg holding on to the tree. At the same time, the old man said to the children, "Beware, my children, I am going to sing so that his left leg shrinks. As soon as it has disappeared, the Mutuama will fall. It will be up to you to pierce it with your arrows," and he started to sing:

> *"Mutuama mama wito wito lapa*
> *Nasawama ke mosusu*
> *Ke mosusu e"*

The Mutuama's left leg disappeared and he fell from the tree like a ripe papaya. The children, encouraged by the old man, shot all their arrows into the Mutuama, who died. Their joy was enormous. The old man then asked that they bring him the *"tukumete"* or a big, sculpted, wooden platter.

"I will cut off his head and take it for myself. You may keep the body for yourselves."

The old man cut the Mutuama's head which he put onto the platter *"tukumete."* Then, the children started to dance around the Mutuama's body. Now, there are no more Mutuamas in Waraolua and the people of Ifira are very happy.

This legend was told in Bislama to Paul Gardissat by the former Chief Minister of the New Hebrides (Vanuatu), George Kaltoi Kalsakau.

Nabanga n°80 (1978)

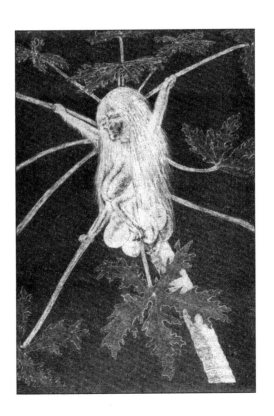

The rat and the octopus
(Ifira)

There was once a rat that lived on the island of Ifira. During a low tide one day, a multitude of sea birds decided to cross the isthmus that separated Efate from Ifira in order to look for the seafood on which they fed. They planned to get to the island by means of a banana leaf that they would use as a canoe. Together, they decided that they would leave at first light the next day. While they were preparing, a passing rat saw them.

"Hey! My friends, I would also like to go with you."

"Alright. We only ask that you bring your own food like we do," they answered.

The next day, as planned, the birds and the rat took to the sea. Then, one of the birds stood up to speak.

"Beware, my friends! When you eat, do not let your crumbs fall on our boat."

A chorus of bird voices answered, "Yes! We all know that!"

The animals continued to row. They were already half way between the two islands when they decided to eat lunch. One of the birds accidentally let some pieces of yam fall on the leaf and, wanting to peck them up, pecked a hole in the boat. The flimsy vessel instantly sank. All of the birds flew off, but the rat couldn't fly. Hopelessly, he started to swim towards the beach. However, there was a high wind and big waves. The waves tired the rat out and pretty soon he was going under every five seconds. Just before he was going to go down for the last time, an octopus crossed his path.

"Help me! Help me! Please!"

"Climb on my back and I'll take you back to Efate."

So, the rat got on to the octopus' back and they swam to Port Pleasant in Port-Vila.

While the rat was on the octopus' back, he noticed that its head went in and out of the water like a submarine. The spectacle of this head that rocked back and forth like a box being tossed around by the waves made him explode with laughter.

He was laughing so much that the octopus asked him, "Rat, why are you laughing like that?"

"I am so glad to finally get back to dry land," he replied.

The journey continued and the rat laughed even harder.

Once they had swum close to the coast, the rat jumped on to the beach.

"Here we are at our destination! You can now return to your home safe and sound," said the octopus.

From the beach, the rat thanked the octopus by saying, "Dear friend, if I was laughing like crazy during the trip, it's because I was watching your ridiculous head floating back and forth in the waves."

The octopus angrily whipped one of its tentacles towards the rat. When it hit the rat, it stuck to his behind and this is how the rat first got its tail. If you look at a rat's tail even today, you will notice that it has a certain resemblance to an octopus's tentacle.

This legend was given by Charles Aiong from Ifira island.

Nabanga n°27 (1976)

Suepus and Atafru
(Pango)

In the olden days, the Port Vila bay was very enticing. This was only normal because the forest covered everything else, even the heights of Bufa. There were a few families on the islet of Imere which is now called Mele. At Blacksands, there were also several families as well as at Tagabe, Tebakor, Fila, and in the hills at Nangire. A little further, Raolua Bay, was as big as Maniura. It was just across from that little bay where Ifira island is today. Like Imere, there were not many people on the island of Ifira. On the other side of this bay, exposed to the southeast winds, was the village of Pango.

This village was a little more protected from the wind. In those days, Pango was in the same place that is now called Epangtui, the old Pango. Across from Pango, on the other side of the bay, the village of Malapoa could be seen. The village was also shielded from the south wind and so, in the evening when everyone was cooking their *laplap,* Pango could see the smoke from Malapoa's fires and Malapoa could see Pango's smoke. This was in the olden days, the days that the missionaries liked to call the "dark times." The people of these villages did indeed live in the blackness of big forests. At this time, only the gardens were cleared or, perhaps, a place to dance. The forest covered everything else and created a deep darkness.

The people of Efate were civilised. Their society was organised. Each village had its *nakamal,* its *farea* and dancing place. Of course, there were wars. They were quite numerous at this time. Erakor had its chief. Pango had theirs. Mele also had their own chief. Fila had theirs. Eratap had its chief and Malapoa had theirs. The chief from Malapoa was terrible, feared in all the other villages. His name was Atafru. Every village was at war with another. The wars were frequent and deadly. In other times, blows were exchanged, discussion was initiated, and pigs were traded. However, the other villages were at war and then were able to settle their disputes. This was not the case with Malapoa.

Atafru, the chief of this village, was horrible. He loved to eat men. He often called the men that he ate his 'crabs.' He had two followers, two warriors who were always at his side. These two warriors watched over him when he went to sea, was off on a hunt, or gathering food in the bush. Atafru commanded wars but rarely participated in them. His warriors, Bismelmel and Bistfarfar, did the dirty work. When they caught a man, they took him to Atafru who happily ate him. However, the warriors were most often hard at working chasing crabs in Pango... that is to say, chasing the men from Pango. Bismelmel and Bistfarfar watched the reef in front of the village closely. When they saw a man, woman, or even a child collecting shells on the reef, they would get into their canoe and go catch the crab. Then, they took it back to Atafru who ate it. Atafru ruled harshly and was bent on exterminating the population of Pango.

"Look! There are still people on the reef! Go, my warriors!"

Bismelmel and Bistfarfar went off and always caught their prey.

"Ha ha ha! How I love the people from Pango! They have such tender flesh. Ha ha ha!"

The people from Pango were naive. They often went to the reef as a family to catch crabs. Atafru would be watching and then send his warriors to capture them. Sometimes the warriors came back with a canoe full of people and Atafru would begin his feasting. From day to day, the population of Pango diminished. No one knew why. No one had seen anything. One day, there was only an old man and an old woman left. Only the two of them had escaped the carnage. They were so scared that they ran away into the bush. There they stayed, doubled over in fear, living on what they could gather. They sometimes killed little birds, but they never went fishing for fear of the reef. These two old people often went to pee into a hole in a rotten tree when they got up in the morning.

One day, a bird came and started to scratch around the trunk of this tree. It found a hole, the hole where the two old people would pee each morning. This bird looked a little like a duck, and it was called a *nambilak*. After the two old people had peed, the *nambilak* started to roll around in the hole, spreading his wings in the urine, and there it laid an egg. A little while later, the egg hatched and a little boy came out. This boy grew. The duck, the *nambilak,* fed the little boy by bringing him something to eat each day. The boy grew and the *nambilak* suddenly realised that it couldn't care for the boy anymore. The food it brought was not enough.

It said, "My child, you are too big now. I am of no use to you now. So, I will leave you to the two old people. They will feed you. Go, my son, and become strong!"

The young boy, used to being raised by the *nambilak,* was a little dismayed at the idea of being raised by the old couple. However, he knew that the *nambilak* could not bring him enough food. So, he went to see the couple.

"I have come to live with you. You will be my parents and you will feed me."

"Yes! We are very happy! A boy! A boy! A little boy who will defend us when he is older! But who are your parents?"

"My mother is a bird. She is a *nambilak*. Do you remember when you would pee each morning in the dead tree? My mother laid her egg there and it hatched in your urine. I come from you, in a strange way."

"Yes! My boy, you will be our son and you will defend us!"

"My mother told me that. She said that I should take care of you."

Time passed. The young boy became a handsome young man. He asked the old couple to make him a bow and he learned to use it by killing all the lizards around their house.

One day, while hunting lizards, he went to the shore and found the elderly couple.

"My parents whom I love, I have come to see the ocean. It is big and seems far away. I would like you to make me a big bow. I want to kill some fish for us."

"Here is the bow that you asked for, my son. You must be very careful. When the tide is low, you may go to the reef to kill fish. But stay on this side of the bay. Never go to the other side near the coast of Pango!"

"I am big now. What could happen to me?"

He had not even passed Pango Point when Atafru saw him.

"My two warriors! Look, there is a crab on Pango reef. There is still one! Quickly! Go!"

Bismelmel and Bistfarfar got into their canoe and went to Pango reef where they hid themselves and watched Suepus. The boy had killed some fish and was attaching them with a vine in order to return to the house. Bismelmel and Bistfarfar followed him. Suepus arrived at the house, happy to put his fish at his parents' feet.

"Look at how big they are!"

"Where did you go?"

"I went to the other side of Pango Point today."

The mother did not even have enough time to scold her son when Bismelmel and Bistfarfar came out of hiding.

"By our ancestors! Suepus! It is Atafru's men!"

"You have come to get me, I suppose. That's good, because you are the strongest. However, give me enough time to prepare a feast and eat it with these two old people who raised me. Come back to get me in two days and I will follow."

The two old people sadly prepared a meal which they ate with their son.

"My parents whom I love, go into the mountains. I will wait for Atafru's men."

"My son, before we leave you to this dirty eater of men, we want to give you our ancestors' club. Here. Take it."

The two old people went off into the bush and Suepus sat down to wait for Atafru's warriors.

When they had arrived, Suepus said, "I waited for you and now I will follow you." They left together and when they had gotten to the shore, Suepus said, "Push the canoe and I will sit in the middle. I don't want to row. One of you will sit in front and the other behind."

Then, they were off. When they had gotten past the reef, Suepus cracked first one and then the other over the head. They both fell into the sea. When Suepus saw their bodies floating, he got them, tied them up to the canoe, and pushed the boat towards the open water. The canoe beached itself on the sands of Malapoa.

Atafru, who had seen the canoe arrive, said, "Go and see if my two warriors have brought my crab! By my ancestors! My warriors are dead! I had finished all the crabs in Pango. There was only one left. Who dared to kill my warriors? Who is he? My men, go tell the chiefs from Lelepa, Nguna, Emao, Emae, and all the other villages from around Efate to come and see me. My anger is great! You hear me? My anger is boiling! My *atavis,* this is the first time that anything like this has happened to me! The last crab in Pango has killed my warriors. I am counting on you for vengeance. We shall chop down ten big trees and make ten big canoes. When they are ready, we will go and kill the last crab in Pango!"

Suepus, in turn, had felled ten big ironwood trees and then climbed high into the hills of Pango to the place called Esseele. From there, he would be able to see the comings and goings of the men from Malapoa. Suddenly, he saw ten canoes full of furious men. The first eight canoes arrived. There were more then one hundred men aboard. Then, Suepus called on his ancestors.

"My ancestors. You who raised me. My ancestors, help me! My ancestors, help me!"

From the heights of Esseele, Suepus threw large stones at the arriving canoes. Some men were instantaneously killed and those that survived were eaten by the sharks. Then, the last two canoes, one containing Atafru, arrived. Suepus again pleaded with his ancestors.

"My ancestors. You who raised me. My ancestors, help me! My ancestors, help me!"

From the heights of Esseele, Suepus threw large stones at the arriving canoes. Some men were instantaneously killed and those who survived were eaten by the sharks. Then, the last two canoes, one containing Atafru, arrived. Suepus again pleaded with his ancestors.

"My ancestors. You who raised me. My ancestors, help me! My ancestors, help me!"

He then threw two stones at the last two canoes to arrive and they sank. The sharks arrived and started to eat all the men aboard.

Suepus said to the sharks, "Don't eat them! Don't eat them! Push them ashore."

The sharks pushed Atafru towards the shore at the foot of Esseele. Suepus went to see him.

"So, Atafru, you wanted to eat the last crab in Pango?"

"Mercy, Suepus! Mercy! Don't kill me."

Suepus took up his club and raised it above Atafru's head.

"You were the one who killed all the people of Pango. You will die now."

"No, Suepus! Don't kill me. I will give you back all the men and women that I have eaten. Let me live."

"Atafru, I want one hundred boys and one hundred girls to repopulate my village. Go now."

Atafru went back to Malapoa unhappy. Then, he spoke to his people.

"My *atavis* from Lelepa, Nguna, Emao, Emae, and all the villages of Efate, I need one hundred boys and one hundred girls to repopulate the village of Pango."

When Atafru had fulfilled his promise, the boys and girls married amongst themselves and filled Pango village with people once again. It was the *nambilak's* son who repopulated the village.

This legend was given in Bislama by Kalmermer from Pango.
Adapted by Paul Gardissat.

Radio New Hebrides

Sokomanu
(Mele)

It was a few days before the independence of Vanuatu. The entire village of Mele was in the big wooden church dating from the beginning of the century. This was a very important event: they were assembled to bless and consecrate a fellow countryman who, in the next few days, would become the President of the Republic of the new State of Vanuatu. The old men, the Matarau, had discussed this during many evenings.

George Ati Kalkoa was not a grand enough name for such an important man. The name of an illustrious ancestor would be more appropriate. Roimata? This title didn't mean much anymore since the coming of the Europeans and certainly since the death of this great chief. Mauitikitiki? This is the name of the one whose name must not be taken in vain. A custom name must be found that could correspond to the importance of the man, the first and the biggest man of the new nation.

Finally, on Saturday, 26 July, at the Farea, Chief Peter Poilapa, son of the revered Chief Kalsautu Poilapa, assisted by the Matarau of the village and in the presence of the whole government, introduced George Kalkoa, who would become *George Ati Sokomanu.*

"Today, your name is Sokomanu," the elder Kalmatak told him. "Here is the lance and the club of your ancestor. You may now rank yourself among the uppermost citizens of the country. We will call you *President Sokomanu!"*

The good Kalmatak, the history of Mele inscribed in his memory, handed to the future President, with a rather theatrical gesture, the insignia of the greatest warriors that the island of Efate could name according to its oral and historical traditions.

Mele Village

In the big bay of Port Vila, the semi-Polynesian group of Mele takes its name from the islet where the original village was established before the arrival of Europeans. The people of Mele called their islet Imere or Imele or Mele (the 'I' or "E" being an article as in Iririki, Ifira, Iruitit or Erakor, Ernangire, etc.). During the first years of their contact with the Europeans, and because of their relative insecurity on the hills of Efate, the people took refuge on their little island. Christianity arrived, security was re-established, the *fareas* were enlarged, and gardens were made on the main land. It was necessary to bring water, firewood, and food from the gardens back to the islet every evening. On the 28th of August 1950, the entire population of Mele moved their village to the main land where it remains to this day. Imere was left in silence. Once again, vegetation covered the *marea,* or dancing grounds.

According to oral tradition, Imere was born underwater. Mauitikitiki, the fisher of islands, arrived with his fishing pole in hand. He threw his line and his hook caught on a rock. Mauitikitiki reeled in his line and pulled lightly. The rock rose up through the water. It was an island, very small, because Mauitikitiki had not pulled hard. It was named Imere. However, that is another story.

From all the oral traditions from Mele, the one that interests us today is that of Sokomanu.

Who was Sokomanu?

Sokomanu Laba was a great "mau," or a great warrior, "Laba" meaning great. It is therefore of Sokomanu the Great that we will speak.

During ancient times, the people from the island of Efate lived in small, disseminated villages in the interior of the island. The chief of each village was assisted by an "atavi" or principle adviser, men of a certain grade, and specialist such as soothsayers, healers, sculptors, and warriors. Discussions were held in the *farea* while dances and tusked-pig killings were held in the *marea* or *"mwalala."* The *"mau"* or warrior ensured the security of the village and the honour of the inhabitants.

Tokay Makau was the warrior or *mau* from the island of Kakula which is in the north of Efate, just across from the village of Paunangisu. Tokay Makau was a strong man who was wise in the ways of village warfare, but he was not an artist. The most beautiful works are reserved for those who have the custom right. Because Tokay needed a lance and because he wanted it to be beautiful, he commissioned one from a village sculptor. The commission for a *"Konokon"* or lance was thus passed to an artesian who started working right away. A long, hard wood was cut, sculpted, and worked to the finest of details. When the lance was finished, the man would rub it down with burnt coconut oil to blacken it and make it shine.

On the fixed day, Sokomanu, who was passing in front of the artist's house, asked, "Friend, that lance is very beautiful. Whom did you sculpt it for?"

"Your friend Tokay Makau will come and get it. The road is long between Kakula and Mele, but he won't be long."

Sokomanu didn't even let him finish his sentence when he responded, "I'll take it!"

"Sokomanu, you are the greatest. However, this lance was a commission made for a friend."

"If I didn't know Tokay Makau, I wouldn't be able to touch this lance. Tokay is my friend. I will take the lance and if he comes, I will talk to him."

The artist, resigned, let Sokomanu the great warrior take the lance. Thus, Sokomanu Laba, proud and majestic, left with the lance *konokon* in his hand. Tokay Makau soon arrived. The meeting was quick and significant. On one side, there was the great *mau* Sokomanu and on the other, the less popular but still powerful *mau,* Tokay Makau. Sokomanu of Mele and Tokay of Kakula, the two warriors were face to face.

Tokay began a gesture that he had not finished when Sokomanu began to explain the situation. Sokomanu didn't want to let his friend begin talking; he must take the upper hand.

"I have wanted this lance for a very long time," said Sokomanu.

"I wasn't aware of the talents of this artist. I heard of him through the "matarau." The beauty of this lance, this *konokon*, surprises me. It is exactly what I'm looking for."

Sokomanu spoke quickly and a lot, all the while looking at Tokay and trying to influence him.

Finally, he said, "I thought you would let me buy it. I have already paid the artist."

Tokay didn't respond so Sokomanu filled the silence.

"I just bought it from the old artist. I paid for it. I gave him pig-tusk bracelets, earrings made from turtle shell, and pieces of rich *tapa* from Erromango. I think that my trade will satisfy the artist who is especially pleased with the *tapa* from Erromango."

When he said the name of this island, Sokomanu looked at Tokay. He wanted to know his reaction. A *tapa* from Erromango! Sokomanu was certainly rich, great, and respected if he possessed a *tapa* from Erromango, that hard and mysterious island from which Roimata and Wotanimanu possibly came. In saying *"tapa* from Erromango," Sokomanu thought that he had won Tokay to his opinion. However, the latter just listened and didn't respond. Sokomanu coughed lightly and continued to count his gifts.

"I added plumes which come from my family on Lelepa."

The list of gifts was long. It was a game. Tokay still didn't speak. This was also a game. Sokomanu played the great and generous. He knew how to give and is certainly the one before whom the smallest *mau* must bow. Who else would own *tapas* from Erromango on the island of Efate?

Tokay resigned himself to a done deed. His displeasure, however, was enormous. Not only was the lance *konokon* commissioned by himself and taken by Sokomanu, his friend, but also by this man of whom he was exceedingly jealous. Hate was born inside Tokay Makau, the *mau* of Kakula. The honour of manhood, the honour of a warrior was a stake, and it had just been ridiculed before the artist.

The old man felt the embarrassment that existed between the two warriors. He looked for an excuse to break the tension. He reflected for a moment and then called to his wife.

"Woman, these men are hungry. Give them something to eat."

Women should not concern themselves with the affairs of men and especially not those of warriors. They may not concern themselves with the affairs of men, but nothing stops them from listening. And women always listen; the wife of the old artist had heard everything. She knew Sokomanu Laba from Mele and Tokay Makau of Kakula.

The tension that existed between the two because of the lance *konokon* bothered her very much. She understood that the discord between these two warriors could start a war between their respective villages. She knew, this old woman, what would happen. The women and the children would be put into an enclosure surrounded by large wooden stakes and be left there waiting for the outcome of the battle. The old woman remembered very clearly her feelings during times like these. Being an intelligent woman and above all used to this sort of disagreement, she, like her husband, tried to minimise the incident. She had prepared a hasty meal for herself, her husband, and her grandson that should have come by. The *laplap* was there being kept warm on the black stones. She took it off of the stones, peeled back the slippery leaves, and brought out pieces of yam.

The old woman said to her husband, "Man, they may eat now."

The old artist had waited for these words before he allowed himself to say, "Come and eat. My wife has prepared a meal for our grandchildren and us. We will share it. Our meal is very simple, but..."

He couldn't find the words to finish his sentence. Thus, he finished by saying, "Eat, then!"

The old man served a piece of yam to each of the warriors. A heavy silence still pervaded the atmosphere. The old woman looked on from a corner of the hut. She knew that a war was brewing.

"Old man," said Sokomanu Laba, "I'm going now."

The old woman brought out a piece of yam wrapped in leaves and gave it to him. Sokomanu Laba then left. Once he had reached the gate in the stone fence that separated the house from the fields and woods where pigs ran wild, Tokay Makau called out to Sokomanu Laba. He wanted to talk to him. The moment was very important and Sokomanu knew it.

"Alright, speak!" he said.

Tokay stood up straight. He was upset, but he had to speak. Between warriors, there must always be an explanation.

"This lance is now called "Nabua Mahot" which means broken road. Our friendship is finished."

The two men looked at each other from either side of the fence. They eyed each other up and down, neither wanting to be the first to look away.

Sokomanu responded, "Tokay, if for you the road is broken, for me the path is burning. I call this lance 'Nabua Vera.' Yes, Tokay, the path is burning, but it is not yet broken. We can still fight!"

War was declared between the *mau* of Mele and those of Kakula. The old artist and his wife who had been there observing the whole exchange understood that war was once again at hand.

"We will never be left in peace. Kakula will call their clans from Nguna and Pele, while Mele will ask for help from Ifira, Tukutuku, Bouffa, and Lelepa. War will start once more and we will be insecure again."

The two *mau* left and took with them their bitter words. It was the end of friendship; war had begun.

The relationships that exist between the islet Mele or Imere and Tukutuku, a little village in the southwest of Efate, are very important because the families from both places are still in contact about fundamental problems such as custom disputes, marriages, and alliances.

Tukutuku, the underworld of death

The canal between Imere and Tukutuku, Devil's Point, has been the subject of many strange stories that people will speak about only under duress. These stories speak of people who return as roaming spirits after their death. Death is always frightening, and these spirits still walk among the living, causing problems.

When a man, woman, or child disappeared from Imere, their spirit would walk for a while, going through different stages that would finally lead them to the Land of the Dead: Tukutuku. Before arriving in Tukutuku, the spirit would be the object of different tests: it would go before the god Soaralema who would verify that it was still holding the woven palm rope used to attach the sacrificial pig during its funeral. It was Soaralema that would allow the spirit to enter into the underwater land that would bring the dead back to life: Bangona.

However, between Imere and Bangona, the road was long. The man would die, his spirit would leave his body, and cross the small stretch of water between Imere and Suango Point. There, a little ways from the alluvial deposits made by the river Teae, was the sacred place, Temate, where the journey to the Land of the Dead would begin. It was there that the spirit of the dead would commence its purification. The inhabitants of Imere could see, at nightfall, a glow coming from the mouth of the river. They could also make out strange noises, the noises of the dead beginning their long journey.

The spirits would leave Temate, follow the black sand beach, and come upon the first rocks: this was Temuri. The ebb and flow of the ocean would vanish into the rocks and reappear as spray, or the thousands of tears shed by the dead for this place. Temuri was the tears of the sea.

A little further was Matnavitunu. In the hot waters that boiled at low tide between the pebbles and the black sand, the spirit would scratch its back by turning over and over in the sand. The hot water once again purified its relaxed body.

After the relaxing hot waters, the spirit would enter an enormous passage hollowed out of a hunk of compact coral. A little *mau,* half guardian, half warrior, would help the spirit to enter the passageway, while another *mau,* at the opposite end, would pull it by its head to help it leave. However, the difficult tests were not finished. Indeed, they had only just begun.

That was Bukura. The spirit would then arrive at Kawene. Kawene is a cave in the rock with a sacrificial table. The spirit is laid on a smooth, white, stone table. The master of this place would tear out its tongue. Blood ran. The spirit could no longer speak and nobody could hear its silenced cries. It would then wash its mouth in the froth of the waves that broke on the white sand of Devil's Point. Continuing on its way, the spirit would take some red burao leaves called "Belelu Nakowia" and wipe its mouth.

It would then arrive in Tukutuku. This was Bangona, the underwater Land of the Dead. In the middle of the bay, at the bottom of the sea, on the marvellously white sand was a mat. This was the red mat at the entrance of Bangona. The dead, tired by so many tests, might then lay down to rest on this red mat. There it would sleep its last sleep. This was the Sleep of the Dead from Efate. Tukutuku possessed at white sandy bay, a red-leafed *burao* and an eternal *banyan.* Here was the *farea,* the village of the ancestors. To the right, towards the point, was a white stone from which one was able to see Retoka. That was Ivai. The god Soaralema lived there. He would verify that each dead was indeed holding the rope from their sacrificial pig, put in the tomb by the family during the funeral.

Those among the dead that tried to trick the god by showing him an ordinary rope would have their skulls smashed by a club so that their blood would run in compensation for the missing beast. After having wiped itself with the red leaves of the *burao,* the spirit would climb to the top of the tree called Sinu. From there, it would call another god, Mataumori, who would send a large wave to take it from the tree to Bangona. The enormous wave would come, envelop the spirit, pull it down into the water, and throw it into the hole of Telalaso. This was the underwater Land of the Dead.

Under the surface of the water, the different levels of Paradise were numerous, each corresponding to the spots of hot and cold water that one feels when swimming near a river. There a new life would start, with paradise being Mangalua Noponopo and hell being Mangalua Vera.

During its new life, the spirit which had come from Imere, after having passed all the appropriate tests, would wait for a long time in a paradise. This was Bangona! This was the underwater Land of the Dead and its entrance, for all the inhabitants of Efate, was at Tukutuku. Tukutuku was, however, also the *farea* of the Roe family.

Tukutuku has a deep, white, sandy bay bordered by casuarinas whose roots penetrate and subsequently destroy the surrounding coral. It is a very welcoming place.

From Tukutuku on board of Tafura

Tukutuku was the village of the Roe family. Roe was the chief of Tukutuku, but this does not mean that he reigned alone and commanded everything. In Vanuatu, no decision can be made without the opinion of others. Roe was there to lean on, to listen to.

He had a large canoe. Its name was Tafura. Roe built it with the help of his friends. It was made of hard wood, hollowed from a *tamanu* or *nabangura* limb. This is a wood of beautiful colour that doesn't crack in the sun. Tafura had a pandanus sail woven in the form of a butterfly wing. The canoe had no deck, only two flat sideboards. It had four crossbars and its wooden floater was called *Nasama*. A second sail was vertically fixed behind the first. Both were preserved from the elements by a cover on each side and a stay at the front. Tafura also had a sort of platform that was used to transport vegetables from the garden so that they wouldn't get wet. Roe's canoe was capable of holding between eight and ten people. It was heavy and during feast or war, Roe flew a banner of dyed and woven pandanus. Roe was not a great seaman, but he knew where the winds came from. He also knew that the winds could take the canoe into extremely dangerous places. He liked to teach his children about the different winds around Efate.

"The north wind is called Tokelau. It comes from Kuwae. Suafate is our wind, that wind comes from the south and penetrates directly into our bay at Tukutuku. Suohit comes from Pango Point and Kandu comes from either Retoka or Lelepa."

Roe liked to say the names of the winds. He rolled them on his tongue like waves roll over the rocks at Devil's Point. Roe commanded admiration from all who listened to him, particularly his ten children. Roe had travelled, and so his children liked him to tell stories of terrible exploding volcanoes, and chiefs who had killed and eaten an entire village.

Roe's youngest child often told him, "Father, tell us the story of Sangalegale. Yes, that little devil with the long hair who always walks backwards! Yes, papa, his children hang from his hair and he has claws on his hands like a flying fox!"

Another said, "When he runs, he throws his "nasusu" or breasts on his back! Papa, tell us the story of the Sangalegale from Emau and talk like the people from Emau, roll your 'r's! Say: Narongorongoroa!"

The ten children of chief Roe would then laugh and admire their father whom they saw as the centre of the universe. Roe always took advantage of these conversations to advise his children.

"If you ever become lost at sea, invoke the name of the god of seamen. Call Atu Na Mauri. He is the spirit that has often helped me to pass Devil's Point without trouble."

Roe told this to his children, his ten squirmy children, who often liked to play together. They would go to the garden and throw reeds at a target, swim in the bay, or handle their father's sail together. The canoe was big, and Roe's whole family could sit inside of it. For years, the children had practiced handling the canoe in the interior of Tukutuku bay. One day, though, they decided to go out into the open sea. The wind was not too strong; Suafate blew lightly. However, Suafate is treacherous on open seas and they also forgot about currents. Indeed, Roe's children didn't understand currents. They knew that the wind was blowing and that they were advancing, but there were no currents in the interior of the bay.

Tafura, its pandanus sail swollen, was no longer following the intended direction. A squall arrived and overtook the canoe. The children, upset, grabbed on tightly and cried out, but the wind carried away their voices. They tried with all of their might to row towards Wo Mati, but the rudder wouldn't work anymore. Under the shell of the canoe, an evil spirit seemed to pulling it adrift into unknown parts. Tukutuku Point disappeared. Retoka, Lclcpa, and finally Moso appeared, came closer, and vanished over the stern of the canoe. The islands flew by and were left behind. The wind Kandu pushed and pushed the canoe while the evil spirit under the canoe pulled and pulled. It was a big adventure. The canoe approached Nguna and finally set ground on chief Mariwota's land.

"My children, what are you doing here without your father? I am a friend of Roe of Tukutuku. You are welcome. However, your arrival has surprised me. One must be very careful when travelling on a sailing canoe like yours! Kandu can blow very strong and carry you to place where you might be killed, eaten, or kept as a slave. You will wait at my house, quietly, and when Tokelau begins to blow again, you will go back to your home. You are all very noisy and I know that I cannot trust you. There are ten of you! I am going to lock you in the *farea*. You will wait for me there. I am going to go to my garden and this evening, when I come back, I will bring food for you."

The chief Mariwota from Nguna knew that the children shouldn't remain playing on the beach. It was an uncertain time, wars were frequent and then children playing around a canoe... well, it could be tempting for a jealous chief.

Everyday, Mariwota went to the garden. This was where he spent the majority of his life. Sometimes he went alone. Often, his wife would come with him, and occasionally, other villagers would help to burn large parts of the bush or big tree roots. The whole village would also participate in the construction of fences that would enclose the growing yams to protect them from the hearty appetite of wandering pigs. Heavy work was always done together.

This day, however, Mariwota went alone and was very preoccupied. He had shut the children in the *nakamal,* he had given them all the necessary advice, but he was still worried. He dragged his feet and pondered. He stopped several times, scratched his head, turned, hesitated, and then continued on his original path all the while trying to see the trees on the mountains of Efate. He thought about his friend Roe, the great Roe from Tukutuku.

"The Roes are a big family, an important family. Why did these children wash up on Nguna and particularly on my land? What would I do if something bad were to happen?"

Mariwota continued to walk. He could not stay near the *nakamal,* guarding the children. They needed to eat! How long would he have to feed ten mouths? The old chief finally arrived at his garden. He shrugged his shoulders and started to dig up sweet potatoes, kneeling and standing, kneeling and standing. He then put them into a pile.

"I have enough problems with my neighbours from Pele. But no, that isn't enough. Now I have ten children to feed and protect. To feed them isn't too difficult, our gardens are big and we haven't had a cyclone for a very long time. But protecting them! Oh, that Nawota the creator would assist me in my old age and give me the courage to protect the lives of these children!"

Mariwota then cut down a big bundle of bananas, fat bananas that were easy to carry and easy to cook.

"Oh, my poor wife! Ten children to feed this evening. You're absolutely worn out but when you get back from your garden, you'll have to start working again!"

The great warrior from the islet of Kakula, Tokay Makau, after his cold altercation with Sokomanu Laba, returned to his land vexed and furious. He, the strongest *mau* from this region in Efate, was completely humiliated.

Sokomanu Laba had said, "NABUA VERA, let's fight!"

Tokay, his muscles strained to the bursting point, paced on Kakula, the islet having become too small for him. "Nabua Vera," he repeated to himself, "I want to fight!" His entire body was shaking with anger, his neck became enormous, his shoulders swelled, his torso rippled, his waist trembled, and his calves lengthened. His anger transformed him and rendered him stronger than he had ever been before. Tokay Makau was handsome, but anger gave him an ugly face and his normally soft eyes became hard and venomous.

The news spread rapidly between Moso, Nguna, Pele, Efate, and Kakula. The small sea canals that separated all these islands were quickly traversed. Only the island of Emau was left in the dark, perhaps because it was further away or possibly because the Tokelau often carried canoes to the other side of the horizon. It was easy, thought, to go between Nguna and Kakula while the distance between Emau and Efate made the journey much more dangerous and thus less frequented by small boats.

Because news travels quickly between Nguna and Kakula, the great warrior from North Efate already knew that locked in Mariwota's *farea* at Utanlang, were the ten children of chief Roe from Tukutuku. The *mau* had heard of these children. Without hesitating, he filled his canoe with *"Leimule"* bananas and left for Nguna, having decided to force the door of Mariwota's *farea*. He left Kakula, followed the coast of Pele, and arrived at Tikilasoa in the early morning where he hid himself among the rocks of Nguna.

While Tokay Makau was paddling along the coast of Pele, an old woman who was gathering shells on the rocks spotted him. As she was hidden, the *mau* didn't see her. The old woman had observed that he paddled abnormally. The man appeared to be furious and heading towards Nguna. He then disappeared and the old woman continued to collect shells.

Tokay Makau went ashore at Utanlang, and knocked on the door of Mariwota's farea. The children were huddled together with fright. The *mau* cried out, broke into the hut, and killed all of the children with his club. He then hung the bunch of *Leimule* bananas above the closed door and left for Kakula once again. The act had been violent and quick.

Mariwota came back from his garden and called to the children. No one responded. He called again; silence. He opened the door to the *farea* and stepped inside to a massacre. The ten children, their skulls cracked open, were there bathing in their own blood. Mariwota was desperate. He ran around hitting the village *tamtam* and calling everyone together.

"Did anyone see a man? It might have been the *mau* from Kakula. Roe's ten children were murdered in the *farea!"*

The whole village was shocked. No one could answer; no one knew anything.

"Atavi, my assistant, take my canoe and go to Pele. See if you can find any information. If our friends on Pele don't know anything, see what you can find in Epau."

The *atavi* or assistant to chief Mariwota arrived on Pele. The news was quickly spread and an old woman who had been sitting in a corner stood up and said, "I was collecting shells on the beach when I saw Tokay Makau in his canoe. He looked furious! He paddled along our island, headed towards Tikilasoa, and then disappeared."

The old woman paused, thought for a couple of seconds, and then resumed her speech.

"I saw him a couple of hours later and was very surprised to see him coming back so quickly. It was him that killed Roe of Tukutuku's children. It was him!"

The *atavi* now knew who had killed the children. He paddled to Nguna. When he got there, he said to his chief, "Mariwota, Tokay killed Roe's children. An old woman from Pele saw him."

The old chief was not surprised, but he was completely demoralised.

"Atavi, take my sailing canoe. Go tell Roe from Tukutuku that his children were killed by the *mau* from Kakula. Tell him that we have cried piteously for them here and that I am not strong enough myself to bring him the news. Tell him too that Tokay is a killer."

When he learned the news, Roe fell to his knees and cried. His ten children were no more.

"Oh, that Nawota would help me to survive," he cried, "and especially that he would help me to take revenge. You, my subjects, send a sprouted coconut to each village on Efate, to each of our clans, to each of our families. I am putting a price on the head of Tokay, and these coconuts will be a symbol of my pledge!"

The wooden drums of Tukutuku resounded throughout the day and the conch shells sent their sounds of grief to every village on Efate. Mourning had come to Tukutuku in the Roe house.

Imere emptied and the inhabitants of Lelepa traversed the sea that separated them from the mainland on canoes weighted down with mats. Everyone was going to the feast for the dead at Tukutuku. Roe cried and let his beard begin to grow on his face. Roe would not cut it as a sign of mourning. The guests came from every part of Efate. An enormous pig was killed and Roe presented the head to Sokomanu's two brothers who had come from Mele.

Sokomanu Laba, the great *mau,* the great warrior of Mele, knew now what had to be done.

"Woman, prepare a small *laplap,* we are leaving," he cried.

Sokomanu and his wife left Imere for the mainland. They went to their garden and unearthed yams. While his wife was digging, Sokomanu went to look for dry coconuts in their small plantation. He found none. He looked again, lifting dry coconut palms from the ground. He found nothing. Only one coconut was there, at the top of a tree. Sokomanu then picked up a shard of pottery from the ground that had come from one of Mautikitiki's vases. He threw it at the coconut, but nothing happened. Furious, he climbed the palm tree and pulled the coconut free and threw it to the ground. His wife brought him three yams. With one brutal wretch, he tried to break them: impossible!

225

The *mau* from Mele flexed his muscles and tried once again to break the fragile yams. He couldn't do it. Now he was satisfied. These were the two signs that he had been waiting for. His triumph over Tokay Makau was assured; the signs from the Land of the Dead had been delivered through the intermediaries of everyday produce. The couple returned to the islet.

Sokomanu's wife, after having peeled the yams with a bamboo knife, opened the coconut to mix its juice with the ceremonial *laplap*. She went to throw the peelings into the sea and saw a canoe coming. From the way the occupant was paddling and from the shape of the canoe, she recognised her brother-in-law.

"He has come from Tukutuku. What news does he bring?"

"My brother, what's happening? Your face is ashen and you won't speak!" said Sokomanu while helping his brother to pull his canoe onto the beach.

The man didn't respond, but threw at the Sokomanu's feet the head of the pig that had been killed at Tukutuku for the funerals.

"Brother, speak, because at Tukutuku people from our clan need me."

The man lowered his head and said, "Sokomanu, Roe's ten children were murdered by Tokay Makau. They were blown off course on Tafura and eventually ran ashore at Mariwota's on Nguna. They stayed locked in Mariwota's *nakamal* at Utanlang for a little while. The *mau* from Kakula learned of their hiding place and while Mariwota was in the garden, he killed them all. An old woman from Pele saw him pass. Roe killed the mourning pig and gave us the head. I bring it now to you."

There on the beach, the great Sokomanu was struck dumb by the news. After having listened, he stood up, looked at his brother, and yelled, "Death! I will kill Tokay Makau and avenge our clan. Go, return to Tukutuku and tell Roe that I am coming. Woman! Take the *laplap* from the hot rocks. We shall eat and then I will go."

After having eaten, Sokomanu Laba prepared himself. He dressed in the most beautiful mats, embroidered with shell money, that wrapped around his waist and accentuated his musculature. His biceps were encircled by armbands. Sokomanu worked a black feather into his hair. He was ready, so he grabbed his comb, *"Seru"*, which carried the same motif as the lance *Konokon*. In an angry gesture, he thrust it into the *natangora* ceiling of the hut and said to his wife, "Woman, look at this comb. It will stay thus until I kill Tokay Makau. If something happens to me, you will see blood appear at the *Seru's* points. That is for you, my wife. Now, let the oldest of my *farea* come."

An old man approached, bent by the years but still respectful of the great Sokomanu.

"I'm listening," said the old man.

"Tasila, you are the oldest and wisest of my *Naflak*. You represent my clan so you must stay on the beach and wait. If I win, I will send you a sign to prove my victory. Tasila, watch closely. I know that you can do this. I am leaving."

Sokomanu got into his canoe. He sat upright and looked at the mountains of Efate that rose above the big plain of Mele. Then, he concentrated himself, took up his paddle, and yelled, "If I am to kill Tokay Makau, then with only one stroke of this paddle, my canoe will be on the mainland. Ancestors, help me!"

With only one small push from the tip of his paddle, Sokomanu's canoe bumped into the shore on Efate.

At Suango Point, the *mau* paddled his canoe and there, on the beach, he prepared to fight. Like all *mau,* the great warriors of Efate, he repeated three times over several metres the methods of handling his arms. The lance was first. It could kill those who would defend the *mau* from Kakula. Sokomanu warmed up. Every muscle in his body was tight. He threw *Konokon,* and the most beautiful lance on Efate stuck in the sand. He repeated this movement three times. He then moved on to the *nalnal* or club. This was the last weapon to be used. It would serve to crush the skull of Tokay Makau. Sokoman backed up and threw the club behind him. It landed in the sand. He repeated this three times. Finally, the *mau* was ready.

The anger of Sokomanu the Great

The *mau* from Mele was ready. He left his island: Imere. He advised his clan to fight for a sure victory. He asked his wife to keep an eye on the comb placed among the leaves of the *natangora* roof. He repeated this three times, a few metres from the arms drill. He had the protection of Nawota, the most powerful god. The *mau* was ready. He could face Tokay Makau. In an impressive feat, he was going to kill the *mau* of Kakula …

The brother of the great warrior departed in another direction; he followed the coast: Bankura, Bangona and, a little further on, Tukutuku Bay. There were many people there: families from Bufa and Rentapao, some from Epau and Erueti, the *naflak* from Malapoa and those from Epangtui. There were family relations, clans and families from far away. They had come for the funeral feasts that lasted ten days. Almost everywhere wide-open, smoking holes could be seen, some of which contained *laplap* on hot stones, while others in which peelings and leaves burned as tradition dictated were empty. The families were seated beneath a large *natapoa;* they awaited others from neighbouring islands to join them in the wailing and grieving, in memory of those who were no more. By the river, under the large *banyan,* groups of men stood beating on wooden drums and an orchestra of *tamtams* resounded throughout the hills. On the *marae,* whose soil had been trampled by thousands of stamping people, group after group of dancers danced, as ten women in a corner of the *nasara* moved sadly, occasionally uttering cries.

While Tukutuku was celebrating the mourning of Roe, Sokomanu's brother, out of breath from his fast walk, burst into the *nasara*. The dancers stopped, the *mau's* brother wanted to speak:

"Brothers! The two *mau* are going to battle and the ground of Efate will tremble. Roe's children will be avenged. Look at the grassy plateau above the bay of Udaone. Watch it closely, in the dry patches where the reeds of the white grass are pushing through."

The dancers listened. The families, the clans, the relations, the elderly, the women and the men all looked in the direction of the white grass. Their eyes were fixed on the coast of Efate that faces Lelepa, Moso and Nguna. It was there that the battle would take place. Sokomanu had departed from Imere at an impressive pace. He had crossed through the forests of Lama, then he glimpsed Moso and Lelepa. He had difficulty breathing and Efate's soil seemed to reverberate under his step. The handsome face of the great warrior was covered with sweat, the fresh sea breeze blew into his lungs which seemed to want to make a reserve of pure air from the Lama mountains. After having got his breath back, he concentrated and looked at Kuwae, which was lost in the clouds, horizon and sea in the distance. One more time he called on Nawota, then he set out at a run, his club and spear in his hand. The gods had given him a power that no-one else could touch. He emerged onto the white grass. The ground was dry and the red soil was completely cracked under the blaze of the sun. Sokomanu appeared, powerful and solemn. He flexed his powerful arms, his face was fearsome, his entire body gave the impression of strength. Behind his path smoke rose, as if there had been fire among the dry grass.

At Tukutuku the people watched and saw the smoke rising in the direction of Udaone bay. They said:

"Sokomanu Laba, Sokomanu the Great is marching. He leaves to fight Tokay Makau. The shock will be terrible. He will certainly make Efate's ground tremble."

The smoke hung, in the air, the *mau* changed direction. He arrived at Tukutuku.
"Tokay Makau killed ten of Roe's children. All of Efate cries and all of the families are in mourning and all of you there are drinking *kava!* That Nawota witnesses your passiveness and punishes you!"

One of the men tried to speak:

"Sokomanu, you are our defender, our warrior, you are the greatest, we have been waiting for you!"

"You could not have been waiting for me while drinking *kava* that calms your anger!"

And the *mau* from Mele took the men's clubs assembled around the coconut cups and, furious, he smashed them.

"Now is not the time to drink *kava*," he said. *"Kava* calms your body and your spirit. It is for times of peace. We need to go to war against Tokay Makau. Leave it!"

The men listened to the warrior and his anger frightened them. They huddled together, one against the other, and looked at their scattered coconut cups and the *kava* juice that spattered onto the ground at Tukutuku. The spilled *kava* juice was an offence. No-one dared tell this to the warrior. Sokomanu continued:

"At the first cock crow, before even the first morning birds have sung, we will leave together. Hear this! Roe's ten children are dead! You have grieved enough! Now we need to react!"

Roe entered onto the *nasara,* his eyes sad and lost in his face. His face was covered in stubble, indicating his great grief. He saw the scared men, the spilled cups of *kava,* the clubs scattered on the ground and the *kava* juice that ran onto the beaten ground. Sokomanu was there, powerful, immense. Everything in him was indignation and rage.

Roe said to the men:

"Listen to him and do what he says. His words are loyal. His anger is justifiable. He has spilled the *kava.* Later he will pay for what he has done. Follow him!"

Sokomanu, after having gotten his men worked up, gave the signal for departure. They left in the direction of Kakula. They crossed dry hills where only reeds and short grasses grow. They passed over Udaone and Saama to arrive at Paunangisu where they used canoes to cross the short stretch of ocean that separated them from their enemy. Tokay Makau's subjects were there on the shore pretending not to know what was happening.

Sokomanu asked the old men, "Where is Tokay's *nakamal?"*

A frightened elder showed him the way. The moment that Sokomanu set foot on the beaten earth of the *nasara,* a conch sounded twice from the shore of the mainland. They were announcing the escape of Tokay and his warriors into the hills of Paunganisu. Furious, Sokomanu and his warriors returned to the island of Efate in pursuit of the cowards.

Once they arrived at Takara Point, Sokomanu told his men, "I know that my enemy usually drinks from a watering hole next to the sea after each combat. This slightly briny water has powers unknown to me. I'm going to wait there. You go that way and try to block his men at the foot of the mountain jutting from the plain where the hot waters smoke between the roots of *buraos."*

The men left their great warrior and went in the direction of the hot water hills, as Sokomanu had told them to do. The *mau* from Mele followed the shore and placed himself near the briny watering hole where Tokay would come and drink.

Tokay was waiting for his enemies. They arrived and the fight started. The *mau* from Kakula killed one man from Tukutuku after the other. Several bodies hit the ground, while the others ran away. Tokay then took his bow, wounded a few and chased the rest.

There was no one left. When he arrived on the shore near the spot where he usually quenched his thirst, he found Sokomanu who yelled, "I have fought in many different places without seeing your face. Now, we meet. Yes, I see that your clothing is torn. You named our lance Nabua mahot but I named it Nabua vera!"

The fight started. It was fierce and the dust flew around them. Sokomanu tried to hit Tokay. He lifted his arms and closed them around his enemy's club. Then, pretending he was hurt, he let himself be flung away. Sokomanu fell to his knees. Tokay took advantage of Sokomanu's weakened position to lift his deadly club above his head. At that very moment, Sokomanu drove his lance through Tokay's body. He fell to the ground. Suddenly, one of Tokay's warriors, his bow taut and ready, shot an arrow at Sokomanu. At the same time, the great warrior's wife saw blood dripping from the comb that he had given her. She knew what it meant. The battle had ended. Tokay's body was brought back to his house. As for Sokomanu, he had told the chief of Tukutuku that his men would return by several different means of transport. Some went by canoe and other returned by the interior of the island. Roe saw a canoe turn Lelepa point and he realised that Sokomanu had been hurt. Despite having some difficulty speaking, Sokomanu announced Tokay's death and his own wound.

Roe told the great warrior, *"Mau,* go to Mele and I will join you tomorrow."

Each man returned sadly to his home. During the night, the fever invaded Sokomanu little by little. The poison on the arrow shot by Tokay's men did its work and tetanus set in.

In the morning, the chief of Tukutuku arrived carrying a cord called Liliko, made from pandanus fibres. This cord knotted here and there around fragments of coral marked the number of presents that Roe had to give for the death of Tokay Makau.

Sokomanu was delirious and death took over slowly. At his side, Roe spoke to Sokomanu who could no longer respond. He grabbed the cord and counted until he reached one hundred. This was the symbol of what he owed to Sokomanu's family for Tokay's death.

Sokomanu closed his eyes. His jaw tightened and he died.

The conches announced the death of the *mau* and the inhabitants of Imere cried hardest of all. They enveloped his body in mats and buried it, the leash of a pig in his hand. This pig would permit him, the great warrior of Mele, to gain entrance into the underwater Land of the Dead, Bangona.

Roe then said to the brothers of Sokomanu, "Your *mau* had avenged my children and now he is dead. In five days, I will come to pay my debt."

The great feasting for Sokomanu's funeral began. The people fed the chief from Tukutuku and then he left. Five days later, he returned with the promised gifts. Ten days later, the people of Efate arrived; many pigs were killed and many *laplap* were made. One hundred days later, the same ceremony was begun again in memory of the great Sokomanu Laba: the great *mau* from Mele that was no longer.

Adaptation from Paul Gardissat based on the original collection of Jean Guiart.

Le Mélanésien n° 1-8 (1980).

Comb *seru*

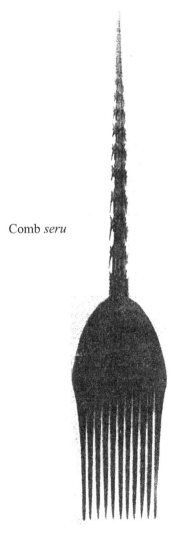

Leikele and Kurunaenae
(Mele)

On Efate, there used to live two old women. The first was named Leikele, and she lived in a big rock at Bakura. The other lived in a hut on the island of Mele. Her name was Kurunanae.

While Kurunanae was a wise old woman full of good sense, the other woman, Leikele, resembled an old ugly witch who was very mean. She had got into the habit of going to the small island of Mele and devouring all the living beings that she could find. That was how she had decimated the whole small island where only Kurunanae now survived.

The witch had aged and her appetite had dampened but no matter, because she was sure that there was no one left on the small island of Mele. Imagine her surprise one evening upon seeing smoke coming from the small island.

"I can't believe it! Alas, there is still someone there. I thought that I had eaten all the inhabitants. I must go see this for myself."

As soon as she had made her decision, she began to act. She seized her magic wand which she used only on special occasions. Arriving on the beach, she hit the ground three times with her wand and the sea, which was at high tide, immediately went down.

"I won't have to do much swimming now," said the old woman as if explaining her actions.

She dived in and swam for a long time. Her old age had sapped much of her strength. Hence, she was very tired when she finally reached the coast.

"I'm going to rest a little before climbing up to that hut where the smoke is coming from."

Leikele dozed a little on the sand and then took up her mission again, pushed by the desire to know the secret of the smoke.

In her hut, Kurunanae heard footsteps. Frightened, she saw Leikele coming up the path. What was she do? Luckily, she too had magical powers. Quickly, she transformed herself into a big, black rock and sat herself next to the fire without taking the time to extinguish it.

A little while later, Leikele arrived in the hut. She inspected and sniffed everywhere, she touched everything, but to no avail. Furious, she turned the whole house inside-out. In a rage, she took the black rock and threw it outside before going out of the hut and yelling, "Hide yourself well because I'll find you eventually!" Hatred burning in her heart, she went back to her house.

Still furious, Leikele decided to return to the small island the next day. Like the day before, she took her magic wand and hit the ground three times. With the third tap, the high tide became low tide and she swam all the way to the small island. Once there, she rested before climbing to the hut. It was again at the last moment that Kurunanae realised that the witch was coming. She quickly transformed herself into a piece of dry wood. Leikele did not discover her and left just as furious as before.

Still angry, Leikele decided to return to the small island again on the third day. Like both times before, she hit the ground three times with her magic wand and high tide became low tide. Leikele swam to the small island. There, she rested a little before climbing to the hut. Like the two proceeding days, Kurunanae was taken by surprise by the arrival of Leikele. Luckily, she was able to transform herself once again. This time it was into a fork that people used to remove hot stones from *laplap*. Leikele discovered nothing and she left just as furious as before.

The fourth day arrived. Kurunanae started to think. Because she had come back twice after her initial failure, she was sure that Leikele would keep coming back until she had caught her prey.

"This time I will be ready," she said to herself.

She then took a piece of sharp wood and started to dig a hole at the end of the path near the beach. This was, in fact, how people used to make holes with only the aid of a piece of wood and a string. Kurunanae dug for a long time. As soon as she had dug a large hole, she tried it.

"This is perfect. I can just fit inside. This is exactly what I need."

Then she started to do the opposite of what she had just done. Kurunanae covered her body with sand. Soon, only her nose was sticking out of the sand to permit her to breath. Thus hidden, she waited impatiently for the witch.

The latter, still furious, decided to return to the small island. Just as she had done before, she hit the ground three times with her magic wand and high tide became low tide. Leikele swam all the way to the small island. There, she rested a little before climbing to the hut. However, when she started walking, she tripped on Kurunanae's nose and fell. Leikele got up, confused.

"I have taken this path three time without tripping and today I fall. Something is not right."

The old woman looked carefully at the ground and discovered Kurunanae's nose which was bleeding from being walked on. Leikele started laughing.

"Ha ha! I told you that I would eventually find you. I haven't even had to look very long for you," and she pulled the end of the nose sticking out of the ground.

Kurunanae was pulled from her hole. In a hurry, Leikele opened her mouth to eat her prey but the other woman stopped her with a wave of her hand and said maliciously, "Listen, don't eat me right away. You can well see that I'm full of sand. You'll break your teeth on me. You must wash me well in the sea before you eat me."

The witch agreed. With one arm, she held her victim while she used the other to quickly wash her. In haste, she open her mouth a second time to swallow Kurunanae but the other woman stopped her.

"No, I'm still really dirty. You're going to hurt your teeth because you have not cleaned me well. Let me go, you'll see, and then I'll be really clean and you can easily devour me."

Without thinking because she was obsessed by the idea of a meal, Leikele released Kurunanae's arm and told her, "Do it quickly, I'm hungry."
Kurunanae's face lit up and "splash," she jumped into the sea. She transformed herself into an adorable little fish. On the small island, Leikele became impatient. She had waited a long time for her prey and little by little she realised what had happened.

"She has made a fool of me," Leikele said.

She became crazy with anger, rolled in the sand, and pulled out clumps of her hair before diving into the sea. She was again searching for her victim. However, Kurunanae was well hidden in the coral and the witch exhausted herself while looking. She ended up being eaten by a shark.

Around the small island of Mele, one can still see the little fish that are called "Kurunanae." It's a fish with a big head and a body full of brown spots. A fish, in any case, that is very, very clever.

This legend was given by a listener of Radio Port-Vila.

The voyage of Atafru
(Erakor)

In ancient times, before the Europeans and their large sailing vessels visited the archipelago, even before the missionaries came to present the Good News and were killed for wanting to destroy and change ways of thinking too quickly, before this new civilisation permeated the Melanesian islands, Erakor was not the large village that it is today. No, before the arrival, in 1858, of Pastor Mackenzie, the village of Erakor was composed of only a few small huts. However, on the hills that are now called Bellevue, there were several villages that went by the names of Epak, Ekpa, and Bufa.

The village of Bufa was the biggest. Like all the villages on the island of Efate, Bufa had its *farea,* its dancing grounds, in the shape of an upside down canoe, covered in reeds with three leaning *tamtams* that often called the villagers to pig killing ceremonies. At Bufa, there were many pigs which were kept in a pen behind dry stones. Each chief had their own pen and their assistants, their *atavis,* had their own smaller pens as well. Now, at Bufa, there are only the remains of these crumbling walls, vestiges of former grandeur.

At Bufa, there was a great chief by the name of Atafru. He was very powerful. He knew everything and everything that he knew was told to him by his *atavis.* However, the great chief had one problem, only one: every night, huge lightning bolts zigzagged through the sky. The thunder rumbled and Atafru, from on top of his hill, looked at the strange horizon.

"Like always, the lightning is coming from Erromango. What a strange thing! If only I knew what this meant! Me, who knows everything and is so powerful! I am humbled before this phenomenon. I don't know where this lightning is coming from..."

"Chief, you should go see. Perhaps the gods have built their *fareas* on Erromango."

"Atavi, you're not thinking, Supwe Na Vanua is on Emae. He is the god of the earth; it is he who is the strongest. He left Erromango a long time ago. No, *atavi,* you are wrong."

"I still think that you should go and see..."

"Atavi, I shall listen to you one more time because past events have shown me that you do not steer me wrong. Tell my people on Erakor to prepare for my departure. Tomorrow morning, I will leave for Erromango. *Atavi,* prepare my leaves and my poisons. Now, leave me alone!"

Atafru, still looking at the lightning on the horizon, was scared by the force of the thunder. He stayed awake the whole night thinking and concentrating.

"Bring me my flute!"

Some young boys brought him his flute and Atafru started to blow into those ten pieces of bamboo connected by a small vine. During the night, the big chief thought and played his flute, planning what he would do while on the water the next day. In the early morning, the chief of Bufa went to Erakor beach. He took a coconut, cut it in two, and formed a small boat with the pieces. Because Atafru was a great chief, he then called on the spirits.

"I want to become very small, small like a flea!"

Atafru got bigger and bigger, blowing up like a balloon. All of a sudden, as if the air was being let out of him, he started to shrink. He shrank and he shrank until he was only as big as a flea. So, he got into the coconut shell and, using it like a canoe, set off for Erromango. In the middle of his voyage, he saw the lightning hanging over that great southern island. He felt he was getting closer. The lightning was brighter and the thunder was stronger. All of a sudden, the coconut was dashed against the coast of the island of Erromango. The chief of Bufa, still tiny, set foot on the land and called the spirits once again. Then, he grew and he grew until he was back to his normal size. Lightning cracked in the sky and pointed the chief in the right direction. Atafru climbed the hills that led into a sudden clearing. There, he saw a strange sight.

In the middle of the clearing, surrounded by mist and moonlight, there was a *nawimba,* a pigeon, an enormous *notou.* It was sitting majestically at the top of a hill surrounded by smaller *nawimbas* that were coming and going, taking care of every whim that the king of the birds might have. Atafru, hidden behind a croton bush, advanced into the smoky environment. A *nawimba* that appeared to be a guardian, the protector of his king, came towards Atafru.

"Stranger, what do you want?"

"I want to approach your chief and to speak with him. I have come from Efate."

"You may approach him, but be very careful. Our queen does not like men from other islands. You have been warned."

Atafru parted the crotons and went into the strange light. At the same time, the queen *nawimba* spread her wings and crowed. A lightning bolt ripped through the sky and the ground started to shake.

"Here is the answer to my night time mystery! Here is the lightning that flashes in the sky above Erromango! Now, I know!"

His eyes still reflecting the strange light, Atafru backed up. He passed close to a young *nawimba* who was a woman soldier there to guard her queen, and in doing so, he looked her in the eyes. The young *nawimba* lowered her head. For the first time in her life, a man had looked at her and she fell in love with him.

Atafru went down to the beach and called the spirits. He became small once again, got into his coconut, and paddled in the direction of Efate. When he got to Erakor,, the chief of Bufa called to his people. The *nakamal* filled quickly with villagers from Bufa, Epak, Elluk, and Ernangire.

"My people, I would like to speak. I have come back from Erromango. I went to see where that lightning that flashes in our sky was coming from. Now, I know the truth. On Erromango, I saw a queen. Yes, a woman! She was a *nawimba* with long, fine wings. Around this queen, lived her subjects, her *atavi,* like us. These were women, *nawimbas,* and some of them were there to protect the queen. Others were cleaning her feathers. They are numerous..."

"Atafru, tell us about the lightning..."

"When the queen wants to stretch, she spreads her wings and crows. At the same time, fire comes out of her feathers, thunder rumbles, and the flashing of her wings turns into lightning."

Time passed. One night, the chief of Bufa and his wife were sleeping in their house. The young *nawimba* who had fallen in love with the chief had escaped from her island. Under the cover of the night, she slid into the house of the one she loved. With her wing, she lightly pushed the chief's wife from her mat and took her place. Every night, this was repeated and the young *nawimba* took the chief's wife's place without anyone noticing. Then, one day, the young *nawimba* became pregnant. Her belly was heavy and she flew low to the ground. Atafru had a little house that was taboo to all except him. In this house was a basket where the chief kept all those secret leaves that gave him his power. The *nawimba* flew low, slid in between the *natangora* leaves and made a nest in the basket. She laid two eggs and then, with a flip of her wing, returned to her queen on Erromango. One day, the young *nawimba* came back. At the same instant, the eggs hatched and two young boys came out. Their mother, the young *nawimba,* took advantage of the chief of Bufa and his wife's trips to the garden to feed her children. They grew and grew.

One day, their mother said, "My children, you are too big now. I am going to leave you. Atafru will feed you. You only have to explain everything to him... everything. I know that he will understand."

The young *nawimba* then left her two boys. Atafru and his wife, just back from the garden, found the two boys.

"What are you doing here?"

238

"Our mother is a *nawimba* from Erromango. She has just left us and has asked you to adopt us."

The chief of Bufa was very happy: he had two sons. To prepare this surprise, he hid them in his house until he felt ready to speak of the event with his people. Finally, he hit the *tamtams* to call his people. When they heard this sound, the people arrived and filled the *nakamal*.

"My people, you will go get yams, taro, and bananas in great quantities. Find dry wood and each one of you will bring a pig. I want to organise a great feast, a very great feast because I am happy."

"What are we celebrating?"

"You will see. Listen to your chief!"

The villagers did as they were told, and the great feast was under way. As soon as everything was ready, the chief again called his people to the *nakamal*.

"We shall wait until my wife arrives."

A little while later, Atafru's wife entered into the communal room, followed by two young boys.

"But...but, who are these young boys?"

"We have never seen them before."

"My people, here are my two sons. The first is named Roe and the other Marak. Rejoice and accept them!"

The old chief Atafru and his wife raised the boys until they were married. Roe eventually had two boys and Marak had two girls. However, one of Roe's boys was a snake and this caused great worry to everyone around.

One day, Roe said to Marak, "Brother, I would like my eldest son to marry your eldest daughter. I would also like your youngest to marry my youngest."

Overhearing this plan, the Marak's eldest daughter said to her father, "I don't want to marry a snake. I want to marry a true man!"

When the younger sister heard her elder sister's complaints, she said, "Don't worry. If you don't want to marry Roe's eldest because he's a snake, I'll marry him. Then, you will marry the second son who was destined to be my husband."

Then, old chief Atafru had the pleasure of marrying Roe's boys with Marak's girls. Everyone was happy and they all danced.

Another day, Atafru asked his people to clear a place to dance under a big banyan tree so that he could organise a party there.

The younger boy said to his brother the serpent, "Brother, we should take our wives to dance in the *nasara.*"

"Brother, you may take my wife and she can dance with you too. Don't forget that I am a snake."

When the dance was over, the snake said to his wife, "Did you enjoy dancing?"

"Yes, the dance was wonderful. But I don't really understand what happened. A man, a very handsome man with light skin, came into the *nasara.* He danced for a very long time. Everyone's eyes were on him. He was so handsome. All of a sudden, he disappeared. No one knew who he was."

Another time, the village organised a second dance. The serpent stayed at home while his wife went to dance. While everyone was dancing, the snake changed skins and became a handsome man. He put some flowers in his hair, put some croton leaves in his belt, and went to dance. When the dance was over, the handsome man left and became a snake once more. Then, he went to sleep.

The next day, the serpent asked his wife, "Did you enjoy the dance?"

"It was great! The handsome man came back. His dancing was wonderfull. But we still don't know who he was..."

Another day, yet another dance was organised. As usual, the snake refused to go. But this time, the snake's wife suspected something.

She said to her sister, "I always go dancing and my husband always stays at home. This time, I will stay with him..."

The woman went back to the house, hid, and watched her husband. The serpent shed his skin and changed into the handsome dancing boy. While he was dancing, his wife took the snake skin and burned it. Then, she returned to dance with the others. Just as usual, a little before the dance was over, the handsome boy returned to the house. However, when he got there, he found only a pile of ashes.

His wife then came in and said, "My friend, you are a real man now. The snake is dead! Come and let's go dancing!"

This legend comes from the island of Erakor.
It was given in Bislama by Liser Sablan.
Adapted by Paul Gardissat.

Nabanga n° 25 (1976)

The origin of clan names
(Efate)

In ancient times, there were two men by the name of Roy, meaning great chief, who lived in Tukutuku on the island of Efate.

One of them was named Roy Lep, meaning the eldest chief, the greatest chief, Marik Roy. The other was named Roy Mur, meaning the youngest chief, the second in command. Roy Lep had a son who was a snake, whereas Roy Mur had two daughters who were fully human. Roy Lep decided to marry off his son, the snake. He went to find Roy Mur and asked him for one of his daughters. Roy Lep gave him his eldest. When he went back home, Roy Lep spoke to his daughter-in-law.

"You know that your husband is a snake, but you have never seen him. He lives on a branch in the *banyan* tree. You must make him something to eat now. When you are ready, your husband will come down from his tree. Don't be frightened when the snake lays his head on your knees to eat."

The new wife did what she was told and prepared the meal. However, when the snake came down from the tree and approached her, despite the warnings of her father-in-law, she was overcome by fear and ran all the way to her father's house. Roy Lep went once again to find Roy Mur. He asked for the hand of the second daughter in marriage for his son, obtained a positive response, took her back to his house, and proceeded to give her the same warning. The new wife prepared the meal, wasn't frightened when her husband came down, and the snake was able to eat.

A little while later, the snake came back, found his wife, and suggested a swim in the ocean. Once in the water, the snake swam away from the woman, went into an isolated spot, shed his skin, and became a man. He went back to his wife and, of course, was not recognised. He was able, though, to convince her of his transformation and both of them, happy as could be, went back to Marik Roy's house. The chief, after hearing the explanation, rejoiced and ordered that a feast be prepared.

A few months later, the woman was pregnant. One evening, she went with her husband in their canoe to fish. But, their departure was witnessed by a woman *lisepsep*. The *lisepsep* are, let's say, a primitive race of human beings with long ears and straggly hair. They look like African monkeys without the hair. They live in the bush, naked, eating roots, plants, and fruit. It is said that some can be found in the island's interior, gifted with great powers, but, for the most part, inoffensive.

The *lisepsep* in question swam to catch up with the canoe. One there, she slipped aboard and, without the husband noticing, pushed the wife over the edge and took her place. This woman *lisepsep* was also pregnant and the husband didn't notice the switch.

However, the woman who had fallen in the water did not drown. She was taken by the current all the way to the island of Emae where a man found her and married her. She gave birth to a boy and eventually had three other boys with the man from Emae. The children grew.

One day, the boys went with some other children from Emae to collect some yams. The four brothers gathered red yams while the other boys gathered white ones. While it was cooking, the *laplap* became entirely red. The four brothers claimed the whole *laplap* for themselves, saying that they were the only ones that gathered red yams. The other children from Emae were indignant.

"You aren't from here. You are eating our yams. Go back to where you came from."

The four brothers went back to their mother's house, told her what had happened and asked, "Where are we from?"

Their mother told them the story and decided to leave Emae. She had her four boys build her a big canoe and on the sail she fixed the insignia of Roy, the sign of the chiefs. She left two sons with her husband on Emae and left with the other two, including her son with Roy.

The canoe set ground on Efate near Tukutuku. Marik Roy's son, whose wife, the lisepsep, was finally getting ready to give birth in a nearby hut, saw the canoe with the sign of Roy. He then understood that it was his real wife who was coming and that the other woman was a usurper. Quickly, he placed dry leaves around the hut where the *lisepsep* was giving birth and set them alight. The hut burnt to the ground. There was only a large stone left of the place where the *lisepsep* had given birth. The occupants of the canoe were well received, the true wife of Marik Roy recognised, and a feast was held. She told her story and was reunited with her husband.

At this time, on Efate, there were many chiefs. However, Chief Marik Roy, chief of Tukutuku, was incontestably the greatest. All the other chiefs obeyed him. When there was a great ceremony, the chief who killed the most pigs was always considered the most important. This was always Marik Roy. The chief of Bufa, Marik Merman, ruled over a greater number of men. Nevertheless, he was of an inferior rank.

To celebrate the return of his daughter-in-law, Marik Roy prepared a great feast to which he invited people from all over Efate and the outlying islands of Emae and Tongoa. The guests each brought a gift: a coconut, a yam, a fish. As a result, each guest was given a name by Chief Marik Roy and it was in this way that clan names were born.

This legend was told by John Iowan from Pango on March 20, 1964.
He had heard this story from his grandfather, Kalsong, the great fire chief of Erakor.

Previously unpublished.

TAFEA Province

The bird woman
(Tanna)

A very long time ago, a man by the name of Ko-oman took up his bow and arrow and went to hunt one morning. A *punung'ha,* a green pigeon with a red breast, was perched on a the branch of a *neses* tree. Ko-oman shot at him and missed. He tried again, and missed yet another time.

He returned the next morning and saw the bird who, before he could shoot, came to perch on the tip if his arrow and, speaking in his language, said, "Don't shoot. Take me with you to the place that I tell you, and I will show you something."

Ko-oman took the bird who then lead him to a spring and told him to go back to his mother's house and then return to this same place the next day. Ko-oman didn't say a word to his mother, went to sleep and then returned to the spring in the morning. As he was looking for the green pigeon, a beautiful young girl approached him and said, "Don't look any further for I am the bird. Take me to your house." Ko-oman's mother was delighted to see her son coming with a woman. She offered the young woman something to eat, but she refused. At this time, gardens were not cultivated and people obtained their sustenance from wild root crops such as *nowitang, nopotem,* or fruits like *nekeriang.* The woman did not want to eat that evening either. However, when night fell she turned her self into the bird *punung'ha* and flew away.

In the morning, she was back. Ko-oman and his mother discovered some root crops in front of the house that they cooked and ate. They were excellent. The woman explained that she had brought them at dawn. This was the yam, called for short *taüiron,* that has been cultivated ever since, making the people forget about the *napotem* and the *nekeriang.*

Every night, the woman became a bird and flew away. In the morning, new provisions were always discovered. It was in this way that she brought sugar cane and different varieties of bananas. Eventually, the woman had a son that she brought up, aided by Ko-oman's mother. When the time of ripe breadfruit came and many had been gathered, the grandmother heard the baby crying, trying to make it understood that his chest was sore.

Instead of calming him, she started to scold him. The mother returned at this exact moment, heard her, and became furious. She took all the breadfruit and threw it all the way to the other side of the sea.

The grandmother saw her and the woman, still unhappy, took her son, put a yam in her basket, and declared that she was leaving because her son had been scolded. She demanded that the grandmother stay and try to marry off her son, Ko-oman, because she would not be coming back. She walked away towards the sea. Ko-oman, who had returned to the house, ran after her and arrived on the coast just in time to see his wife and his son pulled under by the waves.

Overwhelmed with sorrow, he took one of his arrows and ran it through his heart. He was immediately changed into a rock. This rock is still visible at Ipak on the west coast. It is named Ko-oman. His grass skirt still exists as well, as can be seen by the many vines that cover half of the rock. There is also a wild yam that lies on the rock, a descendant of the yam abandoned by the bird-woman, the *punung-ha.*

Legend collected by Josepho Bulesap from the Assessor John (Tanna)
Nabanga n° 6 (04-06-75)

Semusemu, the ogre from Tanna
(Tanna)

A long, long time ago, so long ago that it seems that even the elders of Tanna have forgotten it, the island of Tanna was a well populated island in the south of the New Hebrides. Across from Tanna, there was another island, much smaller in size and population. It was a mountainous island with rivers, many rivers which overflowed during the rainy season and that were dry in times of drought. Covering a part of this island was a certain type of pampas, those long grasses that we call "white grass." Covering the other part of the island were forests, huge, deep forests where men hid. This island was called Aneityum.

In the forests of Aneityum, there lived hidden a terrible man, tall, very tall, with long, natty hair, an immense beard, enormous, piercing eyes, big, hairy ears, and a monstrously dirty body covered in pustules and hair so long that from afar one would think that it was dried reed leaves. Men from other islands thought that this monster was covered in leaves! But no! It was really hair! His hands could crush trees and when he moved, the earth trembled under his feet. This monster that lived on Aneityum was an ogre. His name was Semusemu. Semusemu had eaten the entire population of Tanna. There was no one left. He had eaten the men, the women, the old, the young. He had even eaten the children! Indeed, he preferred children.

The ogre Semusemu had devoured the whole population save one, a woman. Yes, one lone woman had survived the carnage, one only, a young girl. Her name was Naleya. Naleya was a lovely girl who, with horror, had watched Semusemu's feasts. He had come to her village and had eaten her father, mother, grandparents, brothers, and sisters. Everyone had been eaten. Only she had been left in the village. This was when she decided to run, run far away. She hid herself in a hole in a rock and waited. She waited for a long time, and when the ogre finally returned to Aneityum, the ground stopped quaking beneath Naleya's feet and she came out of her hole to find herself alone, alone on the island of Tanna.

One day, Naleya was sleeping in a rock hole near the beach when something strange happened. Next to her, a vine was growing, a vine that is called *"Nolu"* in that region of Tanna. This vine approached her, laid itself on top of her, and Naleya felt something bizarre: the vine entered her. The two coupled. Some time later, Naleya felt her belly swell, and she was sick as women are apt to be during this time. Thus, she believed that she was pregnant.

Indeed, she was pregnant by the vine that grew near the sea, the *Nolu* vine. Nine months after the vine had penetrated her, Naleya gave birth to twins: Kaseasau and Kaniapnin. They were two magnificent babies, two little men from Tanna, happy to be alive and whom their mother watched grow with fear.

"My children, you are so handsome but so alone! What will become of you when Semusemu knows that you exist? What will your lives be like? My children, my little children, you are so handsome!"

The mother and the two boys continued to lead their secret lives. The boys grew and grew. Naleya thought, one day, that they were ready to become men. She took a piece of sharpened bamboo and circumcised them. They had now become men, true men and she turned to thoughts about their future, their education.

"My children, come, I will teach you how to use a bow. You stretch this cord that I have woven from coconut fibres. You put the arrow in the centre, and with your left hand you hold the arrow steady, then with your right, you pull the cord towards yourself using the end of the arrow. Then you let the arrow go. Be careful of your fingers when the cord rebounds. Your turn, Kaseasau!"

Kaseasau shot his first arrow. His mother, very happy, handed the bow to her second son and told him, "Your turn, Kaniapnin! No, don't pull the cord so tightly towards you. Good! Now the arrow…"

And the arrow embedded itself in the bark of a sapling.

"Now, I will teach you to use the spear. Hold it this way, towards the centre, pull your arm back, make this movement with your left leg and throw it in front of you."

One of the twins touched the targeted object, the other missed. The mother, the teacher of her children, said, "Kaniapnin, you threw it well. As for you, Kaseasau, you must practice!"

Every day, at the same time, Naleya taught her children to become warriors. Kaniapnin revealed himself to be the most gifted of the twins. As for their mother, she felt that one day her boys would become strong warriors. And that day arrived. She considered them ready to execute her project and told them of the existence of the man-eater, the existence of the ogre, Semusemu.

"Children, you have grown up. You are circumcised, you know how to use the bow and the spear. I am going to speak with you. A long time ago, on this big island there lived many people. We were very happy when, one day, an ogre named Semusemu came from Aneityum. He devoured our entire family, and I was left alone on Tanna. All alone. All of our ancestors have been eaten. This is why revenge must be taken and I am counting on you two."

The two boys left their home in the north of the island and followed the path Kwotexen, all along the coast. Little by little, they made their way down to Ikamer, their mother sticking lances in the ground at regular intervals along the way. Once they had reached Ikamer, they hid themselves behind some big rocks. The mother drove the last two lances into the black ashes of the volcano, marking the end of the road at Nesey and Nepina. It was also known by the name of the *nakamal* Namreaermene that once sat above this place.

Naleya went and hid on a hill, just behind Loupurmat. There, she lit a fire to cook laplap for her two children. To do this, she rubbed a piece of hard wood against a piece of soft wood and the fire sprang to life.

The ogre Semusemu, living on the island of Aneityum, saw the smoke rise up from Tanna. "Look here," he said, "there's smoke on Tanna! But I have eaten all of Tanna's inhabitants. What's happening?"

Semusemu, angry, crossed the sea in big steps and arrived on the island of Tanna, emitting a cacophony of violent noises. The two children, hidden behind the rocks, felt Semusemu's breath upon them. Kaniapnin, dead frightened, wanted to run away. His brother, Kaseasau, held him by the arm and said, "Don't be afraid. Stay there and we'll see what happens."

At the same time, the ogre arrived, the whole island shook under his footsteps. Kaniapnin threw his lance at him but missed. The youngest did the same and the lance plunged into Semusemu's body; the ogre was wounded but kept advancing towards the boys. Naleya, their mother, who had assisted in the attack from high on her hill, ran towards her children singing,

> *"Narekmil, narekmil,*
> *Kemyako? Kamyako?*
> *Rendo! Rendo!"*

Through her song, the mother was encouraging her children to kill the ogre, the man-eater. However, Semusemu, still upright but covered in lances, continued to advance on the boys saying, "You are running for no reason. Reeds hang from your arses, but I will eat you."

The mother held some reed leaves and a *tapa* belt in her hands that she would shake periodically in the direction of Semusemu, always singing,   .

> *"Narekmil, narekmil,*
> *Kemyako? Kamyako?*
> *Rendo! Rendo! Wou!"*

The ogre continued to approach saying, "You are running for no reason. Reeds can cut your arses, but I will eat you. I will eat you!"

The two boys collected the lances that had been set along the road and threw them. The ogre's body was pierced in many places. He reeled, and at Lamwinu, he vomited his liver. Semsemu's liver is still there today; it has been transformed into a rock.

Semusemu continued to approach, pulling out, one after another, the lances that Kaseasau and Kaniapnin had driven into his body. But alas, Kaseasau had used all but one lance, the last one held tight in his hand. As usual, he was frightened and turned towards his brother to ask, "What should I do, Kaniapnin? This is my last lance!"

Quickly, his brother responded, "You must target his ear, my brother, his ear!"

Kaseasau did exactly as his brother had asked him. He targeted Semusemu's ear, the ogre advancing ever nearer. Kaseasau threw the lance and it hit its mark; Semusemu fell to the ground. The whole island of Tanna shook under his weight.

The two brothers ran away, not able to believe that they had won. A little while later, they timidly sent a red bird, the *bweleng-bweleng,* to see if the monster was really dead. The *bweleng-bweleng* did as it was asked. He went and bit the ogre on the arm. Semusemu did not move. He bit him again. Nothing. Thus, he returned to the brothers to tell them that the ogre was indeed dead.

"He is truly dead!"

However, this was not enough proof to completely reassure them, so the brothers sent another bird, a type of parrot called *Sul.* The *Sul* sat on Semusemu's body and bit him all over his hooked nose. He saw that the ogre did not move and he went back to tell the brothers, "He is truly dead!"

But Kaseasau and Kaniapnin were not yet reassured, so they sent a little bird named Kawia Meta Meta. This one went inside the ogre's opened mouth and came out the other side, carrying a piece of dried, coagulated blood in its beak. This time, the heroes were satisfied.

Then, Naleya arrived, happy and proud of her progeny. She took a piece of sharp bamboo and cut open the ogre's body. Everyone that he had ever eaten came out: the biggest and smallest of animals, men, women, the whole population of Tanna!

Kaseasau, triumphant, gave each man a *nakamal* which he had named, and then he took a palm frond and hit the ground hard until it began to shake.

Thus, the island began a normal life again. Everything reappeared: birds, insects, animals… and especially people!

This legend was told in Bislama by Chief Tuk from Tanna.

Nabanga n°82/83 (1978)

Yasur, "the volcano man"
(Tanna)

Having come from the vast stretches of southern oceans, Yasur started to look for a home suitable to his liking. He tested the depths, here and there, of all possible under-water places but he couldn't find the ideal place anywhere. He thus spent days and nights without any success.

However, one lovely morning, full of ardent desire to find his home at last, he came ashore on the island of Tanna at the point of Loanpakel. Once on dry land, he took the form of a human being so as not to rouse the suspicions of the people living on the island. He criss-crossed the north part of the island, passing seven villages and asking at each one if he could rest there for a while in order to catch his breath. No one was willing to welcome him.

He continued on his way and that night arrived in the village of Namtain which is close to the sea. Yasur saw many advantages to staying there and so once again took the form of a volcano without difficulty. He stayed there for five days and five nights but in the end was not pleased with the place because, several times during the night and day, the sea came and tickled his feet. He decided to find asylum elsewhere.

In the afternoon, when he had become Yasur "The Volcano Man" again, he left the village of Namtain in the north of the island and started to head south-east. He kept on, village after village, Loeasia, Wesisi, White Sand, always prospecting for a suitable place to rest but never finding one. In this way, he arrived at Siwi in the middle of the night.

He saw smoke rising from a small hut and beside it, two old women. The two old women were watching two *laplaps* that they had just put into a traditional oven: that is to say that the *laplap* were well-wrapped with leaves, laid on red-hot rocks, and then completely covered with earth to preserve the heat. Thus, the two *laplaps* looked like two little volcanoes placed one next to the other.

Yasur found the occasion perfect to stop and smoke a pipe before taking up his journey again. With all the charm and politeness required of the situation, Yasur asked the two old women to light his pipe. The two old women, pleased to help a traveller from far away, jumped to his aid and even, when Yasur asked, let him sit in their hut while smoking.

Yasur felt very comfortable next to the two ovens that were giving off an agreeable heat: it was the perfect place for him. In a little while, his desire became truth. The ground shook with such violence that the sound was heard all over the island.

The two old women panicked and ran for the door of their hut only to see Yasur sink quickly into the ground and disappear forever.

The earth was shaking harder and harder and huge cracks were opening at the feet of the two old women. Enormous flames followed by burning lava swallowed up the two old women and their hut, covering them forever.

This is how, at Siwi on the island of Tanna, Yasur "The Volcano Man" was born. If you have the occasion to visit the island of Tanna one day, you will see the conical form of Yasur in the village of Namtain in the north of the island, and at the foot of the volcano Yasur at Siwi, the two *laplap* covered by lava which look like two small volcanoes.

Nabanga n°31 (1976)

The Newak Newak
(Tanna)

At that time, the ancestors' spirits roamed the island of Tanna. Certain spirits wanted to contact the living but could not because they were part of the hereafter. So, invisible, they had to content themselves with following and imitating the living of Tanna.

In the village of Lonelapen, two men were busy cleaning and doing their hair. On the island of Tanna, hair styling was an art and men were often asked to make sacrifices like hiding and not approaching women and girls for months at a time. There was an upcoming feast, and the two men had decided to make themselves handsome. They wanted to wash their hair because they were soon to appear in public. They went to the beach and started to rub their hair with coconut oil. Then, they went to a little beach called Lowanemrapan where they swam.

While they were coming out of the water, they saw a devil that was preparing to swim. It was taking its intestines from inside its stomach. The two men hid and watched the amazing scene. The devil took out its guts, which seemed interminable, and buried them in the sand. Then, he went to swim in order to clean out all the bile in his stomach. When the two men saw that the devil wasn't looking, they dug up the intestines, wound them around a piece of wood, and carried them off. They ran as fast as they could to their village.

When the devil got out of the water, he couldn't find his intestines. He looked everywhere, but in vain. His organs had disappeared. He started to sniff the north wind, but no olfactory clue indicated what direction his intestines had taken. So, he sniffed the south wind, but still had no clue. Then, he snuffled the east wind and realized that this was the direction his intestines had taken. He decided to follow their trail. The minute he left the beach, he started to sing and from the heights of the bush, his intestines answered him. The devil listened attentively to the intestines' song and understood that two men had stolen them. The devil became angry. He started walking again and sang the same song several times. Each time, his intestines answered him.

Thus guided, the devil arrived in the village of Ivunmet. Here, he started to sing again. His intestines answered him from a place near Lonelapen. The devil started forward and eventually came to the Lonelapen *nakamal* where he found the two men. The devil jumped towards the men but, at the same instant, the two men threw its intestines in the fire. The devil died instantly. Its soul walked the path of Hell on Earth into the volcano Yasur where it is still burning today. Its body can still be found in the village of Lonelapen on the island of Tanna. It is now a stone that is called Newak Newak.

This legend was given to Joseph Boulesap by Yapsen Kuras of Lonelapen village.

Nabanga N°101 (1979),

The red fowl and the sea crocodiles
(Aniwa)

Once upon a time, on the island of Aniwa, a red fowl was very bored. She decided to leave her island for the big island of Tanna, arriving by Loanbakel Point. However, the strait was too large and the poor fowl didn't know what to do. She often walked along the coast looking from afar at the island of Tanna with its border of green palm trees, the heavy smoke of its volcano, and it high mountains habitually hidden in the clouds.

Suddenly, she had an idea. At this time, there were many sea crocodiles that lived in and around the blue lagoon of Aniwa. The little fowl went to see them. She said to them, "My dear friends, we shall count how many sea crocodiles and how many red fowl there are on our island."

The sea crocodiles thought for a minute and then responded, "Dear little fowl, what a good idea! But we do not know how to do this."

"Well!" said the red fowl, "we shall start with you, dear sirs. Listen well. You will line up, one behind another, from here to Loanbakel which you see across the way. When you are all in a straight line, head to tail, I will jump from one to another counting."

The sea crocodiles deliberated for a moment and thought, "That fowl from Aniwa is clever!"

"When I have finished counting you," continued the fowl, "we shall count all the fowl on the island. We will then know exactly whether there are more sea crocodiles or red fowl."

"Alright, we shall line ourselves up."

Thus, the sea crocodiles left their lagoon and lined themselves up, head to tail, from Aniwa to Loanbakel Point. The red fowl jumped from back to back, counting quickly and seriously.

"One sea crocodile, two sea crocodiles, three sea crocodiles…," and she continued in this way across the entire strait. Finally, she arrived on the beach at Tanna.

She started to laugh and counted, "One sea imbecile, two sea imbeciles…! What idiots you all are, my dear friends! I was not interested in knowing how many of you there are; I only needed a bridge to get to Tanna. I will call if ever I need you again to get back to Aniwa!"

Alas, the red fowl had spoken too soon. She was still on the back of the last crocodile, who, to hear better, had turned himself around. He opened his mouth as wide as possible and in one foul swoop, pulled out all of her tail feathers.

"Oh!" she cried. "I congratulated myself too quickly!"

The little red fowl, shamed and ridiculed without her tail feathers, ran to hide in the bush. The crocodiles, furious at having been tricked by a fowl, left the south to go live in the north of the archipelago.

This legend was sent in by a Radio Port-Vila listener, Miss Veronique Runa.

Nabanga N° 23 (28/02/76)

The birth of Futuna
(Futuna)

The Polynesian god Maori Tiki, Mauitikitiki of Emao also called Mwatikitiki, lived in Tanna on Mount Melen. He owned an underwater residence called Rueitonga that held the sun and the rain in two prisms. When he wanted to make it rain or to have the sun shine, he opened either one or the other. Rueitonga was located under a rock near the shore. Once a year in September, one could reach it by diving before going through a magic stone ritual. If the year was good, the water in the hole would become clear and the sea swept offerings into it. If the water was murky, the current would sweep the offerings out into the sea and the year would be marked by strife. This happened a long time ago while Kuhngen was creating the earth which was still naked and without bush.

Mwatikitiki lived the rest of the time at Enarupan in the south of the island of Tanna with his wife Perepnap. They didn't have any children and were just becoming worried about this when Perepnap became pregnant.

One night when Perepnap went to lay down on her mat, a woman came to her and said, "Perepnap, the night is very calm. Don't you want to go fishing with coconut palm torches to light our way?"

Under the spell of the engaging voice, Perepnap recognised the devil.
"But I don't know you," she responded, "and I would like to sleep."

The devil insisted and Perepnap, hypnotised, finally gave in. She followed her fully aware of the fact that the only desire of this devilish woman was to kill her. Despite her stupor, she tried to regain consciousness and to stay alert. When the women had arrived at the rocks just before leaving the deep bush, Perepnap turned to pick up a fistful of her ancestral land.
"If I die," she said, "I will die with the memory of what I love."

The devil pressed her, "Come on, what are you doing? Here. Take these coconut fronds! Light them and let's get to fishing quickly!"

They started their hike through the rocks. As they were walking, shells were pushing against the rocks and setting free small avalanches of stone when suddenly the devil went behind Perepnap and pushed her. She slipped on the stones and fell into the water screaming. In the black night, demonic rites mixed with the cries and moans of the unfortunate woman.

The devil yelled, "Here is the most beautiful, the wife of the god now dead and gone! I hope the fish rip you apart and devour you so that your name is never heard again."

Perepnap tried to swim but the night closed in around her and made it impossible for her to find her way. The coast fell further and further away as the current swept her out only to then throw her violently back against the rocks. She tried to hold on but in vain. Each time that she was able to grab a hold of a rock, the devil crushed her fingers.

"No! You cannot hold on to the rocks, wife of the god that I love! Die! Disappear forever! You don't have any chance to save yourself, you are lost! Die quickly so that I never see you again, ever again! Disappear in the waves!" screamed the devil as her laugh pierced the night.

Once again, Perepnap swam, grabbed hold of the rocks, was stepped on, and was taken away by the current. And again, she was thrown back against the reef by the waves. Her hands were bloody and she was losing her breath. Her last try failed as the waves threw her against the stones and her right hand was crushed with even more brutality.

"I told you to die," repeated the woman.

The current pulled an exhausted Perepnap towards the deep. She let herself be taken a little and then tried again to swim with what little of her strength remained.

Seeing her being taken further out, the devil yelled, "I hope the sharks eat you and that you suffer terribly! I am now the wife of the fisher of islands, the wife of Mwatikitiki!"

Remembering that Perepnap was pregnant, she chose a round stone near the edge of the coast, the Tapugha, and swallowed it. Her stomach thus became enormous and she took on the traits of Perepnap.

"I am Perepnap! I am pretty, aren't I? I am the wife of a god!" she yelled dementedly. "You find my belly too big? Maybe, but don't forget that I'm pregnant, pregnant by a god, by Mwatikitiki! " Her crazy laugh rang out again.

She then went to her 'husband.' During this time, Perepnap was swimming towards the deep. The child that she was carrying made her tired. She was on the edge of total exhaustion, ready to give up but she still struggled with all of her might. Her bloodied, crushed fingers hurt her horribly. The saltwater burned her raw flesh. Finally, she couldn't go on.

In a last effort, she cried, "I am truly the wife of the fisher of islands, the wife of the strongest god. I command a reef to break through these waters at this instant so that I may rest myself,"

Perepnap had barely said the words when a reef surged through the waves and lifted her above the water.

Little by little she regained her breath and added, "You, reef, grow a little higher. I want to see an ironwood tree, the Casuarina, that is over there on Enarupan!"

The reef grew a little higher.

"A little higher, I can't quite see the ironwood tree yet," she said.

The reef grew a little higher.

"I think that I can see it. Grow just a little higher. Yes, that's it. I can see it now; you have grown enough. And because I still have a bit of courage left, let's create!"

Perepnap, who was still holding a bit of the ground from Tanna in her left hand, patted it against the newly formed island creating, thus, the ground of the new islet. Then, she laid back and took a deep breath. She stayed this way, alone, on her new island until the day when she gave birth to two twins, Namakia and Nakia.

They grew up. One day, one of the two asked their mother where their father was. Perepnap pointed to the big island that filled the horizon.

"That black dot, the ironwood tree, that's where your father lives."

The two children looked intently at the point on the horizon.

"We don't know much and we would like to know what men have and how they live," said Namakia.

"Would you like to know men?" asked their mother. "On the main land, over there across the way, men use bows, arrows, spears, *nalnals* and canoes."

"Mother, teach us to use these things!" cried the two children in chorus.

Perepnap responded, "Yes, my children, I will teach you everything a man must know. But don't ever forget this, my children," said Perepnap. "You must know how to defend yourself and kill your enemies. If not, they will kill you."

"You must know how to use a canoe to get from one point to another and to fish. The bow is held this way. Look, you stretch it with an arrow, more, even more, and then you aim like this and let go. The spear is different. Be careful because it is bigger and more difficult to throw. You pull back and throw like this. To the *nalnal* now! Always keep it strapped to your back like a walking stick and use it to hit like this. With the canoe, you go fishing. You direct it with a paddle and you turn it like this in your hand."

"Mother, let's go chop down a tree," said one of the children. "We'll hollow it out and make a canoe."

"And when it's done, we'll go see our father," added the second one.

They all left, chose a tree, hollowed it out and when the canoe was finished, Perepnap said, "My children. Your father is a god. I understand your desire, but you will go alone. I won't follow you and I forbid you to come back with him."

"Mother, we will do as you say. We will go to see him and then we will come back to you without him. We promise!" they responded.

The next morning, everything was ready for their departure. Perepnap gave them a *laplap* to tide them over en route, a coconut to quench their thirst and a *kava* plant to bring them healing sleep.

As some last advice, Perepnap said, "My children, be very careful. Always listen to my voice which will follow you during your long journey, your first journey. "

Today, one can still hear Perepnap's voice coming from a hole in the rocks, Tahmichi, that still exist at Mission Bay. On very calm days, the sea goes inside and makes a very particular sound that can be heard from far away. This is the voice of Perepnap.

"When you hear my voice, you may paddle. When the sound of my voice is lost, you will hear the sound of your father's voice, the backwash of the waves on Enarupan. Now, my children, give me a kiss. You may leave."

They heard the voice of Perepnap and the two boys got into their canoe and left the island of Futuna in the direction of Tanna. They paddled, constantly hearing the voice of their mother.

"Look," said one of the two, "the main land is getting closer. I can't hear the voice of our mother anymore. I hear the voice of our father. Listen to the noise of the shore, the waves on the sand. Look at that black dot over there. Let's go!"

The two children paddled but chose the wrong place to moor.

Once again they heard their mother's voice say, "My children, you are going the wrong way. Come back."

They started to paddle again. The voice of their father, the backwash of the waves on Enarupan, was heard above the general din. They finally stepped foot on the island. At dawn, Mwatikitiki's men arrived and asked them what they were doing there. The children answered that they were there to see their father, Mwatikitiki. Despite their initial surprise, the men quickly passed from indignation to anger.

"No," they said, "Mwatikitiki can't be your father. He has a wife but no children."

They then jumped on the boys, ready to kill them. Luckily, the news of their arrival had already reached the ears of the god who then asked to see them. When they presented themselves to their father, the devil who was standing next to him jumped for joy at the thought of fresh meat. She was already imagining the big feast when one of the children spoke.

"I am your son. You are my father. This woman is a devil, a usurper that threw my mother into the waves and swallowed a round stone, the Tapugha, to make you believe that she was your wife, our mother who carried us."

The other child insisted, "Yes, my father. We are your true children, your only children. She is not pregnant; she has only swallowed a round stone. Our mother, your wife, was washed up on the little island across the way, Futuna, where she now lives alone. Acknowledge your children. Stop being tricked. We beg you! You are our father."

"That is perhaps true," responded Mwatikitiki. "You others, go and find some food and bring some dry wood."

The men obeyed and made a big fire.

"The fire is ready. Where is the meat that we are going to roast?"

"Don't worry, you'll see," said the god.

When the fire had gone out, the men took out the stones. Mwatikitiki commanded them to catch the woman, put her in the hole and then to cover her with the burning stones. The devil couldn't escape. She cried in pain and little while later an explosion was heard: the stone in her stomach had burst. Mwatikitiki had his proof.

"It is true, this woman was a devil. How could I have thought that she was pregnant for such a long time? You are truly my sons, but where is your mother?"

The children pointed to the small island across the water, remembering that their mother had forbidden them to bring him back. However, the youngest one insisted.

"He is our father. We shall bring him," he said to his brother.

This is how the three of them found themselves on the way to Futuna. When Perepnap saw them arrive, she turned the island into a desert. The children understood and as soon as they put their feet on the ground, night began to fall. One of the two left for a moment and returned with a *kava* plant that he started to chew. The other then left and came back with a steaming hot *laplap*. All this intrigued their father.

"My wife has not shown herself to me but this *laplap* was made by her. Why this wrath against me?"

Night fell when Perepnap finally appeared and said severely, "You three will sleep together. I will sleep further away."

The children, laying in the hut next to their father, couldn't get to sleep. They thought and thought about what they could do to reconcile their father and mother. The youngest found an solution. He got up, wet his father with urine and waited. Mwatikitiki woke up suddenly.

"Nakia, what have you done? I'm all wet!"

Then he went back to bed. Namakia then approached his father, waited a couple of seconds and employed the same strategy. However, this time, Perepnap saw everything and understood what was happening.

She finally conceded, "Mwatikitiki, my children will not let you sleep peacefully. Come, then, and sleep next to me."

This legend was given in Bislama by Willy Lakai of Futuna,
monitor of the Yohananan Custom School on Tanna.

Nabanga N°108-109 (1979)

The marriage of kava and the coconut palm
(Erromango)

Three spirits live in *kava*. The first of these is a spirit named Melvon Mauripe, the second, Norlemama, and the third, Toretakai. All three are ruled by their chief, the great *kava* spirit, Nelumplenelo, who lives at Isvi (Antioch) in the southwest of the island of Erromango.

One day, Nelumplenelo left his house to cross the island. He wanted to get to a place named Portnarvin in order to commune with the spirit of the sun and rain. This spirit was named Umaeghoghor and was a giant snake that lived in a cave. The two spirits stayed talking a long time. Three young female devils, the spirits of yams, bananas, and taro, along with the girl spirits of Nombo, came to visit the *kava* spirit. The spirit of the yam came forward first and spoke to Nelumplenelo.

"Man, great man, you are very good. I love you. I want to marry you. If you would like, we can first be friends and then get married."

The *kava* answered, "Young woman, tell me, what do you want of me and what will you give me in exchange?"

"I think that you will sleep well next to me. Then, after having drunk of you, men will come to me and serve themselves. The men will eat my flesh and I will heighten your effects on them. Men will feel wonderful thanks to us."

Nelumplenelo answered, "What you propose is very interesting, but you must look for another husband"

Then, it was the taro spirit's turn to come forward.

"Man, great man, you are so good. If we get married, we can first be friends and then be married."

The *kava* answered, "Of course, but first I would like to know exactly what you want and what you propose to give to me?"

"My food is the best. After having drunk of you, men will eat me. Remember, when men clean you, chew you, and then spit you out onto a leaf, it is my leaf that receives you."

The great *kava* spirit replied, "Your offer is very interesting but you must look for someone else to marry. I am too big for you and if you ever had to protect me, you would not be able to do it."

Then, the Fiji taro approached Nelumplenelo and made the same request. The great *kava* spirit refused again.

Moses Jobo, *Mared blong Kava wetem Kokonas*
(colour, acrylon canvas, 200 x 150 cm)

"Sorry, but you look too much like your sister."

Not far from there, at Ifo, a coconut palm spirit named Nambenia was talking to one of her friends, another coconut palm spirit named Iakorau.

"I think that we should go to Portnarvin to visit our friends."

Both of then set off for Portnarvin. On the way, they passed an old woman spirit that lived on top of the Urapia hill. This old woman was called Umlatni.

When the two women arrived at the top of the hill, Umlatni said, "Hey! What are you doing here? Are you taking a walk? Do you want something?"

"Yes, we are taking a walk... a walk to come and see you."

"So, what do you want?"

"We have heard that there is someone important at Portnarvin. Why hasn't he married yet?"

Umlatni said, "Would you like me to go with you?"

Nambenia, the girl spirit of the coconut palm, was delighted and the three of them set off for Portnarvin. They went by Ifo, went down into Ranulevie, and behind the hills of Portnarvin where a great *burao* tree can be seen. The woman stopped here and the coconut palm spirit looked towards Ralponnaghave. The great *kava* spirit from Antioch was there. He was with his friend, Umaeghoghor, the snake spirit of the weather. Nambenia, who was dressed in her best clothes, spoke to Umlatni.

"Could you go and tell them that I would like to marry that man?"

Umlatni went to speak with Umaerghoghor and said to him, "The woman over there would like to know if your friend would like to meet her. She wants to marry him."

The snake passed the message to his friend.

The *kava* spirit called to the woman, "Approach, coconut palm, and tell me why you would like to marry me."

"Here is what I have to offer. After having unearthed you, men will pull off my bark to use in cleaning you. Then, they will begin to chew you. Next, they will put you on my skirt (coconut "cloth," *ninges* in the language of Erromango). They will then take a little of my water and mix me with you. They will press you and pour you into one of my fruit. The man will only have to lift up this coconut to drink you. After that, they will eat my flesh. They will do this to make you happy, and I will be happy too. The man will be drunk and me, I will prolong his drunken state so that he will want to do it again."

265

When the *kava* heard this, he said, "Let us be married!"

The first ceremony was organised. Then, the two spirits, accompanied by Umaeghoghor the snake, went to the place called Malap. It was here that Nelumplenelo and Umaeghoghor shared their first *kava* in a coconut shell. Nambenia started to prepare everything. She used every part of her body in the preparation.

"You may now drink the *kava*," she said.

There were many people there, and a lot of them were jealous that the spirit of the coconut palm had wedded the spirit of *kava*. The young girl devils, driven by Nelumplenelo, protested.

"Why didn't he want us when we proposed to him?"

They fought violently and one of the girls ended up knocking the *kava* spirit's shell of *kava* to the ground. The spirit was furious. He stood to one side and started to cry. He looked at the kava that was slowly being absorbed into the ground. Suddenly, he kneeled down and started to lap up the spilled *kava*. Today, the trace of his knees can still be seen! When he had finished, he took his wife's hand and both of them left for Ralponnaghave. The spirit of *kava* and his wife, formerly of Ifo, still live here today. One can still see traces that the woman left on a stone. They look like the prints of a horse.

That was how *kava* married the coconut palm a very long time ago on Erromango. If you would like to see a stone that had retained the image of the spirit of the palm, go to Portnarvin in the village called Ranulevie. The first shells of *kava* are also at Malap on a black stone.

My story ends here.

This story was given by Jerry Taki, a fieldworker for the Cultural Centre.
It was collected by the Historic and Cultural Sites Register of Vanuatu (VCHSS).

Previously unpublished.

Nalakyang, the ogre
(Anatom)

Without a doubt, all those ogres, all those eaters of man, come from the southern islands. Semusemu came from Aneityum as well as Kampes and Transumas. Aneityum, is the home of all southern devils. The devil Nalakyang also lived on the island of Aneityum at Umej where kauri is now exploited. Nalakyang was a horrible creature. He devoured men, women, and children... especially children. Nalakyang left no one around him alive. Men armed themselves with bows, arrows, clubs, and spears, leaving in groups to try and catch him. Alas, the devil always got away. Nalakyang was stronger and slyer than they were. Often, he would hide himself by a path to spy on children that were playing nearby. The children were, of course, unaware of the danger and Nalakyang went on rubbing his hands together and drooling with anticipation.

"My little children, how beautiful you are and how tasty you will be. Play, play well, my pretties. In a couple of minutes, you will not be laughing as my teeth crush your bones. Go, jump, play, and sing... be happy! But your friend will not forget you! Go, play, sing, sing! Now, you are all mine!"

One day, when the men were thoroughly tired of pursuing the devil without any results, they came up with an ingenious scheme. They cut long poles of bamboo to use as gutters. Then, they laid the gutters at the mouth of a spring and the water flowed along the path they had laid right into the mouth of the ogre's cave. The men waited, armed and ready, hoping that Nalakyang would come out of his hole because he was afraid of drowning. However, the flood did not bother the ogre at all. He just climbed onto higher ground and surveyed the water, munching on his *fehi,* those red bananas that grow near the sky. The *fehi,* called *nalak* in the language of Aneityum, was the ogre's favourite food... after men, of course. Tired of waiting for the monster that never came out of his hole, the men abandoned their siege and went home.

Another time, Nalakyang, wanting to feed on fresh flesh, went to visit a couple of his devil friends. Nasunaleluyang and his wife welcomed him with joy, noticing that their friend paid special attention to their child.

"How cute he is! And how fat!" he exclaimed as if congratulating them on their appetising offspring.

Then, he pretended to admire the weather.

"What a beautiful day! You should go to the garden. While you are there, I'll watch the child."

"No," exclaimed the mother. "We shall bring our son with us."

Nasunaleluyang knew his friend well and understood his intentions. The couple went to the garden with the child. They decided to hide him high up in a kauri tree.

"I know our friend well," the devil said to his wife, "and he will want to eat our son."

The woman put her son high into the tree and told him to be careful.

"Look out for Nalak... his stomach loves children."

Nalak, in turn, looked everywhere for the child, but could not find him.

"Where did he go?" he asked.

He started to get hungry. He turned over every stone in the forest but to no avail. Then, he had the brilliant idea to look high up in the trees and there, up in the kauri, he saw the child. Quickly, he climbed into the tree, jumping from branch to branch. But the branches at the top of the tree were too fragile to hold his weight and he could not reach his prey. Full of rage, he found another strategy: he built a ladder and got the child. The poor boy tried to fight back, but Nalak soon had him in his hands.

"I am going to eat you, my darling little pig," he said with love.

He took his friend's son to his cave, and killed, roasted, and ate him. It was a true feast. Nasunaneluyang and his wife came back to the tree to get the child, but he wasn't there anymore. The wife started to cry and the man, telling her to stay calm, vowed vengeance. He went to see his friend, Natmunel. He was a sly devil, very sly, slyer than that horrible Nalakyang.

"I am very unhappy. Nalak just ate my son. My wife and I are utterly distraught. Can you help us?"

Natmunel told him, "I hate Nalakyang as much as you do and the story that you just told me only confirms my feelings."

They decided to set a trap for Nalak and asked for help from all the devils in the area. Following the plan that Natmunel's brilliant brain had come up with, Nasunaneluyang and he went to get enough lobsters to fill two coconut palm baskets. Then, they transformed themselves into two young boys. Near the ogre's cave, they built a fire. Eventually, the delicate smell of grilled lobsters wafting on the wind came and tickled Nalakyang's nostrils. The monster, driven by his stomach, came slowly out of his cave and followed the smoke.

"Ah, my little children! You are grilling some very nice lobsters... and you are so cute!"

One of the boys explained, "We are already full. If you would like to eat some of our lobsters, we would be happy to give you some."

Because Nalak loved lobster, the boys didn't have to twist his arm. In the blink of an eye, he had eaten three lobsters. He then proceeded to fill his stomach with the rest. After his feast, he yawned and felt like lying down. Because he did not have any friends, no one was there to braid his hair as was the custom in the southern islands.

"We are going to braid your hair!" said one of the children.

"No, it is I who will braid yours," Nalak responded.

But because he was very tired, he finally accepted their offer, laid down, and fell asleep. At that moment, all the devils who were following Natmunel's orders came forward to the place where Nalakyang was sleeping. The children divided Nalak's hair to braid. Each time a braid was finished, a devil grabbed it and pulled it into the bush where he tied it to a tree trunk. From time to time, Nalak felt that the children were pulling a little too hard.

"Be a little gentler, my pretties! Ouch! Be a little gentler!" he murmured.

"You must suffer a little for beauty! You'll see, we are attaching the braids to little vines. You will be very pleased."

Soon, all the braids had been pulled tight by the devils. Quietly, the two children became devils again and hit Nalak with their clubs. Nalak tried to get away, but he couldn't. His hair was tied around trees. The ogre pulled and pulled, finally uprooting the trees. However, at that moment, all the ogres came out of the woods and pierced his body with their spears. Since that day, the island of Aneityum has been rid of Nalakyang.

Story from Anelgauhat on the island of Aneityum.

Nabanga n° 95 (1978)

Appendices

The following story, inspired by a legend from Ambrym "The Lisepsep's son" was written by Didier Daeninckx during his journey to Vanuatu in 2003.

Previously unpublished. story.

The sailor and the children of Ambrym
by Didier Daeninckx

All of this happened several years ago. I was a sailor on a cargo ship that stopped at every port on every island in the archipelago and filled its hull with sacks of copra, bananas, beef, shrimp, and large roots of *kava* to sell in Australia and New Zealand. One day while we were making our way to Port-Vila, the noon sky turned black. A mast-breaking wind rose up and dug trenches in the sea. Then, an ocean of water that had hitherto been hidden in the clouds pelted down upon us. Our boat, though 50 meters long and 20 wide, danced on the waves like a piece of broken coconut shell. Suddenly, the waters opened up and two immense, liquid hands ripped the boat apart. I had only the time to grab a rope and attach myself to a large piece of wood before being thrown, unconscious, into the churning sea. I do not know how much time I spent in the ocean, my skin being eaten by the salt and burnt by the sun, surrounded by the fins of hungry sharks. When a canoe finally approached me, I was almost dead, and the fishermen that hauled me aboard were already discussing plans for my burial when they got back to land. I wasn't moving anymore and the doors to another world were already opening behind my eyelids. The eldest among the fishermen bent over and put his cheek to my mouth, ascertaining that I was still breathing. He turned towards his companions.

"We must take him to the man from Ambrym. Only he can save this man."

They beached their canoe near Pango, wove a sort of hammock with palm spines, banana leaves, and bamboo supports, and gently laid me in it. It was in this contraption that I finally arrived in Port-Vila. They took me inside a *nakamal* built at the top of a hill on the road to Montmartre. A very old man with a dark face haloed by white hair and a beard was squatting by the central fire. The fishermen set me down and left quickly, leaving me alone with the man. He got up and started to cover me in leaves gathered from an unknown tree, all the while intoning words that I couldn't understand. As soon as I had completely disappeared under this mass of vegetation, the redness of my burns faded, all my wounds healed over, and my vigor returned. I was on my feet in an instant. I turned around : the old man had evaporated into thin air.

One of the fishermen, he who had felt my breath against his skin while I languished in the canoe, was waiting for me at the bottom of the hill. As I got closer to him, I asked,

"Who is that man? Where did he go? He saved my life, just as you did, and I would like to thank him."

The old fisherman from Pango sat down on a *nakatambol* stump.

The sailor and the children of Ambrym

"I didn't see anyone... when I went into the *nakamal,* it was empty."

I sat down beside him.

"Yet, it was you who directed the men who were carrying me in the hammock. You knew where you were going..."

The old fisherman shook his head slowly from right to left. He picked up a stick and started to draw on the ground near a colony of ants.

"It was my father and my grandfather that directed my steps... A very long time ago, they told me the story about the child from Ambrym and the voice of the old woman..."

He took a long moment to catch his breath and then started to speak.

"A long time ago, when only trees and flowers grew on the archipelago's islands, well before the advent of houses as we know them today, a young couple lived the profoundest of loves on the island of Ambrym. Happiness defined every moment of their lives spent in the welcoming, colourful environment that surrounded them. They lived on vegetables that they grew and the fish that they caught. One day, their happiness attained a new level when the cries of two children made themselves heard in the small house of wood and leaves. They were the handsomest of children and when they were face to face, one had the impression of looking into a mirror. The father now only took care of the garden, the fishing and the fire, leaving the mother with the twins. He had made two small hammocks that he had strung between the lower branches of a banyan tree in a cool, shady place.

One day, while he was clearing some land that he had already burnt, the father heard one of the children crying loudly. He ran through the forest to ask his wife what the matter was.

'He's cutting his first teeth,' she responded, 'his brother as well, but I haven't heard him, he's been very quiet all day!'

Reassured, the father went back to work without noticing that a woman had approached one of the little hammocks. Unfortunately, she was the wife of the devil that lived in this particular forest. In her arms, she carried her child who was also crying. The woman bent over the hammock to look at the second twin, who slept without making a noise. A large, dreamy smile lit up her face. She couldn't stand crying and had always wanted such a well-behaved child. In a flash, she had taken the sleeping twin, replaced him with her fractious baby and made off towards a nearby curtain of vines.

When the sun had started to slide towards the horizon, the happy couple headed back to their village carrying the two hammocks, completely unaware of the dirty trick that the devil woman had played on them. The young mother had started to prepare the evening meal when the silent twin started to cry with all of his might. The child had just woken up and, in this strange house, did not recognise the familiar odour of the devil's kitchen. The parents went to the mat on which the children were lying and the mother immediately realised that the crying child did not look like his brother. She started to panic.

'Look! That's not our child! That's not him!'

The father came forward for a closer look. Suddenly, he backed up, frightened. For the first time in years, misfortune had marred their perfect happiness.

'Someone has cursed us! We can't keep this child under our roof! You must go quickly and throw him into the sea. Maybe then our true son will be returned to us.'

The young woman, overwhelmed by the situation, wrapped the baby in a small mat and ran towards the shore. Once there, she climbed up onto a large rock that looked out over the bay, closed her eyes and prepared to throw the child into the waves. At this very moment, a scratchy, broken voice spoke up from behind her.

'Don't do that... don't throw him to the sharks. He's my son. Keep him close to you and when he's grown, he will help you, your husband and all those who are in pain... He knows how to stave off death and danger.'

The young woman didn't know whether to obey her husband or to listen to this strange voice coming out of the night. The child's warmth against her breast gave her her answer. She must believe the voice that sounded like so many stones being rubbed together.

She only asked, 'What should I do? He won't eat anything I cook. He doesn't like it; he spits everything out!'

The devil woman answered, 'He likes boiled, mashed bananas mixed with coconut milk.'

The young woman went back home with the child in her arms and explained to her husband what the voice had told her to do. He expressed his relief and admitted that he had gone in search of her for shame of his intial reaction. Then, he went into the forest to get some bananas and coconuts. The child, from that night forward, ceased to cry. Little by little, he became a vigorous young man as handsome as his brother, so handsome that people often mistook them for twins. On the boy's twentieth birthday, his father fell ill and everyone believed that he was not long for this world. The switched son carried the sick man into the *nakamal* and covered him with leaves that he had gathered deep in the forest. The sickness disappeared as if by magic. The next day, the boy got into a canoe and was never again seen on Ambrym. The only thing that is known about him is that he goes from island to island, from Ureparapara to Tanna, from Aneityum to Vot Tande. If someone is in danger, if death is on their doorstep, he hears a small, scratchy voice that directs him to a *nakamal* that no one has ever heard of. Today, you were lucky. He was in Port-Vila..."

A couple of days later, one of my company's boats, on its way to Noumea, docked near the place that tourists leave from in order to savour lobster in the restaurant on *Iririki Island Resort*. I learned from the captain that I was the sole survivor of the wreck. When I tried to tell the story of everything that had happened to me, the Pango fishermen's hammock, the *nakamal* on the road to Montmartre, the blanket of leaves that covered my wounds, I quickly understood that people believed that though my body had survived the accident, my mind had not. I haven't told my story again, not ever, except to this piece of paper on which I put the final full-stop to my memories.

Written at Port-Vila on the 11th of October, 2003 while the sun rose
over Erakor lagoon and dispersed the hazes of kava.

Didier Daeninckx

Radio and the Redefinition
of Kastom in Vanuatu
by Lissant Bolton

In 1991, when working on the island of Ambae in northern Vanuatu, I visited a village called Lowainasasa, a steep climb from the end of the road that skirted part of the island. In the evening a woman called Jennifer Mwera came to talk. The conversation turned to *kastom,* the term used in Bislama, Vanuatu's lingua franca, to denote practices understood to derive from the precolonial past. Yes, Jennifer said, she had heard that *kastom* is the life of the people, she had heard it from the government on the radio. At the time, I was working as a volunteer for the Vanuatu Cultural Centre, setting up a program called the Women's Culture Project, and simultaneously undertaking my doctoral research. In both these roles I was trying to understand what the term *kastom* meant and how it related to people's daily practice. I was struck by Jennifer's comment and her combination of *kastom,* government and radio. Since then I have, in my continuing engagement with *kastom* in Vanuatu, found her remark increasingly significant.

This paper is an attempt to unpack some of the interconnections between *kastom,* government and radio. It is my contention that radio has been extremely important in the formulation of the concept *kastom* and in developing the idea of Vanuatu as a nation. In an area where communications are difficult and where literacy has only begun to be widespread in the last two decades, radio is the preeminent form of communication and engagement over distances. The impact of radio has been substantially enhanced by the model of broadcasting employed until recently in Vanuatu.

The Introduction of Radio Communications

The difficulty of communications in Vanuatu is partly a matter of geography. Most of the islands in the archipelago are small, many are surrounded by open sea, and the terrain of nearly all is rugged, making communication a challenge even within one island. This difficulty is also a matter of language and culture. The nation's population of about 180,000 people speak a total of 113 languages (Tryon 1996, 171); the Anglo-French Condominium Government of the New Hebrides (1906 -1980) complicated the situation further with two languages of administration. Today the islands are linked by the irregular itineraries of small trading vessels known as copra boats, and by a small plane service operated by a government-owned company, and the nation is united in speaking the neo-Melanesian pidgin Bislama. Mail travels to the islands with relative ease, but its delivery within an island is often a matter of happenstance. The two towns-the capital, Port Vila, on the central island of Efate, and Luganville on the northern island of Espiritu Santo-have electric power supplies. Except for irregular power services at some provincial centres, the rest of the country has no access to electricity except where individuals own small generators.[1] Any electrical equipment, such as radios, is dependent on batteries.

Radio was introduced to the New Hebrides during the First World War, when a small radio station that was set up in Port Vila used Morse spark transmitters to communicate with ships and with New Caledonia. A teleradio network was introduced in the Second World War for the purposes of coastwatching. The network, which was controlled by the British government, was set up using the shortwave frequency 6900, just off the amateur radio frequency band, so that amateurs could use their own aerials and equipment to access it. Everyone on the network had to check in to the transmitting and receiving station in Port Vila, known as Radio Vila, morning and afternoon, and were allowed only to pass messages, not to talk among themselves.

---

[1] The smaller provincial centres, such as Norsup and Lakatoro on Malakula, Isangel and Lenakel on Tanna, or Saratamata on Ambae, have some generator-supplied power laid on. This is an irregular service, operating for limited periods at certain times of the day, affected by fuel supply and engine failure. The power is used primarily for lighting. Although generators are used to run video machines in rural areas, I have never seen them used for radios.

Radio and the Redefinition of Kastom in Vanuatu

The coastwatching network became the basis of radio communications in Vanuatu after the war. Although overseas and shipping communications continued to use Morse code, through the next few decades the teleradio network became the lifeline for expatriates living in the archipelago. Certain periods each day were scheduled for specific groups to use the frequency, but outside schedule times, people throughout the region used 6900 to talk to each other. Frank Palmer, who was involved with teleradio for many years from the Second World War, considered that this teleradio network constituted broadcasting in its purest sense (taped interview, 29 Jan 1997). It was, he said, the news broadcast for the country, because those people who didn't have a teleradio license had a shortwave receiver, and could and did listen to 6900, not only to check for messages to themselves and messages being broadcast by Radio Vila each morning and afternoon, but also to hear what everyone else was talking about. Palmer recalled that a planter on Epi called Frank Harvey had speakers for his teleradio set up throughout his house, so that he could listen from morning to night.

This was, of course, an expatriate affair and so were the various early attempts at broadcasting. Before the Second World War, Harvey worked for Radio Vila as an operator. He also had an amateur radio license. At that stage amateurs were allowed to go on the broadcast band, and Harvey broadcast to the immediate vicinity of Port Vila three nights a week for about an hour, collecting and broadcasting local news. When France sent a soccer team to the New Hebrides in about 1948, Frank Palmer broadcast the three soccer matches to the whole archipelago as a one-off event, using his amateur radio setup. Radio Noumea rebroadcast the matches for New Caledonian audiences.

Radio Vila was used, to a limited extent, by the Ni-Vanuatu.[2] Local people did occasionally send messages within the country and used the overseas Morse service, for example, to contact family members studying overseas. Messages in both cases were prepared as telegrams-people went to the Post Office and filled in a telegram form that was then delivered to Radio Vila for transmission. However, few Ni-Vanuatu owned radio receivers, partly because of the expense and difficulty of owning and operating a valve radio, and partly, it can be assumed, because radio was directed at an expatriate audience and involved communication in English and French. Ni-Vanuatu staff were employed at Radio Vila.

It would appear that Ni-Vanuatu started listening to the radio during the 1960s as the result of a number of developments, the first being the introduction of the transistor. Invented in 1947, the transistor not only used less power than the valve (which was until then the essential component of radios for voice transmission) but was smaller, cheaper and more durable. The transistor, which made the cheap radio receiver possible, first came onto the market in the United States in 1953. It was possible to buy transistor radios in the New Hebrides from the mid to late fifties.

Secondly, during and after the Second World War, a number of shortwave radio services developed in the Pacific. Radio Australia, for example, started broadcasting in 1939. It seems that some educated Ni-Vanuatu purchased transistors and listened in the islands to Radio Australia, Radio Noumea and, from its inception in the early sixties, Radio Solomons. Thus, a man in the northern Vanuatu island of Maewo, Chief Shadrach Rasa Usi of Kerebei village, recalled that a radio was first brought to his village by a Ni-Vanuatu schoolteacher in 1955, and that there being no broadcasting in the New Hebrides at the time, they listened to Radio Solomons and Radio New Guinea (interview, 3 Feb 1997). Interest in listening to such services depended in part on a grasp of English or French acquired through mission schooling or employment.

The first broadcasting initiative that most Ni-Vanuatu remember as originating in the country, one remembered with great affection, was a short weekly program recorded in the New Hebrides but broadcast by Radio Noumea. The detail of the transmission through Radio Noumea was perhaps not appreciated, or attended to, by most Ni-Vanuatu listeners-Chief Shadrach, for example, remembered the program as the first broadcast from Radio Vila. The program was prepared by three French men: a businessman, Pierre Bourgeois; the then chairman

---

[2] Ni-Vanuatu is the term used to describe the inhabitants of the archipelago since independence. This discussion ranges in time across both pre- and post-independence eras: for the sake of simplicity I use the term throughout the paper, rather than switching from New Hebrideans to Ni-Vanuatu and back again.

of Vila Town Council, Georges Milne; and a Catholic priest, Father Zerger. It started in about 1960 and was produced for about five years. Each man recorded material that interested him, using reel-to-reel tapes that were then sent to Noumea: programs included local news, music, and stories. George Milne gathered together some of the young men who worked for the Vila Town Council, who formed a stringband that he recorded for the program.[3] Father Zerger, who was partly based in the islands, recorded traditional stories and songs.

Although the program, broadcast for ten to fifteen minutes most Wednesday evenings, was in French, and was intended primarily for French citizens, it made a significant impact on Ni-Vanuatu. The content included material produced by Ni-Vanuatu themselves (the stringband, the traditional stories and songs) and attention was drawn to this content by the theme song that introduced it each week. The song, called Kavelicolico, was sung by a man from Ifira Island (a small island in Port Vila Harbour). This small song is very engaging and tuneful, so much so that the program was known, and is remembered, as Radio Kavelicolico. I have never talked to anyone about the program without them singing the song to me. Paul Gardissat, a Frenchman who subsequently worked for Radio Vanuatu, was working as a teacher on the island of Ambae during this period. He recalled that on Ambae, people hearing the theme would put their ears close to the radio to listen, the quality of the broadcast being poor and requiring close attention. At that period, he said, everybody in the New Hebrides sang the song. Gardissat's understanding is that it was about many small crabs on the beach, which took each other's hands to form a circle, the implication being that people also should be together, hand in hand (taped interview, 14 Feb 1997). Given that the song was in the Ifira language, this meaning was obscure to all but the Ifira Islanders themselves.

Thus, the first broadcast to make an impact on local people in the New Hebrides was one that caught their attention with a traditional song from the region and followed that with other local products deriving from both traditional practice and from contemporary developments-the stringbands. While by no means all Ni-Vanuatu would have understood stories told in French, all would have had access at some level to the music.

Prior to the colonial era, there was a considerable amount of trade and exchange through the region, and in most areas people were familiar with the ideas and practices of groups who lived adjacent to them. Along with exchanges in material items, there was an extensive trade in nonmaterial objects, in rituals, myth cycles, dances, songs and so on. Kirk Huffman, writing about this trade in northern Vanuatu, remarked that in this area rituals "were, and are, thought to have a power and spirit of their own that urges them to get up, move to other areas, to stay there for a while, and then move on" (1996, 190). In other words, while it would be quite misleading to suggest that people throughout the archipelago were familiar with the knowledge and practices of the whole region, it is true to say that the idea of diversity and similarity in local practice was well established, and, moreover, that people were interested in it.

Huffman has argued that interisland trading started to diminish in the 1860s with the arrival of blackbirding ships, which had no compunction in kidnapping the crews of trading canoes found in their path, and was subsequently actively discouraged by missionary, trader and Condominium government pressures. Missionaries discouraged trade in cultural items for reasons of evangelism, traders because indigenous trade in "European" items interfered with their own business, and the Condominium in support of both objectives. As interisland trade diminished, a new means of intergroup communication developed through the labor trade itself. For example, men and a scattering of women recruited for work on the Queensland sugarcane plantations, or on plantations within the New Hebrides, worked side by side and engaged at some levels in the exchange of knowledge and practice. This was the context in which Vanuatu's lingua franca, Bislama, developed. Bislama, a neo-Melanesian pidgin, became the language in which Ni-Vanuatu communicated with each other. People travelled inside and outside the archipelago, were exposed to the diversity and similarities of each other's ways of living, and built a common language.

---

[3] The young men involved included Willie Bongmatur (who subsequently became the first president of the Vanuatu National Council of Chiefs) and Philip Ngungungon, both from Ambrym; Leong Baes from Ambae, who played guitar; and a Fijian called Paul Chino (interview with Willie Bongmatur, 27 July 1996).

Radio and the Redefinition of Kastom in Vanuatu

Into this context of the knowledge of diversity, and the remembered exchange of material and nonmaterial objects, "Radio Kavelicolico" first broadcast what came to be known as *kastom* to the archipelago. There is no documentation for the introduction of the word *kastom* into Bislama, but I suggest that the term originally derives from missionary endeavors to make a distinction between unacceptably heathen practice, and acceptably Christian behavior.[4] The antithesis of *kastom* in this opposition is the Bislama term *skul,* which until the late 1960s referred not so much to school in the English sense, as to the whole missionary project of education. Until the late 1960s the term *kastom* carried a negative connotation - it was used to refer to people who still lived in the bush, in the bad old ways, in the darkness of unenlightened heathenism (see Lindstrom 1982; Jolly 1982). Ni-Vanuatu experience, with rare exceptions, was that Europeans disapproved of and discouraged local knowledge and practice. To radio listeners, therefore, the broadcast of indigenous songs and stories represented an affirmation of local knowledge and practice at a period when such affirmation was not generally expected from Europeans.

There is a further aspect to these early broadcasts. For most Ni-Vanuatu local practice is, in the most fundamental sense, an outcome of the place itself. Joël Bonnemaison argued that on the southern island of Tanna, "in traditional thinking, cultural identity is merely the existential aspect of those places where men live today as their ancestors did from time immemorial" (1984, 118), while Margaret Jolly commented that for the Sa of south Pentecost, land "is thought to be a precondition of human culture" (1981, 269). In the terms of such understanding, radio broadcasts that originate in the archipelago should contain the knowledge and practice that is an outcome of the land itself. Perhaps also because of this identity between place and practice, people such as Chief Shadrach assumed that Radio Kavelicolico derived from the archipelago itself. Interestingly, Radio Solomons broadcast news from the New Hebrides every week during the early sixties, but no Ni-Vanuatu to whom I spoke about the development of radio mentioned these broadcasts, although they did recall listening to the station.

The Establishment of Broadcasting

During the early sixties Radio Vila continued to concentrate on communications, operating all internal public communications, shipping and teleradio, aeronautical communications, and meteorological reporting on the same frequency channel. In addition, the service operated one Morse circuit that was used to transmit to Suva, Sydney, Noumea, Honiara, and Santo in turn (Page 1993, 162). A new communications transmitting station was opened at Malapoa Point in Port Vila in 1965. According to Rex Robinson, then radio engineer, broadcasting was initiated in 1966, to give the joint administration a direct outlet for government information and so relieve the telecommunication service (Page 1993, 164). Broadcasting was the joint responsibility of both governments, although the British were responsible for providing equipment and establishing studio facilities. Each administration had its own Information Office, which produced a newspaper and prepared material for broadcast.

The Broadcasting Service was opened by the Right Honourable Fred Lee, MP, British secretary of state for the colonies, on 2 August 1966. The first British information officer, Michael Leach, recalled that the inaugural broadcast comprised a message from the Queen read by Mr. Lee; an address by General Billotte, the French minister of state for overseas departments and territories, recorded in Paris; and speeches by the French resident commissioner and the acting British resident commissioner, Sir Colin Allan (Page 1993, 172)-an extraordinarily formal lineup for such an otherwise unostentatious beginning.

Initially there was one daily half-hour program, broadcast from the communications transmitter at Malapoa during the lunch hour, when the transmitter was not needed for the teleradio schedule. The program was pre-taped, prepared by the British and the French Information Services, respectively. Broadcasting constituted another arena in which the British and the French could compete. Charlot Long Wah, who worked as a teleradio operator from 1959 to 1963 and was involved in making early recordings for broadcasts, commented that programs involved the endless iteration of French and English viewpoints (interview, 12 Feb 1997). Each government's Information Office employed Ni-Vanuatu staff.[5]

---

[4] I have argued this point at greater length elsewhere (Bolton 1993).

[5] The first Ni-Vanuatu employee of the British Information Office was MacKenzie Tuleo; the first in the French Office was Jean-Baptiste Ramwel. Both men participated in broadcasting: MacKenzie Tuleo, for example, read the Bislama news when it was first introduced.

Michael Leach recalled that early programs included news bulletins in the three languages, a magazine program of interviews with interesting visitors, elaboration of the news, and "items of local culture" (Page 1993, 172).[6] Although there was resistance from the Condominium government to the use of Bislama, by 1971 Radio Vila (as the broadcasting station continued to be called) was using this language to present the news and in other programs. Music included "either tribal chants or local popular music and record requests" (Page 1993, 172). Radio Vila thus continued the practice initiated by Radio Kavelicolico, of broadcasting indigenous knowledge and practice, and thereby providing an implicit affirmation of it by the condominium government.

Government district agents, reporting on the response to Radio Vila in the islands, told Leach that "at transmission times, those with transistor radios, often the village schoolmaster, would hang them in a tree and people gathered around to hear the local news" (Page 1993, 173). In 1971, when the service broadcast for an hour at midday and an hour and a quarter at night, the British administration sent out 300 audience survey forms, of which 67 were returned, representing 54 villages. This sample produced a statistic of seven radios per village, each of which had an average of ten listeners (NHBNS 1971). These statistics are obviously biased in favor of those who were already listening and were therefore interested in completing the survey. Paul Gardissat's experience, while teaching in Ambae and the Banks Islands between 1966 and 1975, was that reception in the remoter parts of the country was not good at all, and that people in these areas were not interested in making the effort to listen to Radio Vila.[7] In 1971 Australia donated a new 2-kilowatt transmitter that was dedicated to broadcasting, and this improved reception in remoter islands to some extent.

Although Radio Vila included "items of local culture" from its inception, the first programs devoted to this subject seem to have been developed in the early seventies. Godwin Ligo, a Ni-Vanuatu from north Pentecost who joined the British Information Office in 1969 (taped interview, 12 Feb 1997),[8] started to make a program called *Taem Nao, Taem Bifo* (The Present, the Past) somewhere around 1970 or 1971. In his work for the British Information Office, Ligo toured Efate and other islands showing films, and wherever he went he took a reel-to-reel tape recorder on which he recorded songs and stories for the program. Recordings were made in Bislama. Later, Ligo said, he found his way to various islands specifically in order to record stories and songs for the program. He would send messages on the radio to announce his arrival and to tell people to prepare stories and songs to record, and then he would go and record them. The program was broadcast on Tuesday evenings and repeated on Thursday evenings, probably not with great regularity. The word *kastom* was at this period still tainted with a negative connotation - *kastom* was still the negative opposite to the positive of Christianization and development.

Ligo said that until 1974 or 1975, Ni-Vanuatu were interested in listening to the radio for two reasons: to hear record requests and to hear indigenous stories and songs. He commented that there was little local interest in the news, whether world news or regional news. People's greatest interest in the news was to hear when officials of the two governments were to visit their village, so that they could prepare a welcome, and then to hear about the event afterward on the radio.

Those Ni-Vanuatu who were able to receive Radio Vila adequately, responded to it from the beginning by engaging with it in correspondence. There was a strong local involvement in record-request programs, as there was also to hearing indigenous stories and songs. This response raises a number of interesting questions about the way in which people are educated to engage with radio. In her analysis of the early years of Australian radio, Lesley Johnson argued that the form in which radio developed during the twenties was not necessarily a given.

---

[6] Charlot Long Wah recalled that the first program broadcast by Radio Vila included some local music recorded especially for the occasion. Long Wah helped MacKenzie Tuleo to record Paul Isono ("the best music man in town") playing his mandolin under the mango tree at the store near the stadium in Port Vila (interview, 12 February 1997).

[7] I interviewed Paul Gardissat twice, on 29 July 1996 and 14 February 1997, and drew on both interviews for this paper.

[8] All quotations from Ligo in this paper were drawn from this interview.

Radio and the Redefinition of Kastom in Vanuatu

During this period, she stated, "not everyone agreed that [radio's] potential as a domestic companion was the best or only way to make use of this technology" (1988, 1). Johnson argued that the characterization of radio as "the-world-out-there brought to listeners in a domestic, private life" is not axiomatic to the medium but is rather a construction that assumes the public and private domains to be already constituted and separate (1988, 45).[9]

The idea of the passive, private listener seems, from the beginning, not to have resonated with Ni-Vanuatu. Insofar as radio already existed in the New Hebrides, it existed as a medium of interchange. While this interchange was predominately the privilege of expatriates, the idea of radio as a means of communication between individuals was well established and was presumably familiar to many Ni-Vanuatu. This idea of exchange would also have been reinforced by the inclusion from the beginning of the record-request program, which provided an avenue for interaction with the radio, and gave people the power to affect what was broadcast by writing in. One might also argue that although by the seventies increasing numbers of Ni-Vanuatu were being educated at primary level, the notion of communication without engagement, which is integral to published text, to books and articles, was not well entrenched. In a primarily oral system, communication always involves response.

A further aspect of this issue is the distinction that can be made between hearing and listening. I draw this distinction from John Potts' analysis of Australian radio (1989, 8). The ear is passive, open to all stimuli. Listening is an active function by which a person tunes in to a particular sound while filtering out extraneous material. Listening is thus the application of hearing. Potts observed that while in the early days of broadcasting, radio was the focal point of a concentrated listening, a different relation to the medium exists in Australia today. Much radio programming, especially for commercial radio, assumes hearing rather than listening. The radio is part of a general flow of background sound. When a person's attention is caught by an item that interests them, hearing becomes listening, a focused attentiveness. In that the Condominium introduced broadcasting to communicate information, radio programming was designed for, and assumed, a listening audience. Keith Woodward, a British residency staff member who oversaw the introduction of radio, said that he "originally envisaged broadcasting as a means of communicating, putting over information about health and agricultural extension work, not as entertainment" (interview, 3 Sept 1993).

In this way, radio in Vanuatu, from its inception until 1994,[10] assumed a listening rather than a hearing audience, and it received it. Ni-Vanuatu listened to the radio both because, at least initially, attentive listening was required to hear information through the static, and also because radio brought them information and ideas to which they did not otherwise have access. An increasingly important aspect of this approach was the development of service messages, by which government, businesses, and individuals communicated with people in the islands and also, sometimes, in the towns. While communicating specifically from one person to another, these messages constituted a kind of news service of the same kind that the teleradio had provided.

Service messages have always been the most listened-to program. Broadcast at least three times a day, they are short messages relating news, making arrangements, and announcing deaths. "Dead messages," which provide details of a death and burial, calling together nominated family members from various parts of the country, and which are signaled by a short theme tune, are listened to with more attention than anything else on the radio. Other service messages relate primarily to transport, of all both individuals and goods. As an eccentric but telling example of this, David Luders, a longtime Vanuatu resident, recalled for me a service message dating from 1978 or 1979. In the message a particular man was instructed to be ready at a named beach on a nominated day, with his blanket and bush knife, so that a Condominium government vessel could pick him up and bring him to Port Vila to serve his prison sentence (pers comm, 16 Nov 1998).[11] Service messages also relate to the shipment of goods, both to and from the islands.

---

[9] Shaun Moores, discussing the social history of radio in Britain, traced a similar process by which radio became identified with domestic space during the twenties and thirties (1988). In Vanuatu, by contrast, as I hope to demonstrate in future work, radio seems to be identified primarily not with the indoors, but with the semi-public space of the hamlet yard and the community space of the men's house.

[10] As discussed at the end of this paper, in 1994 the radio station was incorporated as the Vanuatu Television and Broadcasting Corporation and changed its policy on the presentation of programs.

[11] Luders reported that he checked with David Shephard, a British district agent at that period, who confirmed that the man in question did come to Vila as instructed.

People listened to the radio, both to service messages and to programs. They responded to service messages, as appropriate, with action. They responded to programs with correspondence. According to Ligo, the greater proportion of this correspondence related to the broadcasting of indigenous knowledge and practice. The program generated a form of competitiveness. People would hear a story from another island, or another village on their island, or even from another clan in their own area, that was similar to one they also told themselves, and would write to the radio requesting that their version be broadcast. Sometimes, Ligo said, they would write to say that the version first broadcast had been stolen from them. Or they might write to say that they had the same story in their own island, but that it went further than the story that had been broadcast. Ligo's response was to try to broadcast all versions "so that people could hear the difference." This did not happen so frequently with songs, which were sung in local languages, and therefore not accessible to the majority of listeners.

Ligo's account of response to the radio in the early seventies thus suggests a notion of radio quite different from the one that Johnson has argued developed in Australia in the twenties. Rather than seeing the radio as a way of gaining access to the "world-out-there," Ni-Vanuatu response was concerned mainly with programs that engaged with their own world, the knowledge and practice that arose out of the place itself, and with their own concerns. At the same time, this engagement was with the whole country, rather than that of their own immediate place, creating a sense of a larger unity-a unity not just of the region that people knew through trade and exchange, but of the whole archipelago.

In 1975, French Resident Commissioner Gauger, invited Paul Gardissat to leave the teaching profession and take up a position as "Chief of the Bislama section, French Residency Information Service." Gardissat had previously worked in radio in Algeria. The Commissioner's idea was that Gardissat, who spoke Bislama and had spent thirteen years teaching in the islands, could provide a kind of liaison service for the French government with the Ni-Vanuatu. In the event, Gardissat proved something of a thorn in the side of the French administration, as he was often critical of their approach to the independence movement. Although he was involved in many other aspects of both radio and the French government newspaper *Nabanga,* Gardissat had an extensive knowledge about, and interest in, indigenous knowledge and practice and also began to make programs in this area, broadcasting in both Bislama and French. Ligo and Gardissat both made *kastom* programs for some period, for the British and French governments respectively, but from 1976 Ligo was working as a political reporter, and it is my impression that he paid less attention to *Taem Nao, Taem Bifo* from that time.

Like Ligo, Gardissat received a considerable correspondence from Ni-Vanuatu regarding all his programs, including his *kastom* program. He remembered receiving over fifty letters every day, and has kept some of those letters that interested him. 12 people often sent traditional stories to be broadcast. Thus, for example he has a letter dated 3 May 1976, from Taes Thomson from Hokua village, northwest Santo, written in English, which begins, "It is my own pleasure to write you this Custom Story. I'm very interested of listen to the Custom Stories from all the islands in the group. So I would like to tell one story. It's a really true story." Gardissat also sometimes received tapes. Gaetan Bule, from Narovorovo village on Maewo, sent a cassette with a letter in Bislama dated 5 December 1975, explaining that it contained a recording of a dance called *nalenga,* which had been performed three days earlier at a marriage. Gardissat subsequently developed a system called "walkabout cassettes" by which he sent a tape recorder and tapes to the islands, on request, for people to record stories for broadcast.

Gardissat's approach to the broadcast of traditional material often involved both dramatization and interpretation. He scripted stories and used sound effects and other devices to enliven the account. A longtime resident of Vanuatu (originally from New Zealand) told me that Gardissat's productions were "as good as the BBC" - a high accolade. Gardissat attributed the success of his program at least partly to his attempt to provide some contextualization for the stories, so that people not familiar with the region from which the story came had access to some information that enabled them to understand how the story fitted in.

The issue of understanding traditional stories is relevant. Jean Tarisesei, now a member of the Vanuatu Cultural Centre staff, told me that during the seventies when living in Port Vila and bringing up young children,

---

[12] These letters are kept in Gardissat's personal files and cover the period in which he worked for the radio, 1975 -1986.

she didn't often listen to the cultural programs on the radio (interview, 9 Feb 1997). She was, she said, interested mostly in listening to material from her own island, Ambae, because then she understood what the stories were about. Tarisesei also suggested that the greater number of listeners to the radio were men. She considered that this was because women's domestic duties made it hard for them to sit down and listen to the radio, but a number of other reasons can be hypothesized. One is that the exchange and transmission of local knowledge and practice from area to area had always been primarily the preserve of men, both through the trade networks and also, later, in that most of the people exposed to other places and ideas through the labor trade were men. The discussion and analysis of traditional knowledge and practice was itself a male practice. More importantly, for many years Bislama was a male language. In that women did not travel widely in Vanuatu until some years after independence, and in that men tended to be the members of the community who engaged with visiting outsiders, women did not need to, and often did not, speak Bislama.[13]

Radio, Bislama, and the nation

Gardissat reported that when he first worked on the radio, he was much criticized for his Bislama. At that time the language was not standardized, but existed in a number of versions: plantation Bislama, which was used by expatriates to give instructions to Ni-Vanuatu; French Bislama; English Bislama; and versions of the language specific to certain islands. There seems in particular to have been considerable difference between the language as spoken by Ni-Vanuatu and as spoken by expatriates. Gardissat received criticism on all sides. Had he been Ni-Vanuatu himself, he argued, the Bislama he used would have occasioned no comment, but as a Frenchman, his use of the language raised many issues about the status of the language itself. He was criticized for speaking it at all, and for the way in which he spoke it. French expatriates were incensed because they said he wasn't speaking Bislama but English, while the English accused him of speaking not Bislama but French. Ni-Vanuatu criticized him for using expatriate pronunciations, for example of place names. Gardissat said that his Ni-Vanuatu colleagues at the radio refined and polished his fluency in the language as spoken by local people.

The contribution of radio to the standardization of Bislama (which has been noted elsewhere; compare Jolly 1994, 12), is very important to *kastom*. In order for local knowledge and practice to be presented to an archipelago - wide audience it has to be made at some level comprehensible in a language common to all, that is, in Bislama. Radio both facilitated and developed the presentation of aspects of local knowledge and practice at this level, and was the means of standardizing the terms, and the very words, in which it was communicated. It is the radio, in this sense, that made *kastom* a nationally recognized phenomenon.

Indeed, the very idea of the archipelago as a nation was promulgated by radio.[14] Godwin Ligo, talking about the early effect of broadcasting, said that Radio Vila brought people to understand that Port Vila was the capital of the whole country, and that the name of the country was the New Hebrides. Initially people identified primarily with their own island, and when they heard about Vila it seemed to them to be another country itself, one a person might need a passport to visit.[15] Gradually, however, they began to identify with the nation. This effect of radio was significantly linked to the development of the independence movement in the seventies, and in turn, it was the independence movement itself that increased listenership to the radio. Interest in the radio accelerated greatly after 1974, when the movement for independence began to gain momentum. However much people had or had not listened to record requests and *kastom* programs, at this time they began struggling with the static to hear the latest developments in this eventful period of their country's history.

---

[13] It is hard to tell at present how many women did speak Bislama in the period before independence. Margaret Jolly reported that when she worked among the traditionalist Sa of south Pentecost in 1971, men actively discouraged women from learning Bislama (1994, 8). However, this probably represents only one part of the picture. Dorothy Shineberg has recorded that between six and ten percent of labor-trade recruits between 1865 and 1929 were women (pers comm; see also Shineberg 1999). Those women at least can be assumed to have spoken Bislama or its antecedents.

[14] Edward LiPuma briefly discussed the importance of the media in the creation of "an articulated public sphere" in Oceania (1955, 50 - 51). I would argue more strongly that radio is crucial to the creation of a public sphere throughout Melanesia.

[15] Ligo said a common Bislama expression at that period was "Mi karim paspot blong go long Vila" (I need a [take my] passport to go to Vila).

One of the central concepts in the platform of the indigenous political parties that developed during this era was the notion of the unity of the Ni-Vanuatu as distinct from both the colonial powers. Uniting people who were divided by their mission, education, and employment histories between the British and the French, the nation's incipient politicians made much of *kastom* as representing a unified identity for all the indigenous inhabitants of the archipelago. At this point a kind of national discourse about the importance of *kastom* began to develop. That is to say, radio programs had drawn rural Ni-Vanuatu's attention to the idea that a unity existed in the island-by-island diversity they recognized. As local knowledge and practice are seen to arise out of each place so, in an overarching sense, a nationally characteristic knowledge and practice could be understood to arise out of the whole archipelago. Now politicians drew people's attention to the distinctiveness of that knowledge and practice-kastom -and identified it as an important basis for claims for independence. At the same time many of these politicians established an intellectual rapprochement between *kastom* and Christianity. Instead of being opposed, the two were seen as feasibly coexisting.[16]

The independence movement was marked by contestation not only with the two governments (which had radically different approaches to the granting of independence), but between different local political movements. These coalesced through the late seventies into a coalition of Francophone parties, and an Anglophone party that, in the event, became the first government of independence. As these political parties took shape, one of the points of contestation between them was debate as to which could most legitimately claim to represent and support *kastom.* This discussion and debate took place both in meetings held around the country, as the various political leaders traveled and held meetings widely through the archipelago, and on the radio. Although the condominium practiced censorship by controlling both access to the radio by political leaders and news reportage,[17] discussions about *kastom* -debates about its validity as a basis for independence, and about which political party most legitimately represented *kastom* - were broadcast on the radio. *Kastom* became, in this period, part of the rhetoric of Vanuatu nationalism, part of the way in which politicians and others characterized the nation and affirmed its value and importance.

Here, the difference between *kastom* and indigenous knowledge and practice begins to become clear. The identification of *kastom* as the characteristic that makes the Ni-Vanuatu different, in turn acted on the way in which *kastom* itself was understood. It came to signify that very difference, the practices and characteristics that distinguish the Ni-Vanuatu from other people. No longer characterized as manifesting the darkness of unenlightened heathenism, *kastom* was defined as not only good but as crucially important to the positive characterization of the newly independent nation. A strong association between *kastom* and identity was forged in the rhetoric of this era. *Kastom* was increasingly spoken of as the basis of Ni-Vanuatu identity. This connection is what leads to the formulation Jennifer Mwera quoted to me: *kastom* is the life of the people.

This positive characterization of *kastom* reached a highpoint in December 1979 with the First National Arts Festival, which took place in Port Vila. The festival, which was organized by Godwin Ligo and was named after his radio program, *Taem Nao, Taem Bifo,* brought together performance groups from all over the archipelago who presented to each other songs, dances, magical skills, carving, and more - in a festival in the true sense of the word - an occasion of extraordinary vibrancy and enthusiasm. Writing about the festival a year later, Ligo summed up much of the argument I am making here. The festival, he stated, "has brought about an awareness amongst Ni-Vanuatu of the importance and the vividness of our own culture. There is also a realisation of the importance of preserving and developing culture, custom and traditions as a means of reinforcing national identity. The first Cultural Festival came at a vital moment in the history of Vanuatu, and showed to the world at large their identity, which was their passport through the gate of Independence as 'Ni-Vanuatu' (1980, 65).

Independence was achieved seven months later, on 30 July 1980. Radio Vila, which had been renamed Radio New Hebrides in 1977, became Radio Vanuatu.

---

[16] For accounts of the use of *kastom* by Ni-Vanuatu politicians in the construction of the nation, and the integration of *kastom* and Christianity, see Tonkinson 1982; Facey 1995.

[17] The tradition of government-controlled news censorship continued after independence, and is subject of all the publications on radio in Vanuatu known to me (Manua 1995; Nash ; 1995; Toa 1996).

Radio and the Redefinition of Kastom in Vanuatu

Reinforcing the concept of Kastom

Gardissat's *kastom* program was particularly influential because his interest in local knowledge and practice constituted a reversal of the position that Ni-Vanuatu expected Condominium officials to take. Here was the government on the radio, asserting the importance of local practice. Gardissat had a strong commitment to *kastom* and saw his program as an opportunity to express what he saw as its considerable importance, and to increase comprehension of this evaluation. He attempted to refine the definition of *kastom* by introducing a distinction between it and two other Bislama terms, both also derived from English: *kalja and tredisin.* He used *tredisin* to refer to Ni-Vanuatu practices that have been adopted from elsewhere, such as the singing of New Year *(Bonne Année)* songs, a specialty of the people of Erakor village near Port Vila, and *kalja* to refer to all contemporary practice. He made programs devoted to each of these three terms and attempted to reinforce the distinction between them in a number of different ways.

Here then is an important point concerning the nature of the influence of radio. While Gardissat's three terms were quickly adopted by politicians and other people discussing *kastom* (such as Ligo in the quotation just cited), the distinction between them was never successfully introduced. I have had a number of extensive discussions with people in Vanuatu about *kastom, kalja, and tredisin,* the conclusion to all of which has been that there is no difference between the three. People who use the expression *kastom, kalja mo tredisen* seem to do so to reinforce their emphasis on *kastom* and not to distinguish between the terms. From this it can be argued that radio is successful in introducing new concepts and ideas where there is already an openness to those concepts within the audience. People welcomed the broadcast of *kastom* by the government, and the implicit assurance that it was to be positively evaluated, because they themselves were willing or even eager to adopt that positive evaluation. A definitional distinction between various forms of local practice did not meet with an already receptive audience, and was never established, although the terms themselves were widely adopted.

Gardissat's program had a far wider range than the broadcast of stories and songs, told by Islanders or dramatized with inventive flair. He welcomed researchers working in the country onto the program, and discussed their research with them. This included not only anthropologists, but also archaeologists and biologists. He also made programs about the archipelago's history.

One of the people who appeared on the program was an ethnomusicologist called Peter Crowe, who was working in the north of the archipelago during the seventies. In 1976 the Condominium obtained a grant from the South Pacific Commission to initiate an Oral Traditions Recording Project. This was established under the aegis of the Cultural Centre, an institution that had been founded in 1956 to celebrate the fiftieth anniversary of the Condominium. Crowe selected four village men from islands in northern Vanuatu and trained them in recording techniques at a two-week course held on the island of Ambae. Material they recorded during the course was sent to Gardissat in Vila and broadcast from Radio Vila during the fortnight.

Thus was established a very important link between the work of the Cultural Centre, especially the work of Cultural Centre extension workers known as fieldworkers, and the Radio. Under the direction of Kirk Huffman, who was appointed as the Cultural Centre's first full-time curator from 1977, the Oral Traditions Project developed in scope and importance. Two of Crowe's trainees, James Gwero and Jeffrey Uli Boe, formed the nucleus of a group of over seventy volunteer fieldworkers who continue to work to document and revive knowledge and practice, each in their own village and region. The fieldworkers meet every year for a two-week workshop at which they are trained in all kinds of documentation and recording techniques. At these workshops they also discuss the nature of *kastom.* The Men Fieldworkers Group, which has been meeting annually since 1981, has developed a sophisticated philosophical discussion, both about the nature and content of local knowledge and practice, and about how that relates to the present conditions of education, development, and tourism in the archipelago. A Women Fieldworkers Group was founded in 1994.

The Cultural Centre contributed increasingly to Gardissat's program during the late seventies, until Gardissat relinquished responsibility for it to the Cultural Centre. Huffman mostly edited the program at the Cultural Centre, using recordings made by fieldworkers. Sometimes experienced fieldworkers, such as James Gwero, themselves prepared whole programs based around their own material. The significance of the fieldworker network's contribution to the program is that through it, rural Ni-Vanuatu have continued to have the means to engage with the radio. As service messages and record-request programs (now driven partly through the growing telephone network) have continued to be extremely popular, so interaction with the radio through the *kastom* program was maintained through access to the fieldworkers and the Cultural Centre.

Reinforced by the rhetoric of the government of independence, which continued to affirm *kastom* as central to Ni-Vanuatu life, the Cultural Centre program served to affirm the importance of *kastom,* and was widely listened to. The importance of this became clear to me when I undertook the research I discussed at the beginning of this paper. Wherever I went on Ambae, people were conversant with the concept of *kastom* and with the work of the Cultural Centre. As part of the Women's Culture Project, my colleague Jean Tarisesei and I made programs that derived from our Ambae research. We found that the programs preceded us around the island, so that when we visited new areas people were already aware of our project. More importantly, people were very keen to record stories and songs to be included in the programs, and listened with critical interest to broadcasts, commenting to us, as they had twenty years before to Godwin Ligo, about stories that are "the same but a little bit different."

From 1992 to 1994 Tarisesei herself was responsible for making the *kastom* program as a Cultural Centre staff member. This experience altered her understanding of the importance of *kastom* on the radio. Two decades earlier, as I have mentioned, Tarisesei had been personally uninterested in listening to *kastom.* When she started making programs herself, she began, she said, to realize how many people do listen to *kastom,* and how interested they are in it. People often came to see her at the Cultural Centre to ask her about things they had heard on her program, and if she serialized a story and then for some reason didn't put the next part on the next week, people would come and ask her about it (interview, 9 Feb 997).

In 1994 the Vanuatu Government recreated the radio as a corporation, the Vanuatu Television and Broadcasting Corporation, and commenced charging government departments and nongovernmental agencies for airtime. As a result Radio Vanuatu no longer provided a steady stream of information to Ni-Vanuatu (agriculture programs, women's programs, and so on), as few organizations could meet the prohibitive charges for airtime. Instead, the station began to broadcast increasing proportions of music.[18] At the same time, FM98, a music station modeled on commercial FM popular music stations in western countries, was founded, broadcasting to Port Vila and to Luganville. Both stations increasingly assume a hearing rather than listening model in radio, a development that is far from welcome in the islands, as rural Ni-Vanuatu depend on the radio as the source of all kinds of information.

The Cultural Centre was one of the organizations unable to pay for airtime, and the *kastom* program went off the air. This was not a development welcomed by rural Ni-Vanuatu. Jeffrey Uli Boe, a fieldworker on Maewo, spoke to me about this. He said of his fellow villagers: "They asked me: 'Usually every Saturday evening at six o'clock we wait to hear *kastom* stories and songs. When someone tells a story from his island he sings the song that belongs to it. But now we don't hear this any more. Why not? . . . These things are ours, within *kastom.* Other countries make sure their *kastom* comes out on the radio, how is it that we don't? . . . We must make it alive again'" (taped interview, 4 Feb 1997).[19] Similarly a John Frum cult leader from Tanna, Jif Isaac Wan, sent a news item to the radio during 1996 in which he asked the government to ensure Radio Vanuatu made many *kastom* programs (Jacob Kapere, pers comm, 4 Feb 1997). Rural people feel disenfranchised by radio programming that does not attend to their own knowledge and practice, and to the *kastom* that they have learned to recognize as the basis of their identity.

---

[18] Radio is also, of course, important to the creation of local popular music industries in Melanesia, as Michael Webb demonstrated, largely in passing, in his analysis of popular music in Papua New Guinea (1993).

[19] "Olgeta i bin askim mi, se olsem wanem ia, from we long evri Sarere olsem, long 6 oklok, oltaem mifala i stap reri blong harim ol kastom stori, ol singsing. Taem wan i stori long narafala, olsem long aelan blong hem, gogo nao, i singim singsing blong hem. Be naoia mifala i nomo harim nao. I olsem wanem?. . . From we, oli talem se, evri samting ia i stap long yumi long kastom. From narafala kantri, olgeta i stap mekim kastom blong olgeta i kam tru long radio. Be olsem wanem long yumi? . . . Ating i moa gud we yumi mas mekim i laev bakagen."

Radio and the Redefinition of Kastom in Vanuatu

The decision to conform to western commercial models of radio (which was, I understand, effected by expatriate advisers) fails to recognize the central importance of radio to people living in a primarily oral culture, without other sources of information. Chief Shadrach, praising the radio, said to me that it is a wonderful source of information about weather and tides, and giving notice of deaths. The hearing model of radio assumes, incorrectly in rural Vanuatu, that broadcasting is primarily entertainment, and that information like this can be obtained elsewhere.

Radio has made a profound contribution to the constitution of the nation of Vanuatu. A crucial element of that constitution is the way in which, through the presentation and exploration of local knowledge and practice as *kastom*, radio has linked indigenous projects to the national ideal. The idea of nation is connected not only to education and development, but to local practice, to the history and ritual by which Islanders make sense of their everyday lives. The remotest villager, hearing on the radio that *kastom* is the basis of Ni-Vanuatu identity, is able to perceive him or herself as integral to the nation. Radio could not have achieved this linkage alone. Rather, by affirming publicly something that many people valued privately, it facilitated the development of a region-wide acknowledgment of the nature and importance of *kastom*.

Significantly, there has never been any policy about the broadcasting of *kastom* on the radio. Bob Makin, who was first employed as British radio officer and subsequently appointed as Director of Radio Vanuatu from 1980 to 1991, said that there was never any formal intention on the part of the station as a whole to affirm *kastom*. Apart from the *kastom* program, if the radio was saying that *kastom* is important, he said, that is because people were saying so and the radio reported it (interview, 2 Aug 1992).

The importance of the radio in the redefinition of *kastom* is a function of the way in which radio created a nationally received forum for the communication of ideas. Radio both presented and reinforced new concepts, creating through *kastom* programs an opportunity for rural Ni-Vanuatu to access a national arena, and through it to learn about each other. Although traditional knowledge and practice is being eroded by education, employment, and development, the loss of this program was a disenfranchisement that had the potential to significantly affect the degree to which rural Ni-Vanuatu perceive themselves as partners in the nation. The Cultural Centre fought against the prohibitive fees for their program for a number of years and in 1998 succeeded in gaining a reduction of the fees to a level that they could manage within their overall budget. The program returned to air in mid-1998, in the same Saturday-at-six time slot, re-introducing the Kavelicolico song, retrieved from the Radio Vanuatu archives, as its opening theme. Nothing could more clearly demonstrate the Cultural Centre's assessment of the importance of radio to the ongoing affirmation that *kastom* is, as Jennifer Mwera said, the life of the people.

This paper is based on interview and discussions with many people, whose contribution to it I would like to acknowledge here. In particular I wish to thank Reece Discombe, who introduced me to many crucial actors in the early days of radio in the New Hebrides, and educated me about the technical realities of radio communications. I also thank Frank Palmer, Simeon Kaltonga, Charlot , Long Wah, Chief Willie Bongmatur, Godwin Ligo, Paul Gardissat, Bob Makin, , Darrell Tryon, Kirk Huffman, Keith Woodward, Jennifer Mwera, Chief Shadrach Rasa Usi, Jeffrey Uli Boe, Jean Tarisesei, and Jacob Sam Kapere. All these people provided information which is incorporated into this paper. I would also like to thank a number of Vanuatu Cultural Centre staff and fieldworkers who enhanced my understanding of the role of radio, notably Willie Roi, James Gwero, and Eli Field. This paper has benefited from comments made by a number of colleagues. Here I thank Eric Hirsch, Lamont Lindstrom, David Luders, Klaus Neumann, Miriam Meyerhoff, and Ralph Regenvanu. The paper was first prepared for the Fulbright symposium, Indigenous Cultures in an Interconnected World, held in Darwin in July 1997. I thank Claire Smith for the invitation that stimulated me to write it.

This paper draws on research undertaken in Vanuatu from 1989 to 1998. My doctoral research in 1991 -92 was supported by grants from the Emslie Horniman Scholarship Fund and the Wenner-Gren Foundation for Anthropological Research, while work in 1994 -95 was assisted by the Australian Museum. Research undertaken in 1996 -1998 was supported by the Australian Research Council through the Australian National University, specifically, since 1997, through the Centre for Cross-Cultural Research. I gratefully acknowledge the assistance of all these organizations.

Glossary

ITEM	DEFINITION	LANGUAGE PROVENANCE
abuitok	Chief's sceptre	Mataso
ase mansa	Ceremonial pig tusks	language of Malo
atavi	Chief's adviser	Central Islands
bacon	Dancing ornament	Melsisi
banyan	Strangler fig	English
belelu Nakowia	Red *burao*	Mele
Bislama	Vanuatu Pidgin	English
bubu	Ancestor	Bislama
buluk	Beef	Bislama
burao	*(hibiscus tiliaceus)* coastal burao *(cordia sucordata)*	Bislama
bweleng-bweleng	A red parrot	Tanna
casuarina	*(Casuarina equsetifolia)* ironwood tree, *oktri* in Bislama	language of Tongoa
dong	The name of a ritual dance from Central Pentecost	Melsisi
elder	Elder from the church or tribe	English
fare	Traditional construction	
fehi	A variety of banana	
fela	Cat's cradle	Southern Pentecost vernacular
gaibala	Tongs used to move hot stones	language of Maewo
grass-skirt	Traditional skirt made from frayed leaves	Bislama
hoknait	Owl	Bislama
Iri	Eventail	Language of 'Ambae (Longana)
kaori	*(Agathis obtusa)* a large, hardwood tree	
kawiametameta	Bird	Tanna
konokon	Battle lance or spear	Mele
kumala	Sweet potato	Bislama
Kwaranis	Laplap oven	language of Vanua Lava
laplap	National dish. Pudding made from yam, taro, banana. Baked with meat or fish in a ground oven covered with hot stones.	Bislama
leimule	Variety of banana	Mele
liliko	A small cord made from pandanus used for settling debts	Mele
lisepsep	Creature half-human, half-mythical of small size and long hair. Sometimes having long claws, droopy breasts and ears, this creature is gifted with supernatural strength.	Bislama

Glossary

ITEM	DEFINITION	LANGUAGE PROVENANCE
magha	Short mat made from long *pandanus* fibres used to buy women from Malekula. These mats are never unrolled and are stored in huts.	Language of Mallicolo
man	*Man* Santo: *man* from Santo, *man ples*: indigenous *man*	Bislama
marea or *mwalala*	Dancing grounds (see *nasara*)	Mele
matarau	ancestors	Language of Mele
mau or *maui*	warriors	Mele
meleun	A chiefly rank from Ambrym	Ambrym
mutuama	See *lisepsep*	Ifira
mwaluen	Chiefly rank	language of Malekula (Tomman)
nabanga	Banyan, strangler fig	Bislama
nabangura	*(Calophyllum inophyllum)* see Tamanu	Bislama
nabua mahot	Means " the path is broken "	Mele
nabua vera	Means " the path is burning "	Mele
nadibidou	Red *burao*	Mataso
naflak	A new system of clan organisation of which Roy Mata is purported to have created.	Center islands
nakamal	Communal house	Bislama
nakatambol	*(Dracontomelon vitiense)* Tambol	Bislama
nakavika	Jamalak	Bislama
naluan	Grade taking ceremony	Ambrym
nakiwas	Comb	Mataso
namalao	Bird (land duck)	Bislama
namamao	Tree	Mataso
namambe	*(Inocarpus fagiferus)* Tahitian chestnut	Bislama
namangki	Grade taking ceremony	Bislama
namarae	Eel	Bislama
namatou	Coconut palm	language of Malekula (Tomman)
nambas	Penis sheath	Bislama
nambilak	A land duck	Bislama
namele	Cyca from the fern family. Sacred tree. Its frond is used to symbolize taboos or peace.	Bislama
nananara	*(Gyrocarpus americanus)* tree	Bislama
nandarao	Tree	
nanduledule	Doule	Bislama
naos	Sour apple	Bislama
narbout	Tree	language of south west Malekula
narivirivi	Eventail	Mataso
nasama	Outrigger	Bislama
nasara	Traditional meeting place along with the nakamal. Place of grade taking and dancing that define local custom.	Bislama

290

ITEM	DEFINITION	LANGUAGE PROVENANCE
nasasa	Leaf used as decoration	Bislama
nasese	A type of shell that sticks to rocks	Bislama
nasiko	Kingfisher	Bislama
nasorsor	tree or bush	Gaua
nasusu	Breasts	Mele
natalae	Giant shell also called clam	Bislama
natangora	Ivory palm	Bislama
natapae	Traditional surf board	Torres
natapoa	(*Terminalia catappa*) - tree	Bislama
navara	Germinated coconut	Bislama
navele	(*Barringtonia edulis*) a type of large almond	Bislama
nawimba	Large forest bird also called naotu	Bislama
nawita	Squid or octopus	Bislama
neliku	Sea cucumber	Language of Emae
neses	Tree	Tanna
nolu	Vine	Language of west Tanna
notou	See nawimba	
oute koguona	Sacred place	Language of Ambae (Longana)
pandanus	Coastal tree whose leaves are used to make traditional mats	
pikinini	child	Bislama
por	*Laplap* bag	Language of Vanua Lava
punung 'ha	Green pigeon with a red breast	Language of west Tanna
pupu	Conch used to announce a meeting	Bislama
Ragmuehu	Mythical people of Ambae	Ambae
renmamak kari	" hello my friend "	Language of Pentecost
rupeki	Small *laplap*	Tanna
sangalegale	See *Lisepsep*	Language of Sheperds
savaka	Basket used to preserve food	Language of Ifira
sermop	Means " split chestnut "	Language of southern Pentecost
seru	Comb	Mele
shell	Half coconut shell used to drink kava	Bislama
singwotamarino	Finely woven mats from Ambae	Ambae
siviritot	Means " winged people "	Language of Makura
suf-suf	Variety of banana	South Pentecost

Glossary

ITEM	DEFINITION	LANGUAGE PROVENANCE
Sul	Parrot	Tanna
Talu tuei	Another mythical people from Ambae	Ambae
tamanu	*(Calophyllum inophyllum)* Coastal tree. Its nut was once used to imprison magical fish.	Bislama
tamate	Means " spirit world "	Ambae
tamtam	Slit gong	Bislama
tanmonok	The highest rank for Pentecost chiefs	Pentecost
tapa	Beaten and flattened bark used by the Polynesians as clothing or decoration. On Vanuatu, there exists a form of this tradition on the island of Erromango.	
tapugha	Large stone	Tanna
titamol	see *lisepsep*	Paama
troca	Conical shell	
tukumete	Large wooden plate	Ifira
tupe	vine	Ambae
vermelap	twins	language of west Ambrym
vui	" to come back "	Ambae
waratongoa	Thorny bush	language of Tongoa
white grass	Tall grasses located on plains and near volcanoes	Bislama

The definition in this glossary were taken from the late Terry Crowley's,
(*A new bislama dictionary*), IPS, Fiji, 1995.

Bibliography
Oral traditions of Vanuatu

Agostini, J., *Coutumes et croyances des Nouvelles-Hébrides,* Revue des traditions populaires, 7 : 50-59.

Allen, M., *Male Cults and Secret Initiations in Melanesia,* Melbourne University Press, Melbourne, 1967.

Allen, M., *Matriliny, Secrecy and "Power" in the Northern New Hebrides,* Ms, 1978.

Anonyme, *Les idées de Divinités chez les indigènes de la Nouvelle Calédonie, des Loyalty et des Nouvelles-Hébrides,* Saint Louis, Imprimerie Catholique, 1892. (Compte rendu des conférences ecclésiastiques du Vicariat apostolique de la Nouvelle-Calédonie, 3ème fascicule).

Anonyme, *A legend of Aniwa: Tangaroa Teisauma or Takeira,* New Hebrides Magazine, 5 : 29, 1902.

Anonyme, *Le culte des ancêtres aux Nouvelles-Hébrides,* L'Illustration, 9 janv. , 30, 1904.

Anonyme, *The rat's whiskers,* South Pacific Commission Literature bureau, Presbyterian Church of New Hebrides education committee, 28 p., n.d.

Anonyme, *The Child of the Namele: a story from Maewo.* Port Vila, Ministry of Education (Custom Stories of Our Islands, Series 1, Level B), 1980.

Anonyme, *The Giant of Ra: a story from Mota Lava,* Port Vila, Ministry of Education (Custom Stories of Our Islands, Series 1, Level B), 1980.

Anonyme, *How the Hermit Crab Tricked the Kingfisher: a story from Pentecost,* Port Vila, Ministry of Education (Custom Stories of Our Islands, Series 1, Level B), 1980.

Anonyme, *Nambilak: a story from Tanna,* Port Vila, Ministry of Education (Custom Stories of Our Islands, Series 1, Level B), 1980.

Anonyme, *Rere and the Napau: a story from Nguna.* Port Vila, Ministry of Education (Custom Stories of Our Islands, Series 1, Level B), 1980.

Anonyme, *Tagaro and Merabuto: a story from Aoba,* Port Vila, Ministry of Education (Custom Stories of Our Islands, Series 1, Level B), 1980.

Anonyme, *Suniena Lala Nae Nivenue* (Lewo language, Epi), Vanuatu, Summer Institute of Linguistics, 1983.

Anonyme, *Noanange, stories written in the eastern dialect of north Tanna language,* Ts, produced during a writers workshop hosted by the Summer Institute of Linguistics, 1986.

Apno Y. (ed.), *Stori buk,* TAFEA provincial government, 2001.

Aubert de la Rüe, E., S*ur la nature et l'origine probable des pierres portées en pendentifs à l'île de Tanna (Nouvelles-Hébrides),* L'Anthropologie, 48 : 249-260, 1938.

Bage S., *The legend of Taribuanga and other stories and legend of Vanusiaraga* - Pentecost, book 4 (?), Port Vila, Ts., n.d.

Baker, G. A., *The big leap,* The Australian Magazine, October 14-15:54-60, 1989.

Batick, J-P and J-C Toure, *Ol damej long olgeta olfala ples we I save kamaot sapos ol I wokem rod long Big Bay, Not Santo,* Port Vila, Rejista blong olgeta olfala ples blong Vanuatu, VCHSS, development impact report, namba 9, 1994.

Best, S., *Here be dragons,* Journal of the Polynesian Society, 97(3): 239-259, 1988.

Bonnemaison, J., *The tree and the Canoe: roots and mobility in Vanuatu society,* Pacific Viewpoint, 25(2):117-151, Melbourne, 1984.

Bonnemaison, J., *The tree and the Canoe: roots and mobility in Vanuatu society,* part 2, Pacific Viewpoint, 26(1): 30-62, Melbourne, 1985.

Bonnemaison J., *La dernière île,* Paris, ARLEA/ORSTOM, 1986, 405 p.

Bonnemaison J., *L'Arbre et la Pirogue,* Paris, ORSTOM, 1986.

Bonnemaison J., *Le territoire enchanté croyances et territorialité en Mélanésie,* Géographie et cultures, numéro 3, Paris, 1992.

Bibliography

Bonnemaison J., *Les fondements géographiques d'une identité. L'archipel du Vanuatu,* Paris, ORSTOM, Livre 1, " *Gens de pirogue et gens de la terre* ", 1996, 460 p.

Bonnemaison J., *Les fondements géographiques d'une identité. L'archipel du Vanuatu,* Paris, ORSTOM, livre 2, " *Les gens des lieux* ", 1997, 562 p.

Brunton, R., *Nia's story,* Quadrant, April: 34-36, 1981.

Brunton, R., *A harmless substance? Anthropological aspect of kava in the south Pacific* in J. Prescott and G. McCall (eds.), *Kava: use and abuse in Australia and the south Pacific,* pp. 13-25, Kensington: National Drug and Alcohol Research Centre, University of New South Wales, 1989.

Brunton, R., *Environmentalism and sorcery,* Environmental Backgrounder, 8, 1992.

Capell, A., *The stratification of afterworld beliefs in the New Hebrides,* Folklore, 49:51-85, 1938.

Capell A., *Anthropology and linguistics of Futuna, Aniwa, New Hebrides, Oceania,* Linguistics monograph n°5, University of Sidney, 1958.

Capell, A., *The Maui Myths in the New Hebrides,* Folklore, 71:19-36, 1960.

Capell A, J. Layard, *Materials in Atchin, Malekula, grammar, vocabulary and texts,* in Pacific Linguistics n°20, series D, Australian national university, Canberra, 1980.

Codrington R.H., *Notes on the customs of Mota, Banks islands, with remarks by Lorimar Fison,* Transactions and proceedings of the Royal Society of Victoria, 16:119-143, 1880.

Codrington R.H., *A folk tale from New Hebrides,* Archaeological Review, 2:90-91, 1888.

Codrington R.H., *The Melanesians: studies in their anthropology and folklore,* Oxford, Clarendon press, 1891, 419 p.

Codrington R.H., *Melanesian folk-tales,* Folklore, 4:509-512, 1893.

Collectif, *Tesa ! Mal natrausen* - Erakor, USP centre, Port Vila, 1983.

Crowe, P. (ed.), *Work in the North 1974-77,* reports and other papers of the Northern District fieldworkers Union of the Oral Tradition Project, New Hebrides Cultural Centre, Port Vila, 1977.

Crowe, P., *Recording in the South Seas,* IFPI, News, 4, 1978.

Crowe, P., *Pince son ombilic et le mien vibrera : chant muet, kava et rêves dans la musique mélanésienne,* Anaurio Musical (Barcelona), 39-40 : 217-238, 1985.

Crowe, P., *Copyright and Pacific paradoxes,* Pacific Arts Newsletter, 37-41, 1986.

Crowe, P., *Tagaro seeks Mamalu: Maewo song and migration tradition,* Rongorongo Studies, 1(1/2): 14-21, 35-42, 1991.

Crowley T., *Stories from Paama,* in Oral history, special issue celebrating the independence, vol.8, n°3, Institute of Papua New Guinea studies, Port Moresby, 1980.

Croze, M., *Custom Stories of Our Islands,* Port Vila, Vanuatu Ministry of Education Printery, 1980.

Deacon, A.B., *Notes on some islands of the New Hebrides,* journal of the Royal Anthropological Institute, 59:463-515, 1929.

Déniau, A., *Croyances religieuses et mœurs des indigènes de l'île de Malo, Nouvelles-Hébrides à l'arrivée des missionnaires en 1887* (1ère partie), Missions Catholiques, 21 : 332-370, 1889.

Déniau, A., *Aperçu sur la Religion des indigènes de l'île Malo, Nouvelles-Hébrides,* Saint Louis, Imprimerie Catholique, 1894.

Déniau, A., *Croyances religieuses et mœurs des indigènes de l'île Malo, Nouvelles-Hébrides à l'arrivée des missionnaires en 1887* (2ème partie), Missions Catholiques, 33 : 309-359, 1901.

Dick P., Joseph J., e.a., *Contes et légendes du Vanuatu,* Paris, Centre de relations internationales du Vanuatu, Agence de coopération culturelle et technique, 1985.

Dietschy, H., *Verwandtschaft und Freundschaft : analytische bemerkungen zur Sozialstruktur der Melanesier von Südwest Malekula* in *Südseestudien; Etudes sur l'Océanie, South Sea Studies,* pp. 358-412, Basel, Museum für Völkerkunde and Schweizerisches Museum für Volkskunde, 1951.

Douglas, B., *Autonomous and controlled spirits: traditional ritual and early interpretation of Christianity on Tanna, Aneytum and the Isle of Pines in comparative perspective,* Journal of the Polynesian Society, 98(1):7-48, 1989.

Durrad, W.J., *Notes on the Torres Islands* (part 1), Oceania, 10:389-403, 1939.

Durrad, W.J., *Notes on the Torres Islands* (part 2), Oceania, 11:75-109, 1941.

Durrad, W.J., *Notes on the Torres Islands* (part 3), Oceania, 11:186-201, 1941.

Eddie, T. and Robert N., *Nitae Esge Intas Uja n°1* (Aneytum), Port Vila, Summer Institute of Linguistics, 1989.

Facey E.E., *Nguna voices: texts and culture from central Vanuatu,* University of Calgary press, Calgary, 1988.

Firth, R., *A Raga Tale,* Man, 30:58-60, 1930.

Fox, C.E. and Drew, F.H., *Beliefs and tales of San Cristoval (Solomon Islands),* Journal of the Royal Anthropological Institute, 45(131-228), 1915.

Fox, G.J., *Big Nambas Custom Texts,* Ms, 1978.

Fox G. J., *Big Nambas Grammar,* in Pacific Linguistics, n°60, series B, Australian National University Canberra, 1979.

François A., *Sodosodo Maran Daki, Araki, saot Santo Vanuatu,* par le collecteur, LACITO, 2003.

François A., *Tog Tog i van en... na vap t amag non ige to Motlap lepno Bankis - Vanuatu,* par le collecteur, LACITO, 2003.

François A., *O olmevu ta turmo ta mesem le vonolav Vanuatu - Bankis,* par le collecteur, LACITO, 2003.

Frazer, J.G., *The Belief in Immortality and the Worship of the Dead,* London, 1913.

Galipaud, J-C et al., *Ripot n°3 Tanna : Imayou, Sameria, Manuapen, Isakkey mo Nukunewiaka,* Port Vila, VCHSS, interim report, 1992.

Galipaud, J-C and Kolmas, P., *Ripot n°2 Saot Malekula : Farun mo Taoran,* Port Vila, Rejista blong olgeta olfala ples blong Vanuatu, VCHSS, 1993.

Garanger, J., *Archéologie des Nouvelles-Hébrides : contribution à la connaissance des îles du Centre,* Paris, ORSTOM (publication de la société des Océanistes n°30), 1972.

Garanger, J., *Mythes et archéologie en Océanie,* La Recherche, 3(21), pp. 233-242, 1972.

Garanger, J., *Ethnologie du présent et du passé en Océanie* in *L'Homme d'Hier à Aujourd'hui : recueil d'études en hommage à André Leroi-Gourhan,* pp. 763-773, Cujas, Paris, 1973.

Garanger, J., *Tradition orale et préhistoire en Océanie,* Cahiers ORSTOM, Série Sciences Humaines, 13 (2) pp. 147-161, 1976.

Garanger, J., *Tradition orale et préhistoire en Océanie* in Schuapp, A. (ed.), *L'Archéologie Aujourd'hui,* pp. 187-205, Hachette, Paris, 1980.

Garanger, J., *Archaeology of the New Hebrides: contribution to the knowledge of the central islands,* Sydney, Oceania publications (Oceania monographs n°24), 1982.

Gardissat, P., *Nabanga, une anthologie illustrée de la littérature orale de l'archipel,* éditions des Arts de la Parole, VKS, Port-Vila, 2004.

Gibson, J., *Sofis wetem nakato,* University of the South Pacific Centre, Port Vila, 1988.

Gittings, A., *Tales from the South Seas,* Fiji, Government Printer, 1953.

Godefroy, J., *Une tribu tombée de la lune ou les indigènes de Vao chez eux,* Emmanuel Vitte, Lyon et Paris, 1936.

Gowers, S., *Some common trees of the New Hebrides and their vernacular names,* Port Vila, Department of Agriculture, 1976.

Gravier, C., *Sur le "Palolo" des Nouvelles-Hébrides (d'après les renseignements fournis par le P. Suas, missionnaire à Aoba, île des Lépreux),* Bulletin du Muséum National d'Histoire Naturelle, 30, pp. 472-474, 1924.

Gray, M., *Some notes on the Tannese,* Australian Association for the Advancement of Science, reports of the fourth meeting), 3:645-680, 1892.

Gray, W., *Aniwan folk-lore,* Journal of the Polynesian Society, 3(3):162-164, 1894.

Gray, W., *Four Aniwan songs,* Journal of the Polynesian Society, 3(2):93-97, 1894.

Bibliography

Guiart J., *Sociétés, rituels et mythes du nord-Ambrym, Nouvelles Hébrides* in Journal de la société des Océanistes, t. 7 pp 5-103, Paris, 1951.

Guiart, J., *Le chef de Naxa* in Leroi-Gourhan J et Poirier J. (eds.), *Ethnologie de l'Union Française*, vol.2, pp. 774-775, Paris, 1953.

Guiart J., *Un siècle et demi de contacts culturels à Tanna, Nouvelles-Hébrides*, publication de la Société des Océanistes n°5, Musée de l'Homme, Paris, 1956.

Guiart J., *Espiritu Santo (Nouvelles Hébrides)*, Plon, Paris, 1958.

Guiart, J., *Les Religions de l'Océanie*, P.U.F, Paris, 1962.

Guiart J., *Le dossier rassemblé* in Espirat J-J. et al., *Système de Titres, électifs ou héréditaires dans les Nouvelles-Hébrides centrales d'Efate aux îles Sheperds*, Mémoires de l'Institut d'Ethnologie, Musée de l'Homme, Paris, 1973.

Guiart, J., *Society, Rituals and Myths of North Ambrym (New Hebrides)*, English translation of *Sociétés, rituels et mythes du nord Ambrym (Nouvelles-Hébrides)*, Journal de la Société des Océanistes, vol.7 (7), 1951, pp. 5-103, 1983.

Guiart, J., *The problem of oral tradition and the arts* in Dark P.J.C. (ed.) *Development of the Arts in the Pacific*, pp.9-15, Wellington, Pacific Arts Association (Occasional Papers of the Pacific Arts Association, n°1), 1984.

Guiart J., *L'Océanie*, in *Mythes et croyances du monde*, vol. III, " Afrique noire, Amérique, Océanie ", Brepols, 1991, pp 463-547.

Gunn, W., *Heralds of Dawn: early converts in the New Hebrides*, London,, Hodder and Stoughton, 1924.

Harrison, *Savage civilization*, Alfreda A. Knopf, New York, 1937.

Hébert, B., *Mythe de la nuit : tribu des farea lapa, île de Nguna, Nouvelles-Hébrides*, Etudes Mélanésiennes, 14-17 : 93-94, 1959-1962.

Hébert, B., *" Wota ni Manu " (Ilot Wot ou Ilot Monument)*, Etudes Mélanésiennes, 21-25 : 55-71, 1966-1970.

Howard S. (ed.), *Leth Vekar, castom stori buk*, peace corps, Port Vila 2002.

Huffman, K. (ed.), *Samfala kastom storian blong Vanuatu*, Vanuatu Kaljoral Senta, workshop blong ol fieldworkers, Ts, 1982.

Huffman, K. (ed.), *Workshop blong ol fieldworkers, samfala kastom storian long langwis mo Bislama*, Vanuatu Kaljoral Senta, Port Vila, 1984.

Humphreys, C.B., *The Southern New Hebrides: an ethnological record*, Cambridge, Cambridge University Press, 1926.

Ivens, W.G., *A note on Ambat*, Man, 30(36): 49-51, 1930.

Ivens, W.G., *The place of Vui and Tamate in the religion of Mota*, journal of the Royal Anthropological Institute, 61:157-166, 1930.

Kolmas, P. et al., *Logging in south Erromango: the potential impact on the archaeological, historic and cultural site heritage*, Port Vila, VCHSS, Development impact report n°6, 1993.

Kolmas, P. et al., *Logging in West Malakula: the potential impact on the archaeological, historic and cultural site heritage of Tisvel and Vinmavis*, Port Vila, VCHSS, Development impact report n°8, 1993.

Kolmas, P. and N. Vanusoksok, *Ol damej long olgeta olfala ples we I save kamaot sipos ol I katem wud long Siwo long Emae*, Port Vila, Rejista blong olgeta olfala ples blong Vanuatu, VCHSS, ripot long damej we I save kamaot long divlopmen, namba 5, 1993.

Kolmas, P. and N. Vanusoksok, *Ol damej long olgeta olfala ples we I save kamaot sipos oli mekem Epot, Bungalow mo ples blong seling bot long Port Resolution long Tanna*, Port Vila, Rejista blong olgeta olfala ples blong Vanuatu, VCHSS, ripot long damej we I save kamaot long divlopmen, namba 4, 1993.

Kuautonga, J. et N., *Mashishiki wetem woman we i gat wing, Mashishiki et la femme ailée, Mashishiki and the flying woman*, Oral Arts edition, VKS, Port-Vila, 2003.

Kunike, H., *Dillingavuv: ein märchen den Torres Inseln*, Der Erdball, 3:230-232, 1929.

Lane, R.B., *The Melanesian of south Pentecost, New Hebrides* in Lawrence, P. and Meggitt M.J. (eds.), *Gods, Ghosts and Men in Melanesia: some religions of Australian New Guinea and the New Hebrides*, pp. 250-280, Melbourne, Oxford University Press, 1965.

Langdon, R., *Who was Hiu's prehistoric Michaelangelo?*, Pacific islands monthly, 38(2):91, 1967.

Lawrie, J.H., *The New Hebrideans*, (Aneytum) Scottish Geographical Magazine, 8:303-311, 1892.

Layard J. W., *Stone Men of Malekula, the small island of Vao,* London, Chatto & Windus, 1942, 816 p.

Layard, J. W., *Malekula: flying tricksters, ghosts, gods and epileptics*, Journal of Royal Anthropological Institute, 60:501-524, 1930.

Layard, J.W., *Shamanism: an analysis based on flying tricksters of Malekula*, Journal of Royal Anthropological Institute, 60:525-550, 1930.

Layard, J.W., *The journey of the dead from the small islands of north-eastern Malekula* in E.E. Evans Pritchard et al. (eds.), *Essays presented to C.G. Seligman*, pp.113-142, London, Kegan Paul, Trench, Trubner, 1934.

Layard, J. W., *Der mythos der totenfarht auf Malekula*, Eranos-Jahrbuch, 5:241-291, 1937-1938.

Leckie, J., *Towards a review of history in the south Pacific*, Journal of Pacific Studies, 9:9-69, 1983.

Leo, J., *Atatun Vanua, Avatvotu vilej, Not Pentecost*, Gaiware Bulbulu, n.d.

Leroi-Gourhan A. et Poirier J. (eds.), *Ethnologie de l'Union Française*, vol.2, Paris, 1953.

Lindstrom L., *Achieving wisdom : knowledge and politics on Tanna (Vanuatu)*, PHD Thesis, University of California, Berkeley, 1981.

Lindstrom, L., *Leftamap kastom: the political history of tradition on Tanna, Vanuatu*, Mankind, 13(4):316-329, 1982.

Lindstrom, L., *Manna for man Tanna*, Columban Mission, 67(8):28-31, 1984.

Lindstrom, L., *Spitting and Tannese religion*, Columban Mission, 67(8):19-20, 1984.

Ludvingson, T., *Kleva: some healers in Central Espiritu Santo, Vanuatu,* PHD Thesis, University of Auckland, 1981.

Ludvingson, T., *Healing in central Espiritu Santo, Vanuatu* in Parsons, C. D. F. (ed.), *Healing practices in the south Pacific*, Laie, Hawaii, Institute for Polynesian Studies, 1985.

Luke, H. C. J, *From a South Seas Diary 1938-1942*, London: Nicholson and Watson, 1945.

Luwia M., Leimaya J., Young M., *Suniena lala ne Lewo, ol storian blong Lewo, Epi aelan,* USP centre, Port Vila, 1988.

Lynch J., *A grammar of Lenakel,* in Pacific Linguistics n°55 series B, Australian national university, Canberra, 1977.

Lynch J., Crowley T., *Languages of Vanuatu, a new survey and bibliography,* Pacific linguistics 517, Australian national university, Canbera, 2001.

Mabonlala A., *Dut bi Mama Lelan non Navakni, Contes et jeux d'enfants, Tales and Games for children*, ORSTOM, Centre USP, Port Vila, 1986. (127 p.) Contes de l'île de Pentecôte.

Mabonlala A., *Dut at Apma, Contes Apma, Apma tales*, Port-Vila, ORSTOM, 1986.

Macdonald, A. H., *West coast of Santo: traditions, superstitions, customs etc.*, Proceedings and Transactions of the Royal Geographical Society of Australia, Victoria Branch, 10:43-57, 1893.

MacDonald, D., *Efate, New Hebrides*, Australasian Association for the Advancement of Science, Report for 1892, 4:720-735, 1893.

MacDonald, D., *The mythology of the Efatese*, report of the seventh meeting of the Australasian Association for the Advancement of Science, 7:759-768, 1898.

MacDonald, D., *Native stories of Efate, New Hebrides*, Science of Man, 7:11-13/34-36, 1904.

MacDonald, D., *South sea island mythology,* Journal of the Royal Geographical Society of Australasia, 30:26-44, 1913.

Mael J., Crowley T., *Tunuen telamun tenout voum* - Paama, USP centre, Port Vila, 1984.

Makira Aelan Kaljorel Komiti and W.B. Sperlich, *Na-dolo Na-makir : lanwis blong yumi*, Port Vila, Makira Aelan Kaljorel Komiti, 1986.

Maroi Sore (Trans. W. Gray) *A song of Aniwa, New Hebrides,* Journal of the Polynesian Society, 3:41-45, 1894.

McClancy, J., *Vao concepts*, Res, 2:70-90, 1981.

Bibliography

McMahon, T.J., *Volcano on Tanna island: legend of the giant's looking glass...*, Sea, Land and Air, pp249-251, 1922.

McMahon, T.J., *Tanna island, its interesting volcano*, New Nation Magazine, dec:51-52, 1927.

Mercer P.M. and Moore C.R., *Melanesians in north Queensland: the retention of indigenous religious and magical practices*, journal of Pacific history, 11 (1): 66-88, 1976.

Naiwa, I. et al., *Namsu (stories written in the eastern dialect of north Tanna language)*. Document produced during a written workshop hosted by the Summer Institute of Linguistics, 1986.

Neilson, T., *A legend of Iparé, New Hebrides*, Victorian Review, 8:702-704, 1883.

O'Ferrall, W., *Native stories from Santa Cruz and Reef Islands*, Journal of the Royal Anthropological Institute, 34:227-233, 1904.

O'Reilly, P., *Bibliographie méthodique, analytique et critique des Nouvelles-Hébrides*, Société des Océanistes, Musée de l'Homme (publications de la société des Océanistes, n°6), Paris, 1958.

Paton W.F., *Tales of Ambrym*, in Pacific Linguistics n°10 series D, Australian national university, Canberra, 1971.

Paton W.F., *Customs of Ambrym, texts, songs and drawings*, in Pacific Linguistics n°22 series D, Australian national university, Canberra, 1979.

Rakau, F., *A modern Futuna marriage* in Deverell G. and Deverell B. (eds.), *Pacific Rituals: living or dying?*, pp. 143-155, Fiji, University of the South Pacific and Pacific Theological College, 1986.

Regenvanu, R., *Report n°8, Maewo: Kerepei, Betarara and Nasawa*, Port Vila, interim report of the VCHSS, VCHSS, 1992.

Regenvanu, R. and S., *The story of the Eel and other stories from Uripiv island - Vanuatu, La légende de l'anguille et autres histoires de l'île d'Uripiv-Vanuatu*, éditions des Arts de la Parole, VKS, Port-Vila, 2004.

Riddle T.E., *Some myths and folk stories from Epi, New Hebrides* (part 1), Journal of the Polynesian society, vol. 24:156-167, 1915.

Riddle T.E., *Some myths and folk stories from Epi, New Hebrides* (part 2), Journal of the Polynesian society, vol. 25:24-30, 1916.

Riesenfeld, A., *The Megalithic culture of Melanesia*, Leiden, E.J. Brill, 1950.

Rivers W.H.R., *The History of Melanesian Society*, Cambridge University Press, Cambridge, 1914.

Rivers W.H.R., *The boomerang in the New Hebrides,* Man, 15(59), 1915.

Rivière J.C., *Mythistoire et archéologie dans le centre Vanuatu : l'histoire de Matanauretong* - Tongoa in M. Julien, M.C. Orliac, *Mémoire de pierre, mémoires d'homme*, ORSTOM, n.d.

Rodman, M.C., *Masters of tradition: customary land tenure and new form of social inequality in a Vanuatu peasantry*, American Ethnologist, 11(1):61:80, 1984.

Rodman, M.C., *Masters of Tradition: consequences of customary land tenure in Longana, Vanuatu*, Vancouver, University of British Columbia Press, 1987.

Roe, D. et al., *Report n°1. Nguna: Woralapa-Unakapu*, Port Vila, Interim report of the VCHSS, VCHSS, 1991.

Roe, D., *Report n°4. Erromango: Elizabeth Bay, Potnarvin, Ipota and Ifo*, Port Vila, Interim report of the VCHSS, VCHSS, 1992.

Roe, D. et al. *Report n°1. Nguna: Tikilasoa-Unakapu, Port Vila*, Interim report of the VCHSS, VCHSS, 1993.

Roe D., Regenvanu R., *The anthropology and archaeology of Vanuatu a preliminary bibliography*, working paper of the VCHSS, Port Vila, 1994.

Rory, P.(ed.), *Balbutiements, Aux îles de cendre et de corail, Contes et légendes recueillis par des enfants vanuatais*, Ministère de l'Education, Port-Vila, n.d.

Rory, P.(ed.), *Au pays qui se tient debout, contes et légendes du Vanuatu*, Ministère de l'Education, Port-Vila, n.d.

Rothwell, N., *Keeping the language alive: the voices of Vanuatu are recorded for posterity*, Pacific Islands Monthly, May: 14-15, 1988.

Sherkin, S., *Kastom stori mo laef histri blong ol pipol blong Mataso aelan*, VKS, Port Vila, 1999, 198 p.

Schutz, A., *Nguna Texts*, (Oceania Linguistics Special Publication n°4) University of Hawaii press, Honolulu, 1969.

Simeoni, P., *Buveurs de Kava*, thèse 3ème cycle en géographie, Université Paris IV Sorbonne, Paris, 2003.

Speiser, F., *Two years with the natives in the Pacific*, Mills and Boon, London, 1913.

Speiser F., *Ethnology of Vanuatu, an early twentieth century study*, University of Hawaii press, Honolulu, 1923.

Sperlich W.B., *Na-makir texts of Central Vanuatu*, University of Auckland, department of anthropology (working papers in Anthropology, Archaeology, Linguistics, Maori Studies, n°74) Aukland, 1986.

Spriggs, M., *"Their patrimonial soil they rudely till'd": taro irrigation in Oceania*; Year one report, Fieldwork report, Department of Prehistory, research school of Pacific Studies, Australian National University, 1979.

Suas J.B., *Mythes et légendes des indigènes des Nouvelles-Hébrides (Océanie)*, 1ère partie, Anthropos, tome 6, pp. 901-910, Vienne, 1911.

Suas J.B., *Le septième jour aux Nouvelles-Hébrides*, Océanie, Anthropos, tome 7, Vienne, 1912.

Suas J.B., *Mythes et légendes des indigènes des Nouvelles-Hébrides (Océanie)*, 2ème partie, Anthropos, tome 7, pp. 33-66, Vienne, 1912.

Suas J.B., *Notes ethnographiques sur les indigènes des Nouvelles-Hébrides*, Anthropos, tome 9, pp. 241-260, 760-773, Vienne, 1914.

Suas J.B., *Mythes et légendes des indigènes des Nouvelles-Hébrides (Océanie)*, 3ème partie, Anthropos, tome 10-11, pp. 269-271, Vienne, 1916.

Suas J.B., *Tamate (esprits) ou tamatologie des Lolopuépué (Oba, Nouvelles-Hébrides)*, revue Anthropos, tirage à part, tome 16-17, pp. 240-246, Vienne, 1921-22.

Tabi Resis, *Dut a le kidi*, - Pentecost, USP centre, Port Vila, 1985.

Tattevin E., *A l'ombre des ignames : mythes et légendes de l'île de Pentecôte*, Les Missions Catholiques, n°47 pp. 213, 226-227, 233-237, 1915.

Tattevin E., *Sur les bords de la mer sauvage, Notes ethnologiques sur la tribu des Ponorwol*, 1ère partie, Revue d'histoire des missions vol. 3, pp. 370-413, Paris, 1926.

Tattevin E., *Sur les bords de la mer sauvage, Notes ethnologiques sur la tribu des Ponorwol*, 2ème partie, Revue d'histoire des missions vol. 4, pp. 82-97, Paris, 1927.

Tattevin E., *Sur les bords de la mer sauvage, Notes ethnologiques sur la tribu des Ponorwol*, 3ème partie, Revue d'histoire des missions vol. 4, pp. 407-429, Paris, 1927.

Tattevin E., *Sur les bords de la mer sauvage, Notes ethnologiques sur la tribu des Ponorwol*, 4ème partie, Revue d'histoire des missions vol. 4, pp. 557-579, Paris, 1926.

Tattevin E., *Organisation sociale du sud de l'île Pentecôte*, revue Anthropos tome 23, Vienne, 1928.

Tattevin E., *Mythes et légendes du sud de l'île Pentecôte*, 1ère partie, revue Anthropos, tome 24, pp. 983-1004, Vienne, 1929.

Tattevin E., *Mythes et légendes du sud de l'île Pentecôte*, 2ème partie, revue Anthropos, tome 26, pp. 489-512, Vienne, 1931.

Tattevin E., *Mythes et légendes du sud de l'île Pentecôte*, 3ème partie, revue Anthropos, tome 26, pp. 863-881, Vienne, 1931.

Thieberger, N. (ed.), *Lis blong ol storian mo wok long lanwis*, Vanuatu Kaljoral Senta, Port Vila, 1997.

Thieberger N., *Natrausen nig Efate, stories from south Efate*, Vanuatu, Melbourne, Ts., VKS, 2000.

Tonkinson, R., *Kastom in Melanesia, introduction*, Mankind, 13(4):302-305, 1982.

Tonkinson, R., *National identity and the problem of kastom in Vanuatu*, Mankind, 13(4):306-315, 1982.

Tryon, D. (ed.), *Ples blong ol pig long kastom laef long Vanuatu*, Port Vila, Vanuatu Kaljoral Senta, 1992.

Van den Broek, G.J., *Leven en Dood van Ambat en Kabat: structurele analyse van mythen van de Nieuwe Hebriden*, thèse conservée à la Bibliothèque nationale de Vanuatu, 1981.

Vienne B., *Gens de Motlav, idéologie et pratiques sociales en Mélanésie*, ORSTOM, Paris, 1984.

Bibliography

Viralalao E., *Dekundekuni Ta - Ambae*, USP centre, Port Vila, 1981.

Vuti, J.A.(ed.), *Tavue: a collection of short stories from east Aoba*, Port Vila, Malapoa college, n.d.

Walsh, D.S. and Lini, W.H., *Veveven bwatun tauvwa, ata la vanua Raga: a story about the beginning of creation from Raga island* in Hollyman J. and Pawley A. (ed.), *Studies in Pacific Languages and cultures in honour of Bruce Biggs*, pp. 361-382, linguistic society of New Zealand, Auckland, 1980.

Ward, G.K., *Work of an archaeologist in the New Hebrides*, English draft of chapter *"Wok blong faendemaot fasin blong man long taem bifo"* in Bruntn, R. et al., Man, langwis mo kastom long niu Hebrides, 1978, n.d.

Watt-Leggatt, T., *Malekula, New Hebrides*, Australasian Association for the advancement of Science, report for 1892, 4:697-708, 1893.

Wright J., Wimbis F., *The two little boys and the snake*, W. W. publication, Australie, 1997.

Yoshioka, M., *The Marriage system in north Raga*, Vanuatu, Pre-publication Ts, Faculty of Liberal Arts, Shinshu University, 1985.

Yoshioka, M., *The marriage system in north Raga*, Vanuatu, Man and culture in Oceania, 1:27-54, 1985.

Yoshioka, M., *The story of Raga: a man's ethnography on his own society.* (1) *The origin myth*, Journal of the Faculty of Liberal Arts, Shinshu University, 21, 1987.

Sand drawings

Reference related to Vanuatu sand drawings collected by S. Zagala, Dro long graon blong Vanuatu, VKS, 2001.

Anonyme, *New Hebrides Ground Drawings*, paper read at the annual meeting of the northwest Anthropological Association, Ellensburg, Washington, April 8, 1976.

Batick R., *Drawing competition*, Port Vila, ministry of Education, 1995.

Cabanne J.P., *De poussière et de sable, dessins géométriques de Vanuatu*, édité par l'auteur, 1994, ORSTOM.

Cabanne J.P., *Les dessins sur sable de Vanuatu, un art de la parole*, in F. Angleviel (éd.) *Parole, Communication et symbole en Océanie*, l'Harmattan, Paris, 1995.

Cabanne J.P., *Ululan, les sables de la mémoire*, éd. Grain de sable, Nouméa, 1997, 77p.

Deacon, B., *Geometric drawings from Malekula and other islands of the New Hebrides*, The journal of the Royal Anthropological Institute of Great Britain and Ireland, vol. 64, pp 129-175, 1934.

Deacon B., *Malekula a vanishing people in the New Hebrides*, Routledge, London, 1934.

Huffman K., *Si tuh netan' monbwei: we write on the ground: sand drawings and their associations in northern Vanuatu*, in Bonnemaison, J.(ed.), *Arts of Vanuatu*, Crawford house, Bathurst, pp. 247-253, 1996.

Layard, J. W., *The labyrinth in the megalithic areas of Malekula, the Deccan, Scandinavia and Scotland: with special reference to the Malekulan geometric drawings collected by Deacon*, Man, 35 (10), 1935.

Layard J. W., *Maze dance and the ritual of the labyrinth in Malekula*, Folklore 157, 1936.

Layard J. W., *Stone men of Malekula*, Chatto and Windus, London , 1942.

Rodman, William L., *When questions are answers: the message of anthropology according to the people of Ambae*, in American anthropologist, vol. 93, n°2, 1991.

Tailhade, H., *Ululan : dessins sur sable de l'île de Pentecôte*, Port-Vila, non édité, 1983.

Tailhade H., *Tu : dessins sur sable de l'île d'Ambrym ouest et nord*, Port-Vila, non édité, 1983.

Tailhade H., *Tambours sculptés - dessins sur sable*, Institut de Technologie de Vanuatu, Port-Vila, 1983.

Taylor, J., *Unpublished field notes*, produced in the Raga district of North Pentecost while conducting research toward a PhD in anthropology at the Australian National University, 1999-2001.

Wilson, M., *Unpublished field notes*, produced while conducting research toward a PhD in archaeology at the Australian National University, 1995-2001.

Zagala S., *Drao long graon blong Vanuatu*, VKS, Port Vila, 2001.

Contents

Disclaimer *5*

Foreword *8*

Preface *9*

Maps *10*

TORBA Province *15*

Maraptit the traveller (Hiu) *17*

The legend of Kwat (Mota) *22*

The devils' nasara from Sarevugvug (Vanua Lava) *28*

Wenagon and his two daughters (Gaua) *32*

SANMA Province *35*

The Namalao Cave (Santo) *37*

The tamed lisepsep of Santo *40*

Maliu the fisherman and the giant eel (Santo) *44*

The legend of the namarae from Santo *46*

The legend of Taribowe (Santo) *49*

The life and death of Mol Malamala (Malo) *53*

The legend of the new moon (Malo) *55*

The legend of the fisherman and his five children (Malo) *57*

PENAMA Province *59*

Ulunwel and the devils (Pentecost) *61*

The legend of the moon and the sun (Pentecost) *64*

The story of Tabi and Bule (Pentecost) *65*

Barkulkul the God (Pentecost) *68*

The legend of old Wakos (Pentecost) *72*

The story of two brothers Taisamul and Fassel (Pentecost) *77*

The legend of the namarae from Pentecost *82*

Muehu Katekale, the unsatisfied (Ambae) *85*

The legend of Tagaro (Maewo) *89*

How Tagaro beat Mweragbuto the traitor (Ambae) *93*

The legend of kava (Maewo) *96*

MALAMPA Province 101

Ambat and Nevinbumbaau (Malekula) 103
The two Lindenda (Tomman) 111
The legend of Tolambe Islet (Vao) 114
The pig of the islet of Vao (Vao) 116
The birth of the sea (Malekula) 121
The dwarves of Malekula 124
The legend of the carnivorous stone (Ambrym) 126
The snake of North Ambrym (Ambrym) 129
The legend of the Vermelap stones 137
The lisepsep's son from Ambrym 140
The Titamol (Paama) 142
The namele's child (Paama) 144

SHEFA Province 147

The old man and the bananas (Epi) 148
The prisoner of the stone (Epi) 149
The legend of Sakora and Tiara (Makura) 151
The magic shell (Makura) 161
The legend of Kuwae (Tongoa) 163
Six brothers and the snake (Tongoa) 167
Mauitikitiki, the fisher of islands (Emae) 169
The myth of Sina (Emae) 179
Seganiale, the Forari devil (Mataso) 185
Wotanimanu, the rock monument (Mataso) 188
Nising and Turig (Mataso) 192
The legend of Sosolobeng (Mataso) 197
The Mutuama of Ifira 203
The rat and the octopus (Ifira) 208
Suepus and Atafru (Pango) 210
Sokomanu (Mele) 215
Leikele and Kurunaenae (Mele) 232
The voyage of Atafru (Erakor) 235
The origin of clan names (Efate) 241

TAFEA Province 243

The bird woman (Tanna) 245
Semusemu, the ogre from Tanna 246
Yasur, the volcano man (Tanna) 251
The Newak Newak (Tanna) 253
The red fowl and the sea crocodile (Aniwa) 255
The birth of Futuna 257
The marriage of kava and the coconut palm (Erromango) 263
Nalakyang, the ogre (Anatom) 267

Appendices 271

The sailor and the children of Ambrym by Didier Daeninckx 273

Radio and the Redefinition of Kastom in Vanuatu by Lissant Bolton 277

Glossary 289

Bibliography 293

Contents 301

For more information to order, contact:

Vanuatu Cultural Centre
Oral Arts Project
P.O. Box 184, Port-Vila
VANUATU - South Pacific

Tel : (678) 22129 / 22721
Fax : (678) 26590

Email : vks@vanuatu.com.vu